HOW PUBLIC POLICY
IMPACTS RACIAL INEQUALITY

MEDIA AND PUBLIC AFFAIRS

ROBERT MANN, SERIES EDITOR

HOW
PUBLIC POLICY
IMPACTS
RACIAL INEQUALITY

EDITED BY
JOSH GRIMM
AND
JAIME LOKE

LOUISIANA STATE UNIVERSITY PRESS
BATON ROUGE

Published by Louisiana State University Press
Copyright © 2019 by Louisiana State University Press
All rights reserved
Manufactured in the United States of America

DESIGNER: Michelle A. Neustrom
TYPEFACE: Chaparral Pro

LIBRARY OF CONGRESS CATALOGING-IN-PUBLICATION DATA

Names: Grimm, Josh, 1980– editor. | Loke, Jaime, 1979– editor.
Title: How public policy impacts racial inequality / edited by Josh Grimm
    and Jaime Loke.
Description: Baton Rouge : Louisiana State University Press, [2019] | Series:
    Media and public affairs | Includes index.
Identifiers: LCCN 2018052210 | ISBN 978-0-8071-7070-0 (pbk. : alk. paper) |
    ISBN 978-0-8071-7168-4 | ISBN 978-0-8071-7169-1
Subjects: LCSH: United States—Social policy. | United States—Race
    relations. | Racism—United States. | Discrimination—United States.
Classification: LCC HN65 .H5968 2019 | DDC 305.800973—dc23
LC record available at https://lccn.loc.gov/2018052210

The paper in this book meets the guidelines for permanence
and durability of the Committee on Production Guidelines for
Book Longevity of the Council on Library Resources. ∞

CONTENTS

HOW PUBLIC POLICY
IMPACTS RACIAL INEQUALITY

INTRODUCTION

JOSH GRIMM AND JAIME LOKE

On July 15, 2017, an all-too-familiar tragedy played out in Minneapolis when forty-year-old resident Justine Damond called authorities to report what she thought was a rape occurring in an alley outside of her home. Police arrived to investigate, and not long afterward, Damond was dead from a gunshot wound to the abdomen, killed by one of the officers on the scene. Over the next few days, statements were released on both sides, police initially positing fears of ambush before promising justice, the victim's family telling the world about their loss of a caring, kind woman who was going to get married in less than a month. Inevitably, it was revealed that police body cameras were not recording when Damond was shot. This came just weeks after the officer who shot and killed Philando Castile (and was caught doing so from multiple camera angles) was acquitted of manslaughter charges. Again, the narrative was one that had been seen time and time again, with one important difference: the victim was a white woman, the officer a black immigrant.

As with so many things online, outrage ensued. Sensationalistic headlines peppered far-right populist websites. An *InfoWars* headline read: "Washington Post Worries about 'Islamophobia' after Somali Cop Kills White Woman." *The Washington Feed* stated, "Unarmed White Woman Murdered in Minnesota, Dems SILENT after Shooter's ID Revealed." *Freedom Daily* announced, "First Migrant Muslim Police Officer MURDERS Blonde Girl in COLD BLOOD—You Won't Believe DISGUSTING Reason Why."[1] The comments on social media focused on the hypocrisy, with one side pointing out the hypocrisy of commenters attacking the police officer when normally they default to Blue Lives Matter, and the other side explaining that every situation must be judged on a case-by-case basis.

The story is intriguing because it intersects with so many different aspects of race: immigration, politics, class, criminal justice, media portrayals. The policeman's status as a Muslim Somali immigrant seemed to be fused to his name, at least if you were watching conservative news networks; Fox News led almost every segment with his background, while CNN and MSNBC barely mentioned it.[2] Days later, Minneapolis Mayor Betsy Hodges—who had praised Mohamed Noor's work as a police officer—was mocked by Michele Bachmann, who said Noor was an "affirmative-action hire by the hijab-wearing mayor of Minneapolis."[3] Damond's story was laced with socioeconomic status markers— she lived in an "affluent neighborhood," she was a yoga instructor, she taught meditation. And the understanding of the story can vary wildly based on which news outlet was the source of information. Overall, the story captures the complicated pervasiveness of racial prejudice in the United States.

Racism is a constantly shifting, socially constructed phenomenon through which stereotypes are created or reinforced by the perceived connection between skin color and a culturally homogenous set of characteristics regarding behavior, attitudes, and beliefs. While race is a social construct,[4] it has real effects,[5] reflecting the unequal levels of power between racial groups.[6] Race was constructed biologically, meaning certain traits (laziness, stupidity, aggression, and so forth) were defined as inherent in people of color—and therefore absent in whites.[7] Race becomes less a category and more a form of power that can, at times, be wielded by people of color but is most often relegated to whites. Despite the claims of many politicians, pundits, and even the occasional researcher, racial prejudice remains prevalent in the United States today.

Over the past fifty years, expression of racial prejudice has become more covert. University of Illinois professor Maria Krysan notes that, "In today's contemporary race relations, there's pressure to appear not racist, and embrace racial equality. The more privacy you give a white person to express their attitudes, the less liberal they become."[8] Essentially, rather than the aforementioned biological explanations for observed differences, individuals chalk those differences up to cultural reasons. Devine and Elliot's essential work sought to examine a series of studies to determine if stereotypes were actually fading over time.[9] They added to an established list of stereotypical cues with subtler synonyms to see if attitudes persisted. They found that strong, negative stereotypes still exist toward blacks but that these have changed in form. For instance, when the questions had first been asked in the 1930s, blatant terms for stereotypes registered strong responses that identified blacks with words such as "lazy," "ignorant," and "dirty." By the 1970s, those words weren't registering nearly as many responses; Blacks were still being associated with stereotypes, but it was through subtler synonyms, such as "arrogant" and "loud." In their most recent adaptation, Devine and Elliot found that different words ("rhythmic" and "talkative") were still being used to describe all blacks. In-depth interviews have garnered similar results, with respondents speaking with racial code words[10] or sometimes speaking in frankly racist terms by simply prefacing those statements with a disclaimer, such as the dreaded "I'm not a racist, but. . . ."[11]

Racial prejudice studies have also changed by differentiating between implicit and explicit prejudice. Explicit prejudice is typically expressed through actions and is therefore more easily controlled, whereas implicit prejudice manifests itself through subtle behavior and language because it is much more difficult to suppress. The expression of racial prejudice may have become less blatant, but it is no less damaging. John F. Dovidio and colleagues conducted an experiment where whites were asked to evaluate applications to determine which students would be accepted for admission into a university.[12] The experiment included a variety of applicants with varying levels of accomplishment with SAT scores, grade point averages, and involvement in school activities. The researchers found that, regardless of race, if the application was strong, the individual was accepted into the university and, if the application was weak, that person was rejected. However, when the applications were ambiguous (for example, high GPA, low SAT), the white individuals making the decision were significantly more likely to reject black students. When asked about why certain students were rejected, the white subjects often provided conflicting explanations, suggesting that GPA was the most important indicator when referring to the acceptance of a white applicant while saying that GPA was the least important indicator when referring to the rejection of a black applicant. This implicit prejudice was also present when similar experiments were conducted involving joining a fraternity[13] and when applying for a job.[14]

Experiments can lack external validity—especially in the social sciences—which is why real-world examples can help underscore significant findings. The country got a chance to confront its racial biases in the 2016 presidential election in a lengthy campaign filled with racial dog whistles and outright calls encouraging prejudice. Regardless of whether it was the candidate, the message, the opposition, or some combination thereof, race was a significant factor in the outcome. Researcher Thomas Wood conducted an analysis of voter data and found that "racial biases made a bigger difference in electing Trump than authoritarianism," noting that there has not been such a clear statistical divide between racial perceptions and vote choice since 1988.[15]

In establishing how racial prejudice manifests in certain situations, these individual instances reveal hegemonic relationships by examining the use of racism as a strategy for maintaining power. Bonilla-Silva argues that color-blind racism is prominent in current societal conditions and that this strain of racism maintains white privilege without the fanfare.[16] Through this practice, whites embrace "sincere fictions" that allow for a denial of racial inequality.[17] According to Joe R. Feagin and Vera Hernan, sincere fictions are "personal and group constructions that reproduce societal myths at the individual and group level."[18] Scholars insist more attention needs to be paid to these types of unequal power relationships (and their persistence) by looking at systematic racism, which is an institutional form of racism that has consistently benefited whites in the United States. Arguing that this country is one of the few in the Western Hemisphere built on such extreme levels of injustice (most notably, slavery and elimination of Native Americans), Feagin posits that whites have all benefited (in one form or another) from racism.[19] At a time when racism is changing and becoming more difficult to locate, these social structures of power need to be understood as consistent.

Tackling these social institutions can be daunting. Identifying the issues surrounding inequality across racial lines, accepting that those issues exist, identifying the cause of those issues, and implementing changes to correct those injustices represent a significant barrier to meaningful change. However, such change can be brought about through public policy. Scholars have a difficult time agreeing on a single definition for public policy, in part because it's such a broad topic. Speaking generally, public policy is what "government (any public official who influences or determines public policy, including school officials, city council members, county supervisors, etc.) does or does not do about a problem that comes before them for consideration and possible action."[20] Thomas A. Birkland notes that, although policy is created by governments, it's the "public and private actors who have different interpretations of problems, solutions, and their own motivations."[21] In other words, while policy is the government's to make, ideas from the public can significantly influence the form that legislation ultimately takes. "Policymaking is part of an ongoing process that does not always have a clear beginning or end, since decisions about who will benefit from policies and who will bear any burden resulting from the policy are continually reassessed, revisited and revised."[22]

This volume addresses issues related to race and public policy. The book is meant to be a broad yet in-depth examination and analysis of the state of race in the United States, focusing on race through the lens of public policy, with the aim of connecting the institutional nature of racism to continuing and sometimes explosive unrest. This book is a result of the John Breaux Symposium, an annual academic event where one important issue is selected and discussed in detail. This year's topic, race and public policy, featured multiple panels discussing various aspects of how race is viewed and understood, including a round table of community leaders, journalists, and activists, along with a panel of academic experts discussing a variety of areas of expertise. This book stems from the latter.

Chapters included here include a mix of original research as well as essays. Based off the panel of experts, each chapter is written by a scholar who explores one aspect of race: segregation, politics, health, media, immigration, law, crime, and wealth. This book is intended to be broad—in that it covers several subjects—but also thorough, offering in-depth analysis on a variety of issues essential to understanding the intertwined, ongoing role of race and public policy.

Shaun L Gabbidon begins with a review of data exploring racial profiling before examining police killings. Gabbidon provides the historical foundations and contemporary issues tied to the practice and pays particular attention to key policies that have been crafted to remedy these concerns. He focuses specifically on the continued vigilance to maintain the balance between public safety and civil rights while still holding enforcement entities accountable.

Jackelyn Hwang, Elizabeth Roberto, and Jacob S. Rugh argue that residential segregation remains an unfortunate fixture that helps to define the American racial landscape. It is difficult to assess at times because traditional measures and methods for examining the problem overlook important aspects of segregation that characterize the metropolitan landscape in which we live today. Despite some improvement since legislation was introduced to reduce segregation roughly fifty years ago, the problem persists.

Srividya Ramasubramanian provides an overview of how race and public policy are shaped and molded by mass media in a variety of different ways due to the vast array of workers, owners, and content within media. Given the exponential expansion of media through its users, audiences have more access and influence now than ever before, all of which will continue to play an important role in public policy.

Holley A. Wilkin discusses barriers and solutions to issues surrounding race and health, with an emphasis on challenging health disparities brought on by a variety of factors, both environmental and behavioral. Through her examination of lead poisoning, tobacco, and improving access to healthy foods, Wilkin takes an in-depth look at how policy decisions have impacted overall health equity.

Mary E. Campbell and Sylvia M. Emmanuel discuss how those policies attempting to address inequality often neglect to take into account multiracial individuals and groups. By studying legal precedent, they show how problematic policies could be revised to be more inclusive.

Josh Grimm places Donald Trump's immigration policies—planned and implemented—in the larger historical context. By understanding not only the pieces of legislation passed throughout U.S. history, but also the impact of those policy decisions, Grimm provides much-needed background to help recognize patterns and trends manifesting themselves once again in the ongoing discussion on immigration.

Lori Latrice Martin examines the public policies that helped to create wealth inequality along racial lines, dating back centuries. This will help in understanding how current polices are perpetuating racial wealth inequality and black asset poverty. Martin calls on scholars to seriously consider the role of race in maintaining this inequality along racial lines.

Ismail K. White, Chryl Laird, Ernest McGowen, and Jared Clemons argue that variation in black support for many important political issues can be explained at least in part by the degree to which blacks attend to political messages originating from black indigenous information sources. Analyzing data from the 1996 National Black Election Study (NBES), they test the effects of exposure to mainstream and black political communication on black Americans' assessment of an ostensibly nonracial institution, the U.S. Central Intelligence Agency (CIA). The results from this analysis highlight the role that attention to indigenous political communication can play in shaping the opinions of racial and ethnic minorities.

As this is an interdisciplinary text, you might notice inconsistencies between chapters in terminology used to describe different racial and ethnic groups. However, you'll notice a similarity of themes across the disciplines, particularly in terms of inequality and racism. Through examining a variety of issues across a wide range of topics, we hope to offer a comprehensive picture of race and public policy in the United States.

NOTES

1. According to the story, the reason Noor killed the forty-year-old "blonde girl" is because Muslims have issues with women. Saved you a click.

2. Nina Mast, "Fox News Is Unusually Focused on the Nationality of the Officer Who Shot Justine Damond (He's Somali-American)." *Media Matters,* July 20, 2017, www.media matters.org/blog/2017/07/20/fox-news-unusually-focused-nationality-officer-who-shot -justine-damond-hes-somali-american/217317.

3. Miguel Otárola, "Back in Spotlight, Michele Bachmann Praises Trump, Addresses Minneapolis Police Shooting of Justine Damond," *Star Tribune,* July 20, 2017, m.startribune .com/bachmann-praises-trump-blasts-political-correctness/435517653/?section=%2F.

4. Michael Omi and Howard Winant, *Racial Formation in the United States* (New York: Routledge, 2014).

5. Eduardo Bonilla-Silva, *Racism without Racists: Color-Blind Racism and the Persistence of Racial Inequality in America* (Boulder, CO: Rowman & Littlefield, 2017).

6. Ashley W. Doane and Eduardo Bonilla-Silva, eds. *White Out: The Continuing Significance of racism* (New York: Routledge, 2003).

7. Omi and Winant, *Racial Formation.*

8. Anna Maria Barry-Jester, "Attitudes toward Racism and Inequality Are Shifting," *FiveThirtyEight* June 23, 2015, fivethirtyeight.com/datalab/attitudes-toward-racism-an d-inequality-are-shifting/.

9. Patricia G. Devine and Andrew J. Elliot, "Are Racial Stereotypes Really Fading? The Princeton Trilogy Revisited," *Personality and Social Psychology Bulletin* 21, no. 11 (1995): 1139–50.

10. Amanda Lewis, *Race in the Schoolyard: Negotiating the Color Line in Classrooms and Communities*. (New Brunswick, NJ: Rutgers University Press, 2003).

11. Bonilla-Silva, *Racism without Racists*.

12. John F. Dovidio, Samuel E. Gaertner, Kerry Kawakami, and Gordon Hodson, "Why Can't We Just Get Along? Interpersonal Biases and Interracial Distrust," *Cultural Diversity and Ethnic Minority Psychology* 8, no. 2 (2002): 88.

13. John F. Dovidio, Kerry Kawakami, and Samuel L. Gaertner, "Implicit and Explicit Prejudices and Interracial Interaction," *Journal of Personality and Social Psychology* 82, no. 1 (2002): 62.

14. Dovidio et al., "Implicit and Explicit Prejudices."

15. Thomas Wood, "Racism Motivated Trump Voters More Than Authoritarianism." *Washington Post*, April 17, 2017, www.washingtonpost.com/news/monkey-cage/wp/2017/04/17/racism-motivated-trump-voters-more-than-authoritarianism-or-income-inequality/?utm_term=.c33d3464bba6.

16. Bonilla-Silva, *Racism without Racists*.

17. Hernan Vera and Andrew M. Gordon, *Screen Saviors: Hollywood Fictions of Whiteness* (Boulder, CO: Rowman & Littlefield Publishers, 2003), 15.

18. Joe R. Feagin and Vera Hernan, *White Racism: The Basics* (New York: Routledge, 2000), 26.

19. Joe Feagin, *Systemic Racism: A Theory of Oppression* (New York: Routledge, 2013).

20. Project Citizen, "What Is Public Policy?" Center for Civic Education, www.civiced.org/pc-program/instructional-component/public-policy.

21. Thomas A. Birkland, *An Introduction to the Policy Process: Theories, Concepts, and Models of Public Policy Making* (New York: Routledge, 2015).

22. Project Citizen, *What Is Public Policy*.

RACE, POLICE MISCONDUCT, AND PUBLIC POLICY

Focus on Racial Profiling and Police Killings

SHAUN L. GABBIDON

INTRODUCTION

Since the founding of the United States, the American Justice System (AJS) has been a place where concerns tied to race/ethnicity, class, and gender have persisted.[1] Ironically, the problems that emerged in the AJS were not new. European countries had long identified racial/ethnic disparities in crime statistics.[2] In fact, European thinkers such as Cesare Lombroso and his followers attributed these disparities to physical and biological differences among the races.[3] Such thinking arrived in America and produced the eugenics movement and the push to sterilize inferior "stocks." Conversely, another cadre of European thinkers pointed to sociological factors as holding the key to explain racial disparities.[4] Similarly, a host of American thinkers latched onto this thinking and, most notably, William Edward Burghardt Du Bois in Atlanta[5] and Robert Park in Chicago[6] led serious research-based efforts to better understand racial disparities in the AJS. Upon further exploration of the situation, scholars began to take a closer look at the actual agencies of the AJS to determine their role in both creating and magnifying racial/ethnic disparities.

Much has been written about the ills of the AJS. In particular, race-centered scholarship has grown tremendously in the past thirty years.[7] This scholarship has pointed to racism as one of the leading contributors to the existing racial/ethnic disparities in arrests, sentencing, and correctional populations. While much of the existing literature reemphasizes the concerns related to these disparities, much less of the extended discussion focuses on the public policies that have either directly or indirectly contributed to the observed disparities. Police departments and their officers are the most visible aspect of the criminal justice system. Consequently, the police have received the brunt of the animus tied to concerns related to racial/ethnic disparities in the AJS.

A review of data will illuminate one of the most controversial aspects of police misconduct: racial profiling. An examination of police killings will follow. Each of these sections provide the historical foundations and contemporary issues tied to *profiling and police killings* and pays particular attention to key policies that have been crafted to remedy these concerns.

POLICE MISCONDUCT: RACIAL PROFILING

BRIEF HISTORY

Racial profiling has a long history in the United States. Dating to the slave era, racial profiling was widely practiced by slave masters and supported by local police agencies. Slave masters typically were tasked with tracking down escaped black slaves. Moreover, slave owners often cooperated with one another to retrieve runaway slaves. These slave patrols were the first form of racial profiling in which black slaves were specifically targeted. Slave patrols were followed by the creation of formalized slave codes.[8] These race-specific practices ushered in the enactment of "criminal law and procedure applied against enslaved Africans. The codes, which regulated slave life from cradle to grave, were virtually uniform across states—each with the overriding goal of upholding chattel slavery."[9]

In the past three decades, there has been increased attention on police misconduct. One specific concern that has garnered additional attention is racial profiling, the practice of targeting racial/ethnic minorities for increased stops on highways, in retail stores, at airports, and on the streets.[10] Prior to the terrorist attacks of 9/11, there was considerable scholarly attention devoted to understanding the racial dynamics of traffic stops. In fact, a decade prior to 9/11, Roger Wilkins, an African American attorney from Washington, D.C., challenged the Maryland State Police concerning their nonconsensual search of his car during a traffic stop. The case, *Wilkins v. Maryland State Police* (1993), began the wave of litigation that uncovered discriminatory traffic stops in several states along the I-95 corridor, including Maryland, New Jersey, and Florida. During this period, researchers consistently found that African Americans were stopped and searched at higher rates during traffic stops for speeding than their white counterparts—who were found to speed at rates equal to African Americans.[11] Consequently, several northeastern states were court mandated to annually collect data on the nature and scope of traffic stops.

Despite some forward movement with the revelations about disproportionate traffic stops based on race, the case of *Whren v. U.S.* (1996) provided officers with additional latitude in the decision to make traffic stops. The case involved Michael Whren, who was in his pickup truck that was stopped at a stop sign. He was looking down at the passenger seat when an officer approached; Whren immediately made a turn without signaling and headed away from the stop sign. Officers stopped him on the pretext of not signaling. During the stop, the officers searched the vehicle and found illegal drugs. Both Whren and his passenger were arrested and subsequently convicted. Whren alleged that the stop was based on racial bias, but to prove this the Supreme Court suggested that Whren would have to prove that the primary reason the police stopped him was because of his race—something the officer would have had to admit. Whren lost the case, and police agencies rejoiced in the confirmation of their ability to use pretextual stops to conduct searches that had the ability to uncover illegal drugs and other contraband.

The terrorist attacks of 9/11 brought profiling at airports into the spotlight. Given the backgrounds of the terrorists, there was a heightened emphasis on scrutinizing passengers from the Middle East and those of the Muslim faith. Notably, public-opinion polling following the attacks found limited support for the use of racial profiling; even so, the public was most supportive of racial profiling at airports or the specific use of ethnic/racial profiling,[12] as opposed to retail settings and traffic stops.[13] Despite the heightened concerns about racial/ethnic profiling at airports, the main concerns tied to profiling during traffic stops resulted in the Department of Justice producing the most comprehensive data on public perceptions of police stops both on the streets and during traffic stops. Today, every three years, there are national data collected by the U.S. Census Bureau that provide estimates on the context of encounters involving the police and the public.

PERCEPTIONS OF POLICE BEHAVIOR DURING POLICE CONTACT

In response to legitimate concerns expressed by largely racial/ethnic minorities regarding police bias during traffic stops, the Bureau of Justice Statistics partnered with the U.S. Census Bureau to collect data on the context surrounding police stops. Beginning in 1999, the Police-Contact Survey (PPCS) has been collected every three years and is conducted in conjunction with the annual administration of the National Crime Victimization Survey.[14] The data are based on citizens' contacts with the police during the previous twelve months. In total, the 2011 PPCS sample included 49,246 persons whose responses were weighted to provide a national population estimate for police-public contacts covering more then 241 million people. Using the estimates based on the sample, there were nearly 63 million people aged sixteen and older who had contacts with the police in 2011. This represented nearly one-quarter of the U.S. population. Of these contacts, nearly half (49 percent) were initiated by the police, contacts referred to as involuntary.[15]

Involuntary contacts are typically initiated as a result of a traffic stop (42 percent), street stop (2.3 percent), or an arrest or other contact (5 percent). The PPCS data provide a clear picture that citizens felt that the police behaved properly and respectfully in the majority of the traffic (86.4 percent) and street (65.9 percent) stops. When disaggregated, the percentage of the public that felt the police were not respectful (9.0 percent) or did not behave properly (9.6 percent) during traffic stops paled in comparison to the same responses for street stops, 22.9 percent and 24.5 percent respectively.[16] A deeper examination of the data reveals distinct differences between the perceived police contacts of racial/ethnic groups. In particular, there are small differences between racial/ethnic groups pertaining to perceptions of police behaving properly during traffic stops. Except for American Indians (74.2 percent) and blacks (82.7 percent), all other racial/ethnic groups were above 85 percent in their agreement that the police behaved properly during traffic stops. Conversely, the street-stop data provide stark perceptions particularly between blacks and all other racial/ethnic groups. Of the fewer than 1 percent of people in the United States that ever encounter a street stop, less than 40 percent of blacks felt that the police behaved properly during the contact. Nearly two-thirds of Hispanic respondents expressed the same sentiment, while all other racial/ethnic groups were over 75 percent.[17]

One significant concern of most observers of police behavior is the legitimacy of police stops. Legitimacy generally translates into the notion that people trust and have confidence in officers to carry out their duties fairly. The PPCS data also provide some sense as to whether citizens felt police legitimacy was present during their contact with law enforcement. The data revealed that blacks expressed the least confidence that their stop was legitimate (67.5 percent), with Hispanics next at 73.6 percent, and whites at 83.6 percent. The low level of perceived legitimacy was consistent across nearly every type of reason specified by the police for the stop, as highlighted in table 1.1. Interestingly, among the lowest level of confidence for perceived police legitimacy among blacks was for stops that were alleged to have been initiated for seat-belt or cell-phone violations (63.8 percent). Concerns about the use of seat-belt laws as a pretext to target minority drivers isn't a new accusation. In recent years, for example, Florida has uncovered racial disparities in stops based on seat-belt violations.[18] Across the state, research has found that such stops are conducted upon black drivers at a rate ranging from two to four times as often as white drivers—even though black and white drivers fail to use seat belts at the same rate.

Another aspect of police legitimacy that has entered the limelight pertains to whether the racial dynamics of the officer and the driver matter. The PPCS data found that, when the driver and officer were of the same race, the stops were considered legitimate 83.3 percent of the time, while when the nature of the stop was interracial the stops were considered legitimate 74.4 percent of the time. More detailed data found that "A similar percentage of white drivers believed the reason for the stop was legitimate, regardless of whether they were stopped by white, Hispanic, or black officers."[19] Black drivers perceived the same level of legitimacy when stopped by white and black officers (approximately 70 percent); in contrast, the perceived legitimacy of stops among black drivers was at its lowest level (47 percent) when stopped by Hispanic officers.

POLICE POLICY AND CITIZEN RESPONSE

In response to concerns about stops, there have been policies put in place to achieve enhanced police accountability. In particular, besides

Table 1.1. Perception That Reason for Traffic Stop Was Legitimate among Drivers Aged Sixteen or Older, by Race or Hispanic Origin of Driver and Reason for Stop, 2011

Reason for traffic stop	Percent of stopped drivers				
	All	White[a]	Black/African American[a]	Hispanic/ Latino	Other[a, b]
Any reasons police gave for the stop	100%	100%	100%	100%	100%
Speeding	46.5	50.1	37.7	39.2	37.3
Vehicle defect	14.1	12.7	19	16.5	14.6
Record check	9.7	9	14	9.7	9.9
Roadside sobriety check	1.3	1.6	.4!	1.0!	1.0!
Seat-belt or cell-phone violation	6.6	6.6	6.5	6.5	7.4
Illegal turn or lane change	7	6.6	7	7.1	10.8
Stop light/other light violation	6.7	6.1	5.5	9.9	9.4
Other reason[c]	5.1	4.7	5.3	6.8	5.2
Police did not give reason for the stop	3.1	2.6	4.7	3.3	4.2!

Reason for traffic stop	Percent reporting stop was legitimated[d]				
	All	White[a]	Black/African American[a]	Hispanic/ Latino	Other[a, b]
Any reasons police gave for the stop	80%	83.6%	67.50%	74%	78%
Speeding	87.1	89.6	72.8	83.1	87.3
Vehicle defect	81.2	86.4	69	74.4	79.3
Record check	80	80.9	83	70.7	81.2
Roadside sobriety check	79.4	86	—!	56.6!	68.1!
Seat-belt or cell-phone violation	79.7	84	63.8	77.3	69.0!
Illegal turn or lane change	73	75.4	65	72.6	67.1
Stop light/other light violation	68.4	68.8	69.2	63.6	74.6
Other reason[c]	59.1	65.2	21.6!	61.9	67.8!
Police did not give reason for the stop	44.6	51	36.5!	18.3!	59.8!

! Interpret with caution. Estimate based on ten or fewer cases, or the coefficient of variation is greater than 50 percent.

— Less than 0.05%.

[a] Excludes persons of Hispanic or Latino origin.

[b] Includes persons identifying as American Indian, Alaska Native, Asian, Native Hawaiian, or other Pacific Islander, and persons of two or more races.

[c] Denominator includes approximately 3 percent of white, 6 percent of black, 3 percent of Hispanic, and 4 percent of other race who did not know or did not report whether the reason for the stop was legitimate.

[d] Includes reasons such as reckless driving, littering, failure to yield, following too closely, obstructed license plate, and noise violations.

Source: Based on persons for whom the most recent contact with police was as a driver in a traffic stop. Bureau of Justice Statistics, National Crime Victimization Survey, Police-Public, www.bjs.gov/index.cfm?ty=dcdetail&iid=245.

the data being collected in the PPCS, police agencies continue to track the nature of stops. In the past the main source of this was dashboard cameras. During the 1990s, when there were increasing concerns about racist police encounters, "dashboard cameras emerged as a new method for capturing the real-time encounters between police and citizens."[20] While the use of dashboard cameras was not initially received with open arms by police officers, researchers have found "that the cameras led to increased officer safety and accountability and reduced agency liability."[21] Consequently, police agencies are now big supporters of dashboard cameras. Today, the use of body-worn cameras by the police is being championed as the newest approach to track police behavior when they are carrying out all their duties—not just those captured by dash cameras. In fact, a recent statewide poll of Pennsylvanians found that 88 percent were in support of the use of body cameras.[22] Why so much support for body-worn cameras? A recent National Institute of Justice report summarizes both the perceived benefits and concerns with the technology.[23]

It is believed that body-worn cameras not only increase transparency, they also increase police legitimacy. In short, citizens have much more confidence that the police will fairly carry out their duties when they wear body cameras. White also points out that, when police wear body cameras, there is a civilizing effect on both the police and citizens.[24] Multiple studies have shown reduced complaints from citizens and fewer instances of police use of force in jurisdictions that employ body cameras.[25] Additional studies have also shown that video data from body cameras provide the evidentiary proof required to "expedite resolution of citizen complaints or lawsuits and that improve evidence for arrest and prosecution.[26] Finally, there is also emerging evidence from studies in the United Kingdom and the United States that body cameras provide unique opportunities to better train the police.

In contrast to these positive benefits tied to the use of body cameras, there have been some notable concerns and problems as well. Privacy concerns top the list of issues with the use of body cameras. Citizens are concerned that the vast array of traumatic incidents that the police encounter on a daily basis will be captured on video. These include all sorts of emergencies and issues that would expose the privacy of victims. Similarly, the police are placed in a situation in which their privacy will also be impeded. Moreover, they may encounter situations in which they should have turned off their body cameras and unintentionally capture events that will later be used in cases. Or, they may be held liable in cases where wiretap laws preclude the taping of certain incidents without the consent of all parties. Officers are also placed at risk because of health and safety concerns tied to wearing body cameras. Specifically, they are susceptible to neck injuries as a result of the weight of the camera and potential electrical shock.[27] Finally, the financial investment involved in requiring officers to wear body cameras has been prohibitive in some jurisdictions ($800 to $1,000 per camera).[28]

Racial/ethnic minorities responding to concerns tied to police-public encounters have largely been driven by an increased vigilance about how to handle encounters with the police. On the individual level, parents have been having "the talk" with their children, especially their young, black, males. This activity typically involve sitting down with your children and outlining the proper way to handle encounters with the police. National organizations such as the National Association for the Advancement of Colored People (NAACP), the National Association of Black Law Enforcement Officers, the American Civil Liberties Union (ACLU), and others have put out "how to" or "what to do" guides to increase the potential for harmless and positive encounters with the police.

The PPCS data provide a glimpse of the nature of police stops from the view of those being stopped. Despite the long history of concerns regarding police stops, the numbers suggest there is much to be done to achieve the police legitimacy that police agencies desire. The use of body cameras and the "talks" tied to handling police-citizen encounters represent two ways in which society and parents have tried to minimize negative encounters with the police. Another area of concern related to police misconduct has been police killings.

POLICE MISCONDUCT: POLICE KILLINGS OF RACIAL/ETHNIC MINORITIES

BRIEF HISTORY

The killing of minorities by law enforcement personnel most certainly has its roots in the colonial era. Black slaves were the subject of plantation justice at the hands of their masters—who served as the first line of enforcement—throughout the slave era.[29] This system provided slave masters with absolute power to mete out punishments with impunity. Over time, slave masters and local jurisdictions came together to ensure the survival of the slave system through the development of codes that regulated the lives of slaves. These slave codes included an abundance of restrictions on the slave population and specified how to treat every aspect of slave behavior. These codes included many statutes that allowed jurisdictions to execute slaves not only for insurrections but also for actions such "burning a house, bar, stable, outhouse, corn or hay crops."[30] These slave codes were enforced by slave patrols, which are believed to be the first form of policing in the United States.[31]

CONTEMPORARY SITUATION

Reminiscent of an earlier period in American history, the so-called "national police crisis of 2014–2016" involving the killing of young black males at the hands of the police garnered international attention.[32] While the sporadic killing of blacks by the police had attracted national attention in the past, the numerous killings of black men often captured on video created a furor over police use of deadly force, especially involving black men. Seeking to determine the extent of police killing of citizens in general, observers turned to the national statistics kept by the Federal Bureau of Investigation (FBI). Unfortunately, the FBI data are woefully inadequate, and even former FBI director James Comey admitted as much, stating that the lack of information on police killings of citizens is "ridiculous" and "embarrassing." At some point, he further acknowledged that the United States likely has better data on cinematic ticket sales than police killings. Table 1.2 provides the FBI figures on police killings. It suggests that, from 2008 to 2014, there were no more than five hundred killings per year by the police.

In the wake of the killing of Michael Brown in Ferguson, Missouri, on August 9, 2014, the public and journalists began to question the accuracy of the FBI figures. In fact, two newspapers, the *Washington Post* and the *Guardian,* decided to collect more complete data on police shootings in America. Their efforts involved the use of news reports, public records, Internet databases, and original reporting (based on Freedom of Information Act requests). This approach resulted in conflicting numbers regarding the FBI official statistics on police killings and their more detailed numbers. The *Washington Post* data from 2015 uncovered 990 citizens killed by the police. Similarly, the *Guardian* found that, in 2015, there were 1,134 citizens killed by the police.[33] These conflicting numbers were just the beginning of the controversy. As more unarmed citizens were being killed at the hands of law enforcement, journalists began to examine the data in more detail.

Detailed analyses of the *Guardian*'s 2015 data show that the racial distribution of police killings was as follows: 29 percent of the victims of police killings were African American, 14 percent Latino, and 50 per-

Table 1.2. Justifiable Homicides by the Police, 2008 to 2014

Year	Number of justifiable homicides
2008	378
2009	414
2010	397
2011	404
2012	426
2013	471
2014	444

Source: FBI, ucr.fbi.gov/crime-in-the-u.s/2014/crime-in-the-u.s.-2014/offenses-known-to-law-enforcement/expanded-homicide.

cent non-Hispanic whites. Of particular significance to the mounting concerns regarding police killings was whether officers were killing unarmed suspects. The *Guardian*'s research found that 32 percent of the African Americans who were killed by the police were unarmed. The percentage of unarmed police killings involving Latinos was also elevated at 25 percent, while unarmed whites were killed at the lowest rate (15 percent). Considering these figures, writers from the *Guardian* noted that, in the first twenty-four days of 2015, there were 59 people killed by the police in the United States, while in the last twenty-four *years,* 55 people had been killed by the police in the United Kingdom.[34] Admittedly, there are differences between these two countries; nonetheless, the stark differences in the number of citizens dying at the hands of law enforcement in the United States is cause for concern. Observers of police killings in the United States might argue that, because of the ever-present risk that law enforcement officers face on a daily basis, the current level of police killings might be justified. To investigate this supposition, one needs to examine how many police officers are killed and assaulted each year. These figures can be found in the FBI's annual Uniform Crime Reports. In addition, the Officer Down Memorial Page website provides an unofficial count of the number of police-officer deaths in the line of duty.

OFFICERS KILLED IN THE LINE OF DUTY

The FBI data on officers killed in the line of duty do not appear to justify the number of police killings of citizens. In 2015, there were 41 police officers feloniously killed in the line of duty. This was preceded by the following three years in which 51 (2014), 27 (2013), and 48 (2012) officers were killed in the line of duty. The data from the Officer Down Memorial Page is a bit more extensive and includes deaths that might have been accidental or were related to 9/11 illnesses. This data source provides the following alternative numbers: 2012 (140), 2013 (127), 2014 (151), and 2015 (141). It is likely that these numbers will increase in 2016 as a result of the increasing number of retaliatory attacks on police that followed police killings across the nation. One such attack occurred in Baton Rouge, Louisiana, in July 2016, and left 3 officers dead. Another key statistic to determine whether there might be some evidence as to why American police might kill civilians is the number of officers assaulted in the line of duty. One thing is clear from the FBI data on this subject: there are a substantial number of officers assaulted every year. In 2012, there were 52,901 officers assaulted in the line of duty. The subsequent years leading up to the present were quite similar in numbers: 2013 (49,851), 2014 (48,315), and 2015 (50,212). Taken together, these figures really don't answer the question whether the annual number of citizens killed by the police is justified—based on the number of officers killed and assaulted in the line of duty. At best, the data suggests that more research needs to be conducted to determine the full set of circumstances under which citizens are killed by police officers.

MAKING SENSE OF THE CURRENT STATE OF POLICE MISCONDUCT

Similar to other contentious issues tied to the American Justice system, there tend to be multiple narratives proffered to make sense of the existing state of things. Police misconduct is no different. On one side of the discussion, there are scholars who quickly point to the Uniform Crime Reports' annual arrest statistics as providing evidence for why officers are more likely to profile and kill minorities—especially African Americans and Hispanics.[35] Current homicide statistics, for example, show that blacks represent 51.1 percent of the arrests for homicides in the United States.[36] In addition, they represent 53.5 percent of robberies and 29.5 percent of burglaries.[37] This trend has persisted for decades and has left many minority neighborhoods unsafe and the focus of elevated levels of police attention.[38] Thus, it is in these same neighborhoods where the majority of the racial profiling and killings of minorities by the police occur.

This persistent finding has led some scholars to look beyond racism as the reason for the increased encounters between minorities and the police. More specifically, a consistent lineage of scholars including William Wilbanks, Robert Regoli, Heather MacDonald, John Paul Wright, and Matt DeLisi have all pointed to the overrepresentation of racial/ethnic minorities in crime as being the reason why they are often on the receiving end of negative encounters with the police.[39] Wright and DeLisi argue that, because of these increased interactions, research studies have found race differences in "the use of disrespect towards the police, use of suspicious behavior toward police, holding of negative attitudes toward police, perceptions that police act improperly, and perceptions that police behave improperly during traffic stops."[40] In short, these scholars believe that it is the behavior of racial/ethnic minorities and the level of crime in their communities that have produced racial/ethnic disparities in the AJS—that often begin with disparate arrests.

On the other side of the debate, scholars have made sense of police misconduct targeted at racial/ethnic minorities based on racial bias being at the heart of the issue.[41] This narrative relies on the belief that racism has long influenced outcomes in the AJS. At the core of this narrative is the sentiment that there is a lingering belief, originating in slave-era America, that racial/ethnic minorities—especially African Americans—are innately criminal and violent.[42] This continuing legacy has produced stereotypical views of African Americans in general—but males in particular.[43] The aforementioned legacy has produced fearsome stereotypical images of African Americans that are etched in the minds of justice-system officials, including the police, who tend to be hypervigilant when interacting with African Americans. Powerful research both by noted communications scholars and by psychologists have supported the perpetuation of stereotypes by mass media and the influential role that stereotypes can play in the actions of criminal justice professionals.

Scholars from multiple disciplines have analyzed the content of assorted types of media to determine the nature of the presentation of racial/ethnic groups. This illuminating research has analyzed television shows and news programs. Mary Beth Oliver produced an early study that analyzed the popular reality show *Cops* to determine, among other things, the representation of racial/ethnic minorities in the show as both offenders and police officers. Oliver found that "white characters more often appeared as police officers than they did as criminal suspects, whereas black and Hispanic characters more frequently appeared as criminal suspects than they did as police officers."[44] Additional researchers have studied crime dramas, including *NYPD Blue* and *Law and Order,* and found that "Minorities are disproportionately more likely to be cast as offenders than their white counterparts. This is especially true on 'Law and Order,' where African American offenders are 1.75 times as likely to be shown in handcuffs then white offenders, almost 5 times as likely to be shown as an offender than a victim, and 3.57 times as likely to be shown as an offender than an attorney."[45]

In addition to examining the depictions of racial/ethnic groups, media scholars have also examined whether the viewing of such programs influences perceptions of fear. Sarah Eschholz, for example, found that "the racial composition of television offenders significantly increased fear of crime."[46] Using both student and police professionals as subjects, psychologists have also weighed in on whether stereotypes have the power to influence actions. Joshua Correll and colleagues conducted a series of simulations to determine whether the decision to shoot in certain situations "was influenced by the stereotypic association between African Americans and violence."[47] In this particular research, the authors found: "In four studies, participants showed a bias to shoot African American targets more rapidly and/or more frequently than white targets. The implications of this bias are clear and disturbing. Even more worrisome is the suggestion that mere knowledge of the cultural stereotype, which depicts African Americans as violent, may produce Shooter Bias, and that even African Americans demonstrate the bias."[48]

This body of research provides some evidence that the stereotypical imagery that dates to the slave era not only persists but also likely does play a role in how racial/ethnic minorities are treated in encounters with law enforcement. It clearly helps to make sense of the most recent crisis of high-profile police killings that likely began with the killing of Trayvon Martin in Sanford, Florida (killed by a neighborhood watch person), and increased in significance with the killing of Michael Brown in Ferguson, Missouri, and additional tragic deaths in Baltimore, New York, Baton Rouge, and other cities across the United States. Almost daily, from 2014 to 2016, the news media coverage was punctuated with stories of police officers killing suspects. The cell-phone videos of these incidents regularly went viral on the Internet and sparked outrage among citizens in general, but African Americans in particular.

The outrage among African Americans resulted in the social activism that led to the development of the Black Lives Matter movement in 2012. This movement describes its purpose as "an ideological and political intervention in a world where Black lives are systematically and intentionally targeted for demise. It is an affirmation of Black folks' contributions to this society, our humanity, and our resilience in the face of deadly oppression."[49] At its height, the movement led protests after the killing of Trayvon Martin by George Zimmerman, who was serving as a neighborhood watch person, and other black men who were killed at the hands of law enforcement. Since its founding, the movement has expanded its focus. Whenever there is a controversial act committed against black citizens by the police, the Black Lives Matter followers engage in organized protests. Most of the protests have been peaceful, but some of the demonstrations have turned violent. The movement was countered by the founding of the Blue Lives Matter movement in 2014, following the Michael Brown killing. The mission of this movement is "to honor and recognize the actions of law enforcement, strengthen public support, and provide much-needed resources to law enforcement officers and their families."[50] These two organizations have become focal points on both sides of the debate surrounding police misconduct.

CONCLUSION

The United States has a long history of police agencies mistreating racial/ethnic minorities. This has been the case since the slave era, when masters dictated every aspect of the lives of slaves—including the distribution of plantation justice. This also involved the formation of slave patrols, which were among the first official forms of policing. While much has changed since the colonial period, it is apparent that in the twenty-first century there remains a lot of work to be done to reduce or eliminate the encounters that produce police misconduct perpetrated against racial/ethnic minorities. Despite the continuing concerns, some policy initiatives are promising.

During the Obama administration, the Attorney General's Office under the leadership of Loretta Lynch made a concerted effort to negotiate consent decrees with troubled police agencies across the country. These consent decrees mandated training and other corrective actions to reduce the potential for additional instances of police misconduct. More recently, President Trump's attorney general, Jeff Sessions, has moved to revisit these consent decrees. Sessions believes that such decrees not only hurt the morale of police officers, but also reduce their willingness to engage in certain crucial policing activities that impact on their effectiveness.[51] Pointing to the fourteen cities under consent decree, including Baltimore; Ferguson, Missouri; and Cleveland, Sessions believes that the notable increase in crime in these cities is directly tied to the monitoring involved with the decrees.[52] The effectiveness of the consent decrees has not been evaluated. Thus, it is possible that, with the current negative sentiment towards them, there will be a move away from them before any long-term evaluative studies are conducted. There has been little formal discussion from the current administration about the use of body cameras. With recent body-camera research providing evidence that "police officers speak significantly less respectfully to black than to white community members in everyday traffic stops, even after controlling for officer race, infraction severity, stop location, and stop outcome,"[53] it remains a promising way in which to monitor police behavior. Despite this recent finding, it remains to be seen whether such technology—that involves additional scrutiny of the actions of police officers—will be supported under the Trump administration.

Another issue addressed by the Obama administration was the pursuit of better data tied to policing—something mentioned in the well-received *President's Task Force on 21st Century Policing* released in 2015. Currently, the FBI is in the process of overhauling its data-collection system on police killings. Along with data on police shootings, deaths that result from the use of Tasers and any other form of force will also be tracked.[54] In addition, the Department of Justice's Community-Oriented Policing Division started the Police Data Initiative. This initiative includes the collection of data on traffic stops, searches, and other activities from more than 130 police departments. The collection of such data offers the opportunity to provide additional insights to assist in resolving current and future police-misconduct issues.

It will take continued vigilance to maintain the balance between public safety, civil rights, and overall accountability. This has always been a challenge—especially in underprivileged racial/ethnic minority communities that have been targeted for additional police attention because of the high crime rates in such areas. Despite the high levels of crime, like all citizens, racial/ethnic minorities deserve respectful and competent policing.

NOTES

1. Samuel Walker, Cassia Spohn, and Miriam DeLone, *The Color of Justice: Race, Ethnicity and Crime in America*, 5th ed. (Boston: Cengage Learning, 2018).

2. Adolphe Quetelet, *Adolphe Quetelet's Research on the Propensity for Crime at Different Ages* (Cincinnati, OH: Anderson Publishing, 1984).

3. Shaun L. Gabbidon, *Criminological Perspectives on Race and Crime*, 3rd ed. (New York: Routledge, 2015).

4. Charles Booth, *Life and Labour of the People in London*, vol. 8. (London: Macmillan and Co., 1903).

5. W. E. B. Du Bois, *The Philadelphia Negro: A Social Study* (1899; rpt. Philadelphia: University of Pennsylvania Press, 1996); Shaun L. Gabbidon, *W. E. B. Du Bois on Crime and Justice: Laying the Foundations of Sociological Criminology* (London: Routledge, 2015); Earl Wright, *The First American School of Sociology: W. E. B. Du Bois and the Atlanta Sociological Laboratory* (New York: Routledge, 2017).

6. Martin Bulmer, *The Chicago School of Sociology: Institutionalization, Diversity, and the Rise of Sociological Research* (Chicago: University of Chicago Press, 1986).

7. Shaun L. Gabbidon and Helen Taylor Greene, *Race and Crime*, 4th ed. (Thousand Oaks, CA: Sage Publications, 2016); Walker, Spohn, and DeLone, *The Color of Justice.*

8. Gloria J. Browne-Marshall, *Race, Law, and American Society: 1607–Present*, 2nd ed. (New York: Routledge, 2014).

9. Katheryn Russell-Brown, *The Color of Crime* (New York: New York University Press, 2009), 14–15.

10. Brian L. Withrow, *Racial Profiling: From Rhetoric to Reason* (Upper Saddle River, NJ: Prentice Hall, 2006).

11. Charles R. Epp, Steven Maynard-Moody, and Donald P. Haider-Markel, *Pulled Over: How Police Stops Define Race and Citizenship* (Chicago: University of Chicago Press, 2014).

12. Deborah J. Schildkraut, "The Dynamics of Public Opinion on Ethnic Profiling after 9/11: Results from a Survey Experiment," *American Behavioral Scientist* 53 (2009): 61–79; Kelly Welch, "Middle Eastern Terrorist Stereotypes and Anti-Terror Policy Support: The Effect of Perceived Minority Threat," *Race and Justice* 6, no. 2 (2016): 117–45.

13. Shaun L. Gabbidon, George E. Higgins, and Matthew Nelson, "Public Support for Racial Profiling in Airports: Results from a Statewide Poll," *Criminal Justice Policy Review* 23, no. 2 (2012): 254–69.

14. Lynn Langton and Matthew R. Durose, *Police Behavior During Traffic and Street Stops, 2011* (Washington, DC: U.S. Department of Justice, Office of Justice Programs, Bureau of Justice Statistics, 2013).

15. Ibid.

16. Ibid.

17. Ibid., 3.

18. American Civil Liberties Union, *Racial Disparities in Florida Safety Belt Enforcement* (2016), www.aclu.org/report/racial-disparities-florida-safety-belt-law-enforcement.

19. Langton and Durose, *Police Behavior*, 6.

20. Michael Douglas White, *Police Officer Body-Worn Cameras: Assessing the Evidence* (Office of Justice Programs, U.S. Department of Justice, 2014), 11.

21. Ibid.

22. Jennifer Gibbs, Timothy Servinsky, Nicole Sturges, and Stephanie L. Wehnau, *Pennsylvanians' Perceptions of Police Body Worn Cameras: Research brief* (2017), csr.hbg.psu.edu/Portals/44/Research%20Brief_Body%20Cams_Feb%202017_Final.pdf.

23. White, *Police Officer Body-Worn Cameras.*

24. Ibid.

25. Ibid.

26. Ibid., 7.

27. Ibid., 8.

28. Ibid., 9.

29. A. Leon Higginbotham, *In the Matter of Color: Race and the American Legal Process. The Colonial Period* (London: Oxford University Press, 1980); Russell-Browne, *The Color of Crime.*

30. Higginbotham, *In the Matter of Color,* 132.

31. Sally E. Hadden, *Slave Patrols: Law and Violence in Virginia and the Carolinas* (Cambridge, MA: Harvard University Press, 2001).

32. Walker, Spohn, and DeLone, *The Color of Justice.*

33. Jon Swaine, Oliver Laughland, Jamiles Lartey, and Ciara McCarthy, "Young Black Men Killed by US Police at Highest Rate in Year of 1,134 Deaths." *Guardian,* December 31, 2015, www.theguardian.com/us-news/2015/dec/31/the-counted-police-killings-2015-young-black-men.

34. Jamiles Lartey, "By the Numbers: US Police Kill More in Days Than Other Countries Do in Years," *Guardian,* June 9, 2015, www.theguardian.com/us-news/2015/jun/09/the-counted-police-killings-us-vs-other-countries.

35. Matt DeLisi, "Where Is the Evidence for Racial Profiling?" *Journal of Criminal Justice* 39 (2011): 461–62; Heather MacDonald, *The War on Cops: How the New Attack on Law and Order Makes Everyone Less Safe* (New York: Encounter Books, 2016).

36. Uniform Crime Reports, *Crime in the United States, 2015,* ucr.fbi.gov/crime-in-the-u.s/2015/crime-in-the-u.s.-2015/tables/table-43.

37. Uniform Crime Reports, *Crime in the United States.*

38. Darnell F. Hawkins, Jerome B. McKean, Norman A. White, and Christine Martin, *Roots of African American Violence: Ethnocentrism, Cultural Diversity, and Racism* (Boulder, CO: Lynne Rienner Publishers, 2017).

39. Matt DeLisi and Bob Regoli, "Race, Conventional Crime, and Criminal Justice: The Declining Importance of Skin Color," *Journal of Criminal Justice* 27, no. 6 (1999): 549–57; William Wilbanks, *The Myth of a Racist Criminal Justice System* (Monterey, CA: Brooks/Cole, 1987); DeLisi, *Where Is the Evidence?*; MacDonald, *The War on Cops*; Delisi and Regoli, "Race, Conventional Crime, and Criminal Justice"; John Wright and Matt DeLisi, *Conservative Criminology: A Call to Restore Balance to the Social Sciences* (Abingdon, UK: Routledge, 2015).

40. Wright and DeLisi, *Conservative Criminology,* 66.

41. Coramae Richey Mann, *Unequal Justice: A Question of Color* (Bloomington: Indiana University Press, 1993).

42. Hawkins et al., *Roots of African American Violence*; Fox Butterfield, *All God's Children: The Bosket Family and the American Tradition of Violence.* (New York: Vintage, 1995).

43. Mary Beth Oliver, "Portrayals of Crime, Race, and Aggression in 'Reality-Based' Police Shows: A Content Analysis," *Journal of Broadcasting & Electronic Media* 38, no. 2 (1994): 179–92; Lincoln Quillian and Devah Pager, "Black Neighbors, Higher Crime? The Role of Racial Stereotypes in Evaluations of Neighborhood Crime," *American Journal of Sociology* 107, no. 3 (2001): 717–67; Kelly Welch, "Black Criminal Stereotypes and Racial Profiling," *Journal of Contemporary Criminal Justice* 23, no. 3 (2007): 276–88.

44. Oliver, "Portrayals of Crime," 186.

45. Sarah Eschholz, "The Color of Prime-Time Justice: Racial Characteristics of Television Offenders," *Racial Issues in Criminal Justice: The Case of African Americans* (2003): 173–74.

46. Sarah Eschholz, "Racial Composition of Television Offenders and Viewers' Fear of Crime," *Critical Criminology* 11, no. 1 (2002): 53.

47. Joshua Correll, Bernadette Park, Charles M. Judd, and Bernd Wittenbrink, "The Police Officer's Dilemma: Using Ethnicity to Disambiguate Potentially Threatening Individuals," *Journal of Personality and Social Psychology* 83, no. 6 (2002): 1314.

48. Ibid., 1327.

49. Black Lives Matter, "We Affirm That All Black Lives Matter," blacklivesmatter.com /guiding-principles/.

50. Blue Lives Matter, "About Us," bluelivesmatter.blue/organization/.

51. Andrew Kaczynski, "Attorney General Jeff Sessions: Consent Decrees 'Can Reduce Morale of the Police Officers,'" *CNN*, April 14, 2017, www.cnn.com/2017/04/14/politics /kfile-sessions-consent-decrees/index.html.

52. Sheryl Gay Stolberg and Eric Lichtblau, "Sweeping Federal Review Could Affect Consent Decrees Nationwide," *New York Times*, April 3, 2017, www.nytimes.com/2017/04 /03/us/justice-department-jeff-sessions-baltimore-police.html.

53. Rob Voigt, Nicholas P. Camp, Vinodkumar Prabhakaran, William L. Hamilton, Rebecca C. Hetey, Camilla M. Griffiths, David Jurgens, Dan Jurafsky, and Jennifer L. Eberhardt, "Language from Police Body Camera Footage Shows Racial Disparities in Officer Respect," *Proceedings of the National Academy of Sciences* (2017), www.pnas.org /content/114/25/6521.

54. Kevin Johnson, "Feds to Begin Police Shooting Data Collection by 2017," *USA Today*, October 13, 2016, www.usatoday.com/story/news/politics/2016/10/13/police-shootings -data-justice-department/91997066/; Tom McCarthy, Jon Swaine, and Oliver Laughland, "FBI to Launch New System to Count People Killed by Police Officers." *Guardian*, December 8, 2015, www.theguardian.com/us-news/2015/dec/09/fbi-launch-new-system-count -people-killed-police-officers-the-counted.

RESIDENTIAL SEGREGATION IN THE TWENTY-FIRST CENTURY AND THE ROLE OF HOUSING POLICY

JACKELYN HWANG, ELIZABETH ROBERTO, AND JACOB S. RUGH

INTRODUCTION

Fifty years ago, landmark federal legislation passed in the United States prohibiting discrimination by race in housing and lending. Prior to these changes, mortgage lenders could legally refuse to issue loans to minority residents or to residents who sought to purchase homes in neighborhoods with racial minorities, a practice commonly known as "redlining." Moreover, racially oriented covenants that restricted the ownership and sale of homes to members of specific race groups were allowed, and landlords could legally refuse to rent to prospective tenants based on their race.

Many celebrated the passage of the 1968 Fair Housing Act and the 1975 Home Mortgage Disclosure Act, along with the additional legislation intended to advance racial equality in access to opportunities in education and the workplace, as key steps to alleviating racial inequality in the United States. Scholars have long considered residential segregation—the extent to which racial groups reside in distinct places—to be a key barrier to racial equality. Segregation not only prohibits informal social interaction and exposure between members of different race groups that can perpetuate racist attitudes, but it also facilitates unequal access to resources, opportunities, and institutions that can help advance individuals' social and economic mobility.[1] Douglas S. Massey and Nancy A. Denton's *American Apartheid* demonstrates that residential segregation exacerbates racial inequality by concentrating the effect of macrostructural changes, such as the large-scale decline of manufacturing, into areas densely populated by minority residents, who are disproportionately adversely affected by these economic changes.[2] Such concentrated economic effects, they argue, explain the decline in social and economic conditions of minority neighborhoods in urban areas during the decades following the passage of these legislative reforms.

Since the 1970s, the black-white high-school completion and life-expectancy gaps have decreased,[3] and the black middle class has grown substantially.[4] Surveys indicate that negative attitudes towards blacks have weakened and that whites are more willing to live with minorities compared to the 1970s.[5] The United States has also experienced a large rise in Latino and Asian populations since this time following immigration reforms passed during the mid-1960s. These reforms expanded immigration from Latin American and Asian countries, changing the racial and ethnic compositions of neighborhoods, cities, and towns across the country. Indeed, the prevalence of neighborhoods that are homogenously white has declined.[6]

Recent research examining trends in residential segregation since 1970 document substantial declines in black-white residential segregation, as well as the isolation of blacks from other race groups. Does this imply what Edward Glaeser and Jacob Vigdor call "the end of the segregated century"?[7]

Residential segregation remains a defining feature of the American landscape. Indeed, much has changed in the United States since the 1960s and 1970s when key legislative efforts aimed at reducing racial inequality passed, but traditional measures and methods for examining segregation overlook important aspects of the problem that characterize the metropolitan landscape in which we live in today. First, methods of measuring segregation that have dominated research for decades limit analysis to two-group comparisons, but considering multiple race groups together better captures the multiethnic composition of contemporary metropolitan areas. Second, traditional measures are generally aspatial—that is, a place may have the same level of segregation according to traditional measures over time, but the spatial ecology of the segregation may be very different. Third, most studies of segregation trends examine the separation of groups by race or by class, but, changing dynamics of the intersection of race and class necessitate studying the segregation of specific race and class groups, such as poor minorities and affluent whites.

Segregation has changed in form but still persists in the twenty-first century. Changes related to housing policy are associated with changes in segregation, including gentrification, the housing crisis during the Great Recession, and poverty deconcentration efforts in public housing policy. Here we present findings from recent research on these transformations to help explain why segregation persists despite these changes. Our results, combined with recent findings, explore the implications for housing policy in addressing residential segregation today.

TRENDS IN RESIDENTIAL SEGREGATION

In social science research, segregation is most often measured using the dissimilarity index. This index measures the extent to which two groups are evenly distributed across smaller spatial units, such as neighborhoods, within a larger aggregate unit, such as a city or metropolitan area. In essence, this measures the percentage of either group's population who would have to move for each smaller spatial unit to have the same composition of the groups as the larger aggregate unit. Another common measure used to examine a different feature of segregation is the isolation index, which captures the extent to which residents of a particular group are exclusively exposed to other residents of the same group. A score of zero on either index indicates low segregation, and a score of one on either index indicates that two groups live in completely separate neighborhoods.

Figure 2.1 shows the average dissimilarity index between blacks and whites and the isolation index for blacks from 1970 to 2010 for the one hundred largest metropolitan areas, based on their 2000 population. The averages are weighted by each metropolitan area's black population. The figure shows that, since 1970, the dissimilarity index between blacks and whites has decreased steadily, and the isolation index for blacks has exhibited parallel declines. Based on these trends, the segregation of blacks and whites is decreasingly a defining feature of the metropolitan landscape of the United States.

Several trends, however, have occurred during this time that implicate the need to reexamine segregation using new approaches. First, the

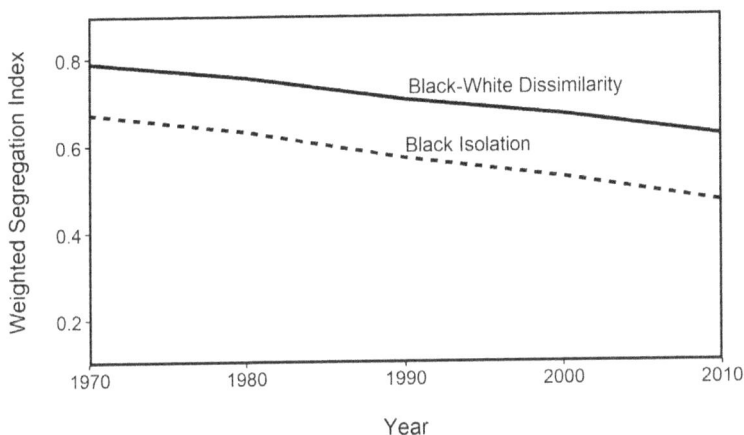

Figure 2.1. Black population-weighted average black-white dissimilarity and black isolation index for 100 largest metropolitan areas, 1970–2010. Calculations use data from the Longitudinal Tract Database (LTDB). Largest metropolitan areas based on population size in 2000. Blacks and whites include Hispanics in 1970.

racial composition of metropolitan areas across the country has transformed dramatically since the 1970s with the growth of immigrants. The passage of the 1965 Hart-Celler Act primarily removed a previous system of imposing quotas based on country of origin, thus opening the doors for immigrants from countries that were discriminated against in the prior system. Figure 2.2 depicts how much the ethno-racial composition of large U.S. metropolitan areas has changed since this period. The figure shows the growing average share, weighted by the total populations of metropolitan areas, of ethno-racial minorities over time across the one hundred largest metropolitan areas with the declining share of non-Hispanic whites. While the share of Hispanics[8] and Asians has grown, the share of blacks has remained relatively steady over time.

Although the Latino and Asian population grew over this time, their segregation from whites has been relatively steady, and these levels are substantially below the segregation levels for blacks. Their isolation from other groups, however, has increased, particularly for Hispanics, reaching similar levels as blacks by 2010.[9] Figure 2.3 displays the average dissimilarity indexes for blacks and whites, Hispanics and whites, and Asians and whites, as well as the average isolation indexes for blacks,

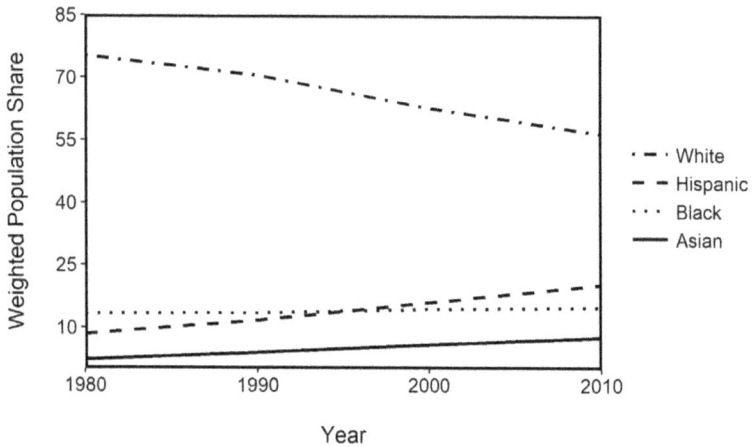

Figure 2.2. Total population-weighted average composition for 100 largest metropolitan areas, 1980–2010. Calculations use data from the Longitudinal Tract Database (LTDB). Largest metropolitan areas based on population size in 2000.

Hispanics, and Asians across the one hundred largest metropolitan areas from 1980 to 2010. Averages for each group index are weighted by the black, Hispanic, and Asian populations, respectively.

While these trends show moderate levels of segregation for Hispanics and Asians, they do not provide information on the degree of segregation considering all groups at once. Most research assessing segregation employs the dissimilarity index and compares two groups at a time. Given the substantial presence of Latinos and Asians in the U.S., two-group comparisons overlook the increasingly complex patterns of racial segregation that characterize metropolitan areas today.[10] A measure that considers all major ethno-racial groups simultaneously can shed more light on the structure of segregation in the contemporary metropolis.

Second, there has been a major shift in the racial and class structure of central cities and suburbs in many metropolitan areas over this period. Central cities during the 1960s and 1970s experienced large-scale population declines and accompanying socioeconomic declines as middle- and upper-income, predominantly white residents continued to move to the suburbs. In recent decades, however, there has been a rising trend of socioeconomic increases in many neighborhoods across large central cities and socioeconomic decreases in many suburban areas.[11]

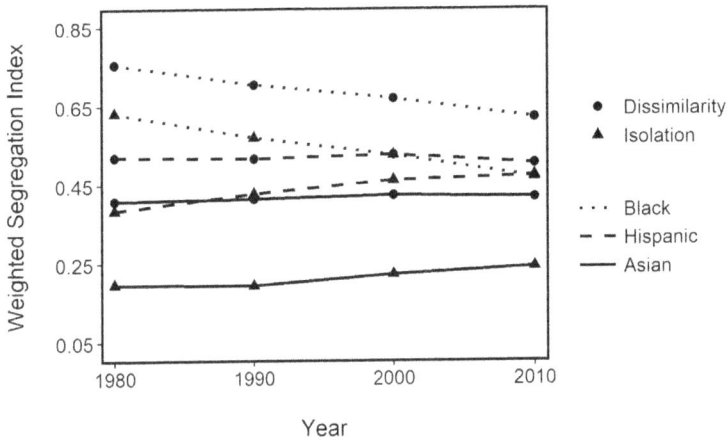

Figure 2.3. Minority group population-weighted average dissimilarity and isolation indices for 100 largest metropolitan areas, 1980–2010. Calculations use data from the Longitudinal Tract Database (LTDB). Largest metropolitan areas based on population size in 2000.

These trends are associated with the rise and spread of gentrification—the process by which low-income central city neighborhoods experience an influx of middle- and upper-class residents and substantial reinvestment, the increasing suburbanization of minorities, and changing settlement patterns of immigrants. Whereas traditional models of immigrant settlement depict immigrants arriving to the urban core and moving to the suburbs as they gain economic mobility, research shows that immigrant groups are increasingly moving directly to the suburbs, forming "ethnoburbs."[12]

Altogether, these changes have restructured the ethno-racial compositions of central cities and suburbs. Figure 2.4 illustrates the changing population-weighted average ethno-racial compositions of the central cities and suburbs across the one hundred largest metropolitan areas from 1980 to 2010. Both cities and suburbs have experienced substantial decreases in their shares of whites. In the suburbs, the share of blacks, Hispanics, and Asians has increased, while central cities have seen increases in their shares of both Hispanics and Asians. Further, Hispanics have become the largest minority population in both cities and suburbs.

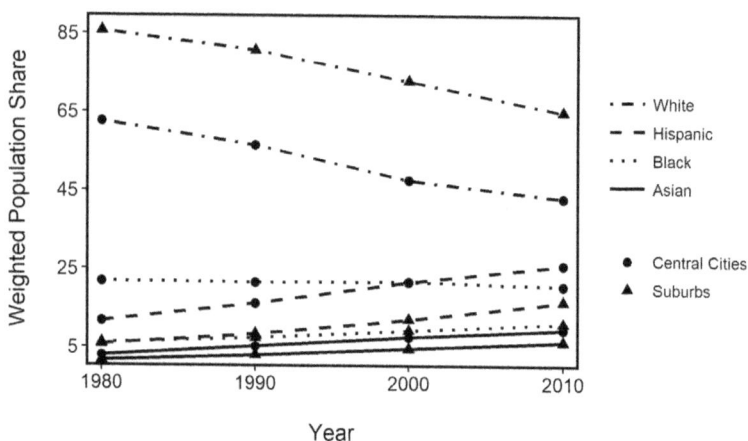

Figure 2.4. Total population-weighted average ethnoracial composition for central cities and suburbs across 100 largest metropolitan areas, 1980–2010. Calculations use data from the Longitudinal Tract Database (LTDB). Largest metropolitan areas based on population size in 2000.

Third, income inequality has increased overall for both black and white families. Using the Gini index—a widely used measure of inequality ranging from zero to one that captures the extent to which the income distribution deviates from the hypothetical distribution in which all families have equal incomes, Sean F. Reardon and Kendra Bischoff find that the Gini index increased from .344 to .384 among white families and from .376 to .436 for black families from 1970 to 2000 across the one hundred metropolitan areas with the largest populations in 2000.[13] Thus, income inequality grew more rapidly for black families—a reflection of the growth of the black middle class during this period.

Related to this trend is the growth in residential segregation by income *within* these race groups. In their study, Reardon and Bischoff measure income segregation using the innovative rank-order information theory index, which measures the ratio of variation in income ranks within neighborhoods (census tracts) to the overall variation in income ranks in a metropolitan area. Income ranks, or percentiles, rather than actual income amounts, are useful because they do not change with changes in the income distribution and are thus comparable over time and across metropolitan areas.[14] Using this measure,

Reardon and Bischoff find that income segregation also increased from 1970 to 2000 and at a much faster rate for blacks compared to whites, particularly during the 1970s and 1980s.[15] These patterns indicate that lower-income black families are increasingly living in separate neighborhoods from affluent blacks.

EXAMINING SEGREGATION IN THE TWENTY-FIRST CENTURY

These trends suggest that we can better understand the structure of segregation today by reexamining segregation in the following ways: assessing multiple ethno-racial groups rather than two-group comparisons, examining different patterns between the central cities and suburbs of metropolitan areas, and considering specific groups identified by both race and class. The measures of segregation that are traditionally used have mathematical properties that limit our ability to examine segregation in these ways. We employ Elizabeth Roberto's measure of segregation—the divergence index—to assess these various aspects of segregation today.[16] Details on calculating the index are in the appendix of this chapter.

The divergence index measures the difference between the composition of groups within a smaller spatial unit, such as neighborhoods, relative to the composition of a large aggregate spatial unit, such as a city or metropolitan area. Thus, it is a measure of how evenly the groups are distributed across space, similar to the dissimilarity index, and more than two groups can be compared at the same time. An additional advantageous property of the divergence index is that it is decomposable. In other words, we can assess components of the measure, such as the degree to which segregation is occurring within or between cities and suburbs. A recent study by Daniel T. Lichter, Domenico Parisi, and Michael C. Taquino demonstrates that, despite overall declines in the segregation of blacks and whites, the black-white segregation has increased *between* municipalities while it declined *within* municipalities from 1990 to 2010.[17] In other words, segregation between blacks and whites has shifted to a different level of geography than in the past: Whereas blacks and whites once lived separately across neighborhoods, they are increasingly living in separate towns, particularly in the suburbs. While Lichter and colleagues decompose an index of diversity, rather than evenness, to assess how the scale of segregation has shifted over time, their study demonstrates the usefulness of examining the components of segregation.[18]

For our purposes, we also examine trends of segregation that consider the intersection of race and class, specifically the segregation of poor residents of each ethno-racial group from nonpoor residents and the segregation of white affluent residents from nonaffluent residents. Given the growth of income segregation particularly for blacks,[19] the growing isolation of Hispanics and Asians,[20] and the continued rise of Latino and Asian immigrants, we expect that poor, minority residents may be becoming increasingly segregated from other groups in the twenty-first century. Further, we suspect that the growth of multiethnic suburbs may lead to patterns of white flight among the affluent within the suburbs further to the "exurban" fringe.

We report measures of segregation across the one hundred largest metropolitan areas with central cities using the divergence index. We use data from the Longitudinal Tract Database for the 2000 and 2010 U.S. Census and American Community Survey (ACS) five-year estimates from 2010 to 2014 (hereafter, 2010). Metropolitan areas are based on the 2009 metropolitan divisions defined by the U.S. Census Bureau, and central cities are defined as the central city, as designated by the U.S. Census Bureau, with the largest population in 2000 in a metropolitan area. The suburbs are defined as the remainder of the metropolitan division that is not part of the central city. We use census tracts based on 2010 U.S. Census boundaries as the smaller spatial unit of analysis.

MULTI-GROUP SEGREGATION

Figure 2.5 displays the average overall divergence indexes in 2000 and 2010 for multiple groupings of race groups across the one hundred largest metropolitan areas and weighted by the total populations of the metropolitan areas. When we examine the standard pairings—blacks and whites, Hispanics and whites, and Asians and whites—we find that segregation decreased for blacks and whites but increased for the other pairs. These trends are similar to those found when using the dissimilarity index to measure segregation. When we consider multiple race groups together, we find that segregation levels are higher than if we

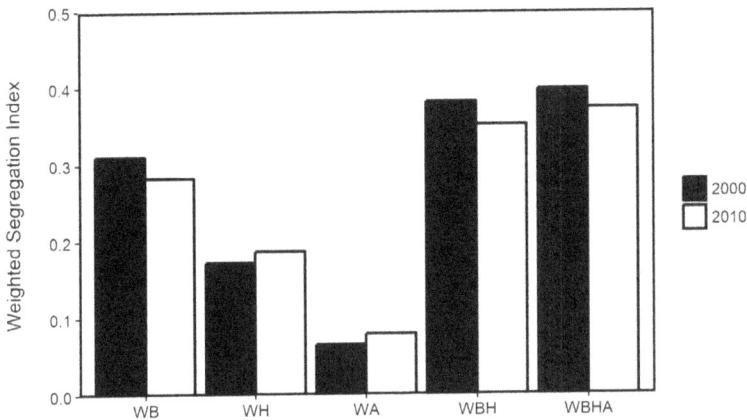

Figure 2.5. Total population-weighted average overall divergence for various groupings by race across 100 largest metropolitan areas, 2000–2010. Calculations use data from the Longitudinal Tract Database (LTDB). Largest metropolitan areas based on population size in 2000.

compare pairs of groups separately. These measures of segregation decrease from 2000 to 2010, but the levels still remain higher than if we had examined only two groups at a time.

THE SEGREGATION OF POOR MINORITY GROUPS
AND AFFLUENT WHITES

Next, we consider the intersection of race and class by examining the segregation of poor blacks, poor Hispanics, poor Asians, and poor whites from nonpoor residents of all ethno-racial groups, as well as affluent whites from all nonaffluent residents. We consider residents to be "poor" if they live in a household with an income below the poverty line in the 2000 Census or 2010–2014 ACS, respectively; we consider residents to be "affluent" if they live in a household with an income four times the poverty line.

Figure 2.6 presents trends in the population-weighted average overall divergence indexes in 2000 and 2010 for these race-class groups across the one hundred largest metropolitan areas.[21] The results show that the segregation of affluent whites from all nonaffluent residents is highest across all group pairings and that the segregation of poor blacks

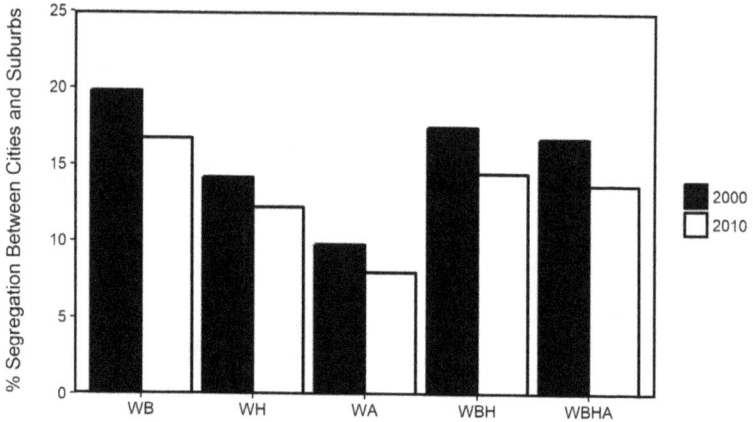

Figure 2.6. Total population-weighted average overall divergence for various groupings by race and class across 100 largest metropolitan areas, 2000–2010. Calculations use data from the Longitudinal Tract Database (LTDB) and 2010–14 American Community Survey (ACS). Largest metropolitan areas based on population size in 2000.

from all nonpoor residents is not far behind. Further, the average segregation level of poor Hispanics from all nonpoor residents increased substantially from 2000 to 2010, while the segregation of poor whites from all nonpoor residents and affluent whites from all nonaffluent residents barely changed.

SEGREGATION BETWEEN OR WITHIN CITIES AND SUBURBS
Next, we decompose the segregation measures for each of the groupings reviewed above and examine the share of total segregation of the metropolitan area that is occurring between the cities and suburbs relative to the share of segregation occurring within the cities and within the suburbs. Figure 2.7 reports trends in the population-weighted average share of overall divergence between the central city and suburbs across the metropolitan areas in 2000 and 2010, depicting race groups in the left panel and race and class groups in the right panel.

The charts indicate that most segregation occurs within cities and suburbs rather than between them. For example, about 20 percent of the overall segregation between whites and blacks occurs between cities

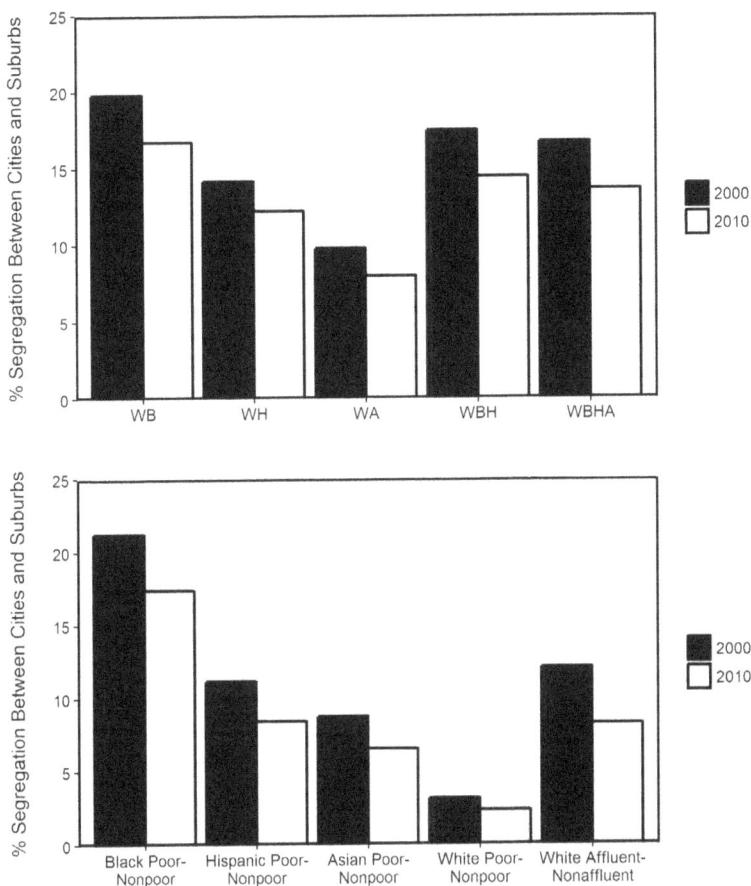

Figure 2.7. Total population-weighted average percentage of overall divergence between central city and suburbs for various groupings across 100 largest metropolitan areas, 2000–2010. Calculations use data from the Longitudinal Tract Database (LTDB) and the 2010–14 American Community Survey (ACS). Largest metropolitan areas based on population size in 2000.

and suburbs; the remainder occurs within cities and within suburbs. The highest share of the overall segregation that is between cities and suburbs is for segregation of blacks from whites and poor blacks from all nonpoor residents for each respective chart. This is consistent with classic depictions of the city-suburb divide. Nonetheless, the share of segregation occurring between subareas declined across all groupings from

2000 to 2010, indicating that each of the groupings became increasingly segregated within the cities and suburbs. Thus, the city-suburb divide along these group dimensions has weakened, pointing to the need to look at trends within cities and suburbs.

SEGREGATION IN THE CITIES AND SUBURBS

Figure 2.8 displays population-weighted average segregation levels within central cities and within suburbs for race groupings for the metropolitan areas from 2000 and 2010, and figure 2.9 is a similar figure for the race-class pairings. The results reveal that racial segregation, particularly for whites and blacks and for multiple race groups, is very high within central cities compared to segregation levels in the suburbs and compared to the segregation of whites from Hispanics and Asians. While the segregation of these groupings with the highest levels declined in central cities from 2000 to 2010, segregation levels increased slightly within the suburbs, particularly for Hispanic-white and Asian-white divergence indexes.

There are also important regional differences (not shown) that reflect different histories of migration among various racial and ethnic

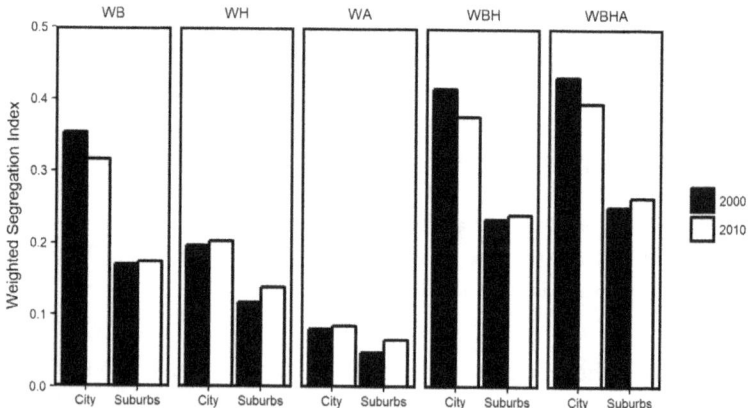

Figure 2.8. Total population-weighted average divergence within central cities and suburbs for various groupings by race across 100 largest metropolitan areas, 2000–2010. Calculations use data from the Longitudinal Tract Database (LTDB). Largest metropolitan areas based on population size in 2000.

groups. For example, in the West, segregation for whites and blacks and for multiple race groups within central cities is far lower than in other regions, while segregation between blacks and whites is much higher in the South in the suburbs. In addition, segregation between whites and Hispanics and between whites and Asians is much higher within central cities in the Northeast and West compared to other regions. In the suburbs, segregation between whites and Hispanics is also higher in these regions, while segregation between whites and Asians is only much higher in the West. Patterns for multiple race groups, nonetheless, are similar across regions.

Figure 2.9 shows that segregation between poor blacks and nonpoor residents is much higher in central cities relative to the suburbs and is much higher relative to the segregation of other poor race groups from nonpoor residents in both central cities and suburbs. Regional differences are also notable. Compared with other regions, in the West, segregation of poor blacks and nonpoor residents is much lower but is much higher for poor Asians in both central cities and suburbs. In the Northeast, segregation of poor Hispanics in central cities is much higher relative to other regions and is high in the suburbs in both the

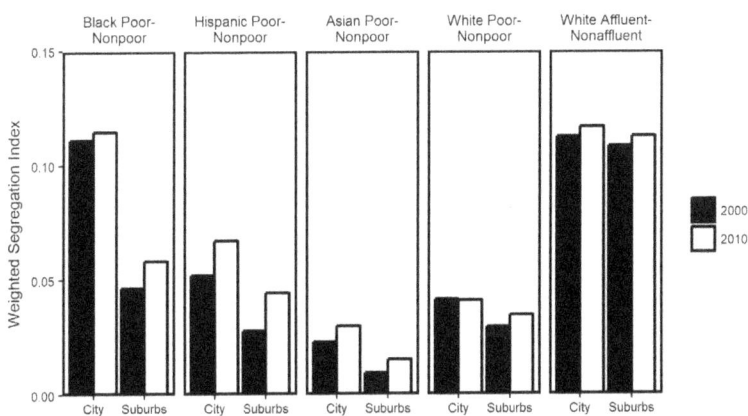

Figure 2.9. Total population-weighted average divergence within central cities and suburbs for various groupings by race and class across 100 largest metropolitan areas, 2000–2010. Calculations use data from the Longitudinal Tract Database (LTDB) and the 2010–14 American Community Survey (ACS). Largest metropolitan areas based on population size in 2000.

Northeast and West. Affluent whites, on the other hand, are highly segregated from nonaffluent residents in both central cities and suburbs. This trend is stronger in the South and West within cities. Poor residents of other race groups have higher levels of segregation in central cities than the suburbs, but the segregation levels are much lower than for poor blacks, with the exception of the West, where the segregation of poor Hispanics is higher. From 2000 to 2010, the average segregation levels increased in both central cities and the suburbs for all group pairs, especially in the Midwest, except for the segregation of poor whites from nonpoor residents, which remained relatively stagnant over the period. This trend is distinct from the one observed for race groupings in figure 2.8, indicating that the intersection of race and class appears to be increasingly important in separating where groups live within cities and the suburbs, while race on its own is becoming less significant. Overall, despite regional variation, the results highlight the increasing isolation of poor blacks in central cities and affluent whites in both central cities and the suburbs.

HOUSING AND THE "NEW SEGREGATION"

Explanations of the persistence of residential segregation in the post–civil rights era generally fall into three categories: socioeconomic differences, housing-market discrimination, and residential preferences. These factors have weakened over time, but our findings show that segregation is higher when we consider multiple race groups and that the share of the overall segregation of these groups is increasingly occurring within suburbs, though it remains much higher in central cities. Moreover, despite improving trends in segregation by race marked by declines from 2000 to 2010, our findings nonetheless show less progress when we consider race and class together. Our results show high levels of overall segregation of poor blacks from nonpoor residents and affluent whites from nonaffluent residents, with large increases in the segregation of poor Hispanics and Asians from nonpoor residents over the decade. These segregation levels are also increasing within both central cities and suburbs, implicating a new pattern of segregation characterized by isolated poor minorities and isolated affluent whites. Maria Krysan and Kyle Crowder argue that the dominant theories explaining the persistence of segregation are outdated and suggest the need to reconsider the assumptions of existing explanations for segregation, such as the assumption that all residents have the same experience and knowledge of neighborhoods when choosing where to live.[22]

The trends we show are likely related to major demographic and spatial shifts in housing that have taken place during the start of the twenty-first century. Next we discuss three major changes related to housing policy—gentrification, the housing crisis, and public housing policy aimed at the deconcentration of poverty—and review recent research that sheds light on how these shifts are related to recent trends in segregation.[23]

GENTRIFICATION

Several changes may be responsible for the increasing prevalence of gentrification in central cities, including shifts in preferences and policies that promote development, large declines in crime in central cities, and increases in high-skilled jobs across cities.[24] Gentrification—marked by the socioeconomic upgrading of previously low-income neighborhoods via the influx of high-income residents and investment—is often portrayed in public discourse and the media as a process of racial change, where primarily affluent white residents of higher socioeconomic status move into poor, minority neighborhoods. If this were occurring, we would expect to find decreases in the segregation between poor minorities from nonpoor residents and segregation between affluent whites from nonaffluent residents in central cities. Our results, however, reveal the opposite trends.

Recent evidence on gentrification provides insights on why we do not see such trends. First, national-level studies show that gentrification in predominantly minority neighborhoods is still a rare occurrence;[25] the primary trajectory of low-income, minority neighborhoods is persistent disadvantage.[26] While Lance Freeman and Tiancheng Cai find an increase in the share of majority-black tracts experiencing an influx of whites that is associated with gentrification from 2000 to 2010 compared to previous decades, this only occurred in about 10 percent of majority-black neighborhoods.[27] Another study finds that neighborhoods in Chicago with greater shares of minorities that are gentrifying or that are adjacent to gentrifying neighborhoods are slower to gentrify than neighborhoods with fewer minorities.[28] Additional findings suggest that the gentrifiers in predominantly minority neighborhoods tend to be middle-class minorities, rather than middle- or upper-class whites.[29] Thus, while the segregation between middle- and upper-class residents from poor residents may be decreasing with gentrification, evidence on the relationship between race and gentrification suggests that gentrification may not be integrating poor minorities.

Alternatively, our results may reflect the product of residential displacement—when the process of affluent whites moving into poor, minority neighborhoods results in the reconcentration of poor minorities and affluent whites as these previously low-income neighborhoods become unaffordable for their preexisting residents and other poor residents. Although residential displacement has been the center of controversies over gentrification, the empirical evidence on whether gentrification displaces residents has been mixed. While numerous qualitative accounts document the displacement of residents and neighborhood-level demographic changes imply the decline of low-income residents, quantitative studies that track individuals over time generally do not find that socioeconomically disadvantaged or minority residents move more from gentrifying neighborhoods compared to those who live in nongentrifying neighborhoods.[30] A recent study, however, finds that socioeconomically disadvantaged residents moving from majority-black gentrifying neighborhoods in Philadelphia do not necessarily move more than those in nongentrifying neighborhoods, but, when they do move, they move to more disadvantaged neighborhoods compared to other movers from nonblack and nongentrifying neighborhoods.[31] These findings suggest that gentrification may have disproportionately adverse effects on residents in poor black neighborhoods and may explain the trends in segregation that we observe.

THE HOUSING CRISIS

The housing boom and bust of the 2000s marks another major occurrence associated with housing policy that had a substantial effect on the residential landscape across metropolitan areas. The housing boom was marked by speculation and lax lending regulations. Whereas banks had historically denied racial minorities access to home mortgages through explicit discriminatory practices such as redlining, the changing structure of the lending industry to mortgage-backed securities during the 1980s and 1990s provided means for lenders and brokers to garner large profits from those at the lower end of the wealth distribution.[32]

This new landscape of lending provided racial minorities with increased access to homeownership, but such access to homeownership was marked by high-risk loans. Indeed, black and Hispanic borrowers were 2.8 and 2.3 times more likely, respectively, to receive high-rate subprime loans compared to white borrowers.[33] On the one hand, the increased access to homeownership for minorities should have reduced segregation levels between blacks, Hispanics, and whites, especially in the suburbs. Our findings show that overall racial segregation levels did decrease for these groups over the decade on average, but this generally occurred within central cities and increased slightly on average in the suburbs.

Further evidence shows that subprime loans were disproportionately concentrated in minority and mixed-race neighborhoods, especially in highly segregated cities and metropolitan areas.[34] In areas with high levels of racial segregation, large residential concentrations of minorities provided a spatial context in which subprime lenders could efficiently target minorities, who had limited access to wealth, alternative lending options, and information networks.[35] Further, most subprime loans were for refinancing rather than home purchases.[36] Thus, subprime lending practices instead concentrated risky loans in areas already concentrated with minorities and, therefore, did not necessarily reduce segregation.[37]

Nonetheless, borrowers with subprime loans were much more likely to default.[38] Thus, the collapse of the housing market resulted in the disproportionately negative fallout for racial minorities and minority neighborhoods. Minorities experienced higher foreclosure rates than whites, and foreclosures were concentrated in minority and mixed-race neighborhoods and more so in highly segregated metropolitan areas.[39] For Latinos, this generally occurred in suburbs experiencing high rates of Latino population growth.[40] To assess the effect of the housing crisis on segregation, Matthew Hall, Kyle Crowder, and Amy Spring analyzed national data on foreclosures from 2005 to 2009 and found that neighborhoods with high foreclosure rates experienced decreases in their shares of whites and increases in their shares of black and Hispanic residents.[41] They further found that the foreclosure crisis slowed declines in racial-segregation levels between blacks and whites and between Hispanics and whites, based on the dissimilarity index.[42]

PUBLIC HOUSING POLICY

As social scientists uncovered the detrimental effects of spatially concentrated poverty during the last quarter of the twentieth century, federal and local public housing policy priorities shifted towards poverty deconcentration and increased their focus on deconcentration at the beginning of the twenty-first century. Such policies include the demolition and transformation of high-rise public housing projects into mixed-income developments, placing project-based housing in higher-income neighborhoods, and an increase in housing choice vouchers, which provide low-income residents with subsidies to assist with rental payments. Given these changes and policy goals of deconcentrating the poor, we would expect that the segregation of poor residents from nonpoor residents would decrease. Our findings, however, indicate otherwise: average segregation levels of poor minority residents from nonpoor residents increased across the one hundred largest metropolitan areas in both the cities and the suburbs and remained relatively stable for poor whites from nonpoor residents.

The shifts in public housing policy were intended to support greater residential integration, but recent studies shed light on why they have had only weak effects in reducing racial and class segregation. In an analysis of the deconcentration of assisted housing units, which includes both vouchers and project-based units, and the concentration of poverty across the one hundred largest metropolitan areas from 1977 to 2008, Ann Owens finds declines in the concentration of poverty, particularly after 2000, but finds that the declines are only modest. In other words, poor residents continued to concentrate in the same neighborhoods over time, despite efforts to deconcentrate subsidized housing.[43] In a separate study on income segregation, Owens finds that, even as the segregation of poor residents declined modestly with the deconcentration of subsidized housing, affluent residents became more segregated.[44]

Additional research finds that poor residents, with or without housing-choice vouchers, disproportionately end up in poor neighborhoods of similar racial compositions from which they moved.[45] Among voucher holders, this pattern is particularly true for blacks and Latinos, who face greater disadvantages throughout the housing-market process, such as discrimination by landlords.[46] Residents moving as a result of the demolition of public housing and who receive vouchers often use their vouchers in the same neighborhood.[47] DeLuca and colleagues find that voucher holders have limited resources, information, and time to search for housing—in many ways a result of administrative barriers in the design of the program, such as excessive waiting times to receive vouchers that can take years followed by a short period to find a place.[48] Further, landlords often engage in strategic practices that attract and keep voucher holders in high-poverty neighborhoods.[49] For example, landlords with properties in poor neighborhoods try to recruit voucher holders because the vouchers guarantee them reliable rental income and often match tenants to properties in particular areas based on their race.[50] Altogether, while recent increased efforts to deconcentrate poverty through public housing programs have led to slight increases in the economic integration of poor residents, there remain several barriers that perpetuate the segregation of poor minority residents from non-poor residents.

SUMMARY AND POLICY IMPLICATIONS

Major changes that, at first glance, should have brought about a major reduction in residential segregation in the post–civil rights era have had limited effects. New measures and methods that adapt to the contemporary racial and socioeconomic context of the United States demonstrate that segregation strongly persists. First, segregation levels are higher when we consider multiple race groups together, rather than only two groups. Second, segregation is increasingly taking place in the suburbs as they become more racially and socioeconomically diverse. Third, consistent with other recent studies on racial segregation, we find declines in the segregation of race groups, but when we consider the intersection of race and class, our findings demonstrate that poor minorities and affluent whites are highly isolated and became increasingly segregated from nonpoor and nonaffluent residents, respectively, from 2000 to 2010 both in central cities and in the suburbs.

These patterns persisted even as gentrification spread throughout cities and neighborhoods, subprime loans were channeled to minority residents, and public housing policies increased their focus on poverty deconcentration. Recent research shows how these shifts in the housing landscape can work in ways that lead to minimal impact in reducing segregation. Given that segregation comes with a host of negative consequences, particularly for the life chances of minorities living in low-income neighborhoods, and reduces intergroup relations, stronger policy intervention is required to promote racial, ethnic, and socioeconomic integration across all neighborhoods. Below, we outline a broad framework for addressing segregation with housing policy. This framework is "place-conscious."[51] In other words, it moves beyond debates in the housing-policy world between people-based policies—those focused on moving poor families into nonpoor neighborhoods (for example, housing vouchers)—and place-based policies—those focused on redeveloping poor neighborhoods. A place-conscious framework, instead, recognizes the need for both types of strategies with the goal of improving individuals' short-term and long-term well-being while recognizing the dynamics of residential mobility and neighborhood change.[52]

First, housing policies should continue to support and expand people-based programs, but these programs need to be modified to improve the residential outcomes, as well as the social and economic outcomes that come with this, for residents who use these programs. The research documents several ways in which the program design and the structure of the housing market inhibits low-income families from moving to neighborhoods with more opportunities and resources, including limited information and time as well as landlord practices.[53] Therefore, these housing programs need to adapt to these realities at scale. Evidence from special voucher programs, such as those that restrict voucher holders to move to low-poverty neighborhoods (for example, Moving to Opportunity), show that alternative strategies can work.[54] Programs need to provide effective guidance and oversight and provide incentives for landlords in socioeconomically advantaged neighborhoods to accept voucher holders so that the program can ensure that its users are moving to places with opportunities and resources and that they have the resources to stay there.

Second, housing policies also need to continue to support and expand place-based programs, but there needs to be a stronger policy focus on diversity and inclusion. People-based policies, if implemented effectively, can move a fraction of people out of poor neighborhoods, but those who remain in these neighborhoods need access to opportunities and resources. Such neighborhoods need substantial place-based investment that can attract residents with higher socioeconomic status. At the same time, these investments need to come with the right policy interventions that allow low-income residents to stay in these neighborhoods, that connect them to the opportunities and resources that come with reinvestment, and that ensure that the development process is inclusive. A mix of regulations and tax legislation, such as protections for low-income homeowners and renters, can prevent the residential displacement—either directly or indirectly—of poor residents. Some examples of such policies and programs include strong affordable housing requirements in new construction or redevelopment (that is, inclusionary zoning), protections for low-income homeowners and renters against substantial price increases through property tax breaks or subsidies, rehabilitation assistance for blighted properties, opportunities for equity building for low-income residents, inclusive community-planning processes, and oversight on predatory landlords and developers. These policies and strategies have been used in cities such as Columbia (Maryland), Oak Park (Illinois), Denver, Seattle, and Salt Lake City where diversity and inclusion have served as guiding principles in the development of their housing policies.

Third, housing policies need to be structured in a way that disincentivizes "white flight" and "white avoidance." Our results documented the increased concentration of affluent whites across the United States in recent decades. Given that 15 percent of households move each year in the United States, decisions about which neighborhoods to enter and which ones to exit play an important role in maintaining residential segregation. Research consistently demonstrates the persistent residential mobility patterns of whites to avoid entry into minority neighborhoods and exit neighborhoods that begin to diversify.[55] Such patterns perpetuate racial segregation. Effective place-based strategies that reduce and ideally eliminate the existence of deleterious social and economic conditions in poor, minority neighborhoods may help to reduce race-based neighborhood stereotypes—when individuals associate minority residents with poor-quality neighborhoods, crime, and declining home values[56]—that promote such processes. But housing policy also needs to remove the ability for affluent residents to use their political advantages to oppose development that prohibits integration (that is, "NIMBY" or not-in-my-backyard–ism). For example, some suburban municipalities prohibit multifamily housing, which often restricts low-income and minority families from entering.[57] Thus, removing or altering zoning and low-density restrictions can help limit the concentration of affluent whites.

Finally, effective housing policy needs to be designed to meet the needs of the local housing market. There is substantial variation in segregation trends across the one hundred largest metropolitan areas, often resulting from distinct histories of economic, social, and political development. Thus, housing policies need to consider the general supply and demand of affordable housing and its quality in a region, as well as the existing spatial patterns of segregation, and should further consider the specific needs of each neighborhood that the policies will affect.[58] For example, in cities in which demand for affordable housing exceeds supply, like San Francisco, regulations that remove supply restrictions across the region are one antidote to relieving these supply constraints; in cities where the supply of affordable housing is plentiful, like Detroit, what is needed is to remove subsidies for fringe development, which promote the continued disinvestment of central cities, and instead to invest in existing areas. The Metropolitan Housing Rule in the Portland, Oregon, region, which requires zoning for large numbers of apartments in suburban cities and counties, is one potentially effective approach for housing markets where demand exceeds supply. Nonetheless, it is imperative that the 2015 Affirmatively Further Fair Housing Rule, which requires jurisdictions receiving federal funds toward housing programs to ensure that their policies promote racial integration, be enforced. Without federal oversight, the free market and local political dynamics will continue to inhibit racial, ethnic, and socioeconomic integration across all neighborhoods and perpetuate inequality by race and class.

APPENDIX

THE DIVERGENCE INDEX

Formally, the divergence index (D) is represented as:

$$D = \sum_{i=1} \frac{\tau_i}{T} \sum_{m=1} \pi_{im} \log \frac{\pi_{im}}{\pi_m}$$

where π_i is the population count for tract i, T is the overall metropolitan population count, π_{im} is group m's proportion of the population in tract i, and π_{im} is group m's proportion of the overall metropolitan population. We can formally decompose D into the sum of two quantities: (1) *macro-D*, the segregation *between* the central city and suburbs, and (2) *micro-D*, the segregation *within* the central city and suburbs. *Macro-D* compares the composition of groups within each subarea to the composition of the overall metropolitan area. *Micro-D* is the population-weighted mean of the segregation of census tracts within each subarea, which is calculated by comparing the composition of the groups of interest in each census tract to the overall composition of the groups of interest across the entire subarea. Therefore, the overall D for a metropolitan area is equivalent to the sum of the *macro-D* and *micro-D*, and the *micro-D* is the population-weighted average D comparing the composition of tracts within the central city to the overall central city composition and comparing the composition of tracts within the suburbs to the overall composition of the suburbs.

NOTES

1. Douglas S. Massey and Nancy A. Denton, *American Apartheid: Segregation and the Making of the Underclass* (Cambridge, MA: Harvard University Press, 1993), 15–16; Camille Z. Charles, "The Dynamics of Racial Residential Segregation," *Annual Review of Sociology* 29 (2003): 167–68.

2. Massey and Denton, *American Apartheid*, 9–16.

3. Pew Research Center, *King's Dream Remains an Elusive Goal; Many Americans See Racial Disparities* (Washington, DC: Pew Research Center, 2013), 2, www.pewsocialtrends .org/files/2013/08/final_full_report_racial_disparities.pdf.

4. Reynolds Farley and William H. Frey, "Changes in the Segregation of Whites from Blacks During the 1980s: Small Steps Toward a More Integrated Society," *American Sociological Review* 59, no. 1 (1994): 28–30.

5. Charles, "The Dynamics of Racial Residential Segregation," 184.

6. John R. Logan and Charles Zhang, "Global Neighborhoods: New Pathways to Diversity and Separation," *American Journal of Sociology* 115, no. 4 (2010): 1091.

7. Edward Glaeser and Jacob Vigdor, *The End of the Segregated Century: Racial Separation in America's Neighborhoods, 1890–2010* (New York: Manhattan Institute, 2012), www.manhattan-institute.org/pdf/cr_66.pdf.

8. Since 1980, the U.S. Census employed the term "Hispanic" to identify persons from Latin American countries or "other Spanish culture or origin, regardless of race," and changed the term to "Spanish/Hispanic/Latino" in the year 2000. When referring to data from the U.S. Census, we use the term "Hispanic" (Cohn 2010). D'vera Cohn, "Census History: Counting Hispanics," Pew Research Center (Washington, DC, Mar. 3, 2010.)

9. Jacob S. Rugh and Douglas S. Massey, "Segregation in Post–Civil Rights America: Stalled Integration or End of the Segregated Century?" *Du Bois Review: Social Science Research on Race* 11, no. 2 (2014): 214–15.

10. Sean F. Reardon and Glen Firebaugh, "Measures of Multigroup Segregation," *Sociological Methodology* 32 (2002): 34.

11. Jackelyn Hwang and Jeffrey Lin, "What Have We Learned About the Causes of Recent Gentrification?" *Cityscape* 18, no. 3 (2016): 10–16; Elizabeth Kneebone and Alan Berube, *Confronting Suburban Poverty in America* (Washington, DC: Brookings Institution Press, 2013), 1–12.

12. John R. Logan, Wenquan Zhang, and Richard D. Alba, "Immigrant Enclaves and Ethnic Communities in New York and Los Angeles," *American Sociological Review* 67, no. 2 (2002): 305–6; Ming Wen, Diane S. Lauderdale, and Namratha R. Kandula, "Ethnic Neighborhoods in Multi-Ethnic America, 1990–2000: Resurgent Ethnicity in the Ethnoburbs?" *Social Forces* 88, no. 1 (2009): 447–49.

13. Sean F. Reardon and Kendra Bischoff, "Income Inequality and Income Segregation," *American Journal of Sociology* 116, no. 4 (2011): 1116.

14. Ibid., 1111.

15. Ibid., 1116.

16. Elizabeth Roberto, "The Divergence Index: A Decomposable Measure of Segregation and Inequality," working paper, 2016, arxiv.org/abs/1508.01167.

17. Daniel T. Lichter, Domenico Parisi, and Michael C. Taquino, "Toward a New Macro-Segregation? Decomposing Segregation within and between Metropolitan Cities and Suburbs," *American Sociological Review* 80, no. 4 (2015): 858.

18. Ibid., 843–73.

19. Reardon and Bischoff, "Income Inequality and Income Segregation," 1116.

20. Rugh and Massey, "Segregation in Post–Civil Rights America," 205.

21. The values of the race-class divergence indexes are substantially lower than those that only consider race because the race-class divergence indexes intentionally combine multiple race groups in the "all nonpoor" and "all nonaffluent" categories for the purposes of this study. Therefore, the race-class divergence indexes do not measure any segregation that may occur between the race groups within each of these categories.

22. Maria Krysan and Kyle Crowder, *Cycle of Segregation: Social Processes and Residential Stratification* (New York: Russell Sage Foundation, 2017), 3–16.

23. Some of the ideas in this section first appeared in the essay by Jackelyn Hwang, "Residential Mobility by Whites Maintains Segregation despite Recent Changes," *The Dream Revisited* (blog) (New York: Furman Center, December 2016), furmancenter.org /research/iri/essay/residential-mobility-by-whites-maintains-segregation-despite-recent -changes.

24. For a review, see Hwang and Lin, "What Have We Learned About the Causes of Recent Gentrification?"

25. Lance Freeman, "Neighbourhood Diversity, Metropolitan Segregation and Gentrification: What are the Links in the US?" *Urban Studies* 46, no. 10 (2009): 2092; Jackelyn Hwang, "Pioneers of Gentrification: Transformation in Global Neighborhoods in Urban America in the Late Twentieth Century," *Demography* 53, no. 1 (2016): 201–3.

26. Ann Owens, "Neighborhoods on the Rise: A Typology of Neighborhoods Experiencing Socioeconomic Ascent," *City & Community* 11, no. 4 (2012): 357; Robert J. Sampson, *Great American City: Chicago and the Enduring Neighborhood Effect* (Chicago: University of Chicago Press, 2012), 97–120.

27. Lance Freeman and Tiancheng Cai, "White Entry into Black Neighborhoods: Advent of a New Era," *Annals of the American Academy of Political and Social Science* 660 (2015): 307.

28. Jackelyn Hwang and Robert J. Sampson, "Divergent Pathways of Gentrification: Racial Inequality and the Social Order of Renewal in Chicago Neighborhoods," *American Sociological Review* 79, no. 4 (2014): 740–44.

29. Derek Hyra, *The New Urban Renewal: The Economic Transformation of Harlem and Bronzeville* (Chicago: University of Chicago Press, 2008); Jeffrey M. Timberlake and Elaina Johns-Wolfe, "Neighborhood Ethnoracial Composition and Gentrification in Chicago and New York, 1980 to 2010," *Urban Affairs Review* 53, no. 2 (2017): 259–66.

30. Lei Ding, Jackelyn Hwang, and Eileen Divringi, "Gentrification and Residential Mobility in Philadelphia," *Regional Science and Urban Economics* 61 (2016): 38–51; Ingrid Gould Ellen and Kathy M. O'Regan, "How Low Income Neighborhoods Change: Entry, Exit, and Enhancement," *Regional Science and Urban Economics* 41 (2011): 89–97; Lance Freeman, Adele Cassola, and Tiancheng Cai, "Displacement and Gentrification in England and Wales: A Quasi-Experimental Approach," *Urban Studies* 53, no. 13 (2016): 2797–814; Lance Freeman and Frank Braconi, "Gentrification and Displacement New York City in the 1990s," *Journal of the American Planning Association* 70, no. 1 (2004): 39–52; Terra McKinnish, Randall Walsh, and T. Kirk White, "Who Gentrifies Low-Income Neighborhoods?" *Journal of Urban Economics* 67 (2010): 180–93; Jacob L. Vigdor, "Does Gentrification Harm the Poor?" *Brookings-Wharton Papers on Urban Affairs* (2002): 133–82.

31. Jackelyn Hwang and Lei Ding, "Unequal Displacement: Gentrification, Race, and Residential Destinations," presentation, Annual Meeting for the *American Sociological Association*, Seattle, August 20–23, 2016.

32. Douglas S. Massey, Jacob S. Rugh, Justin P. Steil, and Len Albright, "Riding the Stagecoach to Hell: A Qualitative Analysis of Racial Discrimination in Mortgage Lending," *City and Community* 15, no. 2 (2016): 119–22; Richard Williams, Reynold Nesiba, and Eileen Diaz McConnell, "The Changing Face of Inequality in Home Mortgage Lending," *Social Problems* 52, no. 2 (2005): 187–90.

33. Debbie G. Bocian, Delvin Davis, Sonia Garrison, and Bill Sermons, *The State of Lending and Its Impacts on US Households* (Washington, DC: Center for Responsible Lending, 2012), 39, www.responsiblelending.org/state-of-lending/State-of-Lending-report-1.pdf; see also Jacob W. Faber, "Racial Dynamics of Subprime Mortgage Lending at the Peak," *Housing Policy Debate* 23, no. 2 (2013): 338–39.

34. Vicki Been, Ingrid Gould Ellen, and Josiah Madar, "The High Cost of Segregation: Exploring Racial Disparities in High-Cost Lending," *Fordham Urban Law Journal* 36, no. 3 (2008): 380–83; Paul S. Calem, Jonathan E. Hershaff, and Susan M. Wachter, "Neighborhood Patterns of Subprime Lending: Evidence from Disparate Cities," *Housing Policy Debate* 15, no. 3 (2004): 615; Jackelyn Hwang, Michael Hankinson, and Kreg Steven Brown, "Racial and Spatial Targeting: Segregation and Subprime Lending within and across Metropolitan Areas," *Social Forces* 93, no. 3 (2015): 1094–99; Derek S. Hyra, Gregory D. Squires, Robert N. Renner, and David S. Kirk, "Metropolitan Segregation and the Subprime Lending Crisis," *Housing Policy Debate* 23, no. 1 (2013): 187–88; Dan Immergluck, "From the Subprime to the Exotic: Excessive Mortgage Market Risk and Foreclosures," *Journal of the American Planning Association* 74, no. 1 (2008): 68–69; Jacob S. Rugh, Len Albright, and Douglas S. Massey, "Race, Space, and Cumulative Disadvantage: A Case Study of the Subprime Lending Collapse," *Social Problems* 62, no. 2 (2015): 196–202.

35. Hwang et al., "Racial and Spatial Targeting," 1084–85.

36. Geetesh Bhardwaj and Rajdeep Sengupta, "Did Prepayments Sustain the Subprime Market?" *CentER Discussion Paper*, No. 2009-38S (2009): 3.

37. Carolyn Bond and Richard Williams, "Residential Segregation and the Transformation of Home Mortgage Lending," *Social Forces* 86, no. 2 (2007): 687–91.

38. Bocian et al., *The State of Lending*, 39; Immergluck, "From the Subprime to the Exotic," 66–70.

39. Matthew Hall, Kyle Crowder, and Amy Spring, "Neighborhood Foreclosures, Racial/Ethnic Transitions, and Residential Segregation," *American Sociological Review* 80, no. 3 (2015): 535–36; Jacob S. Rugh and Douglas S. Massey, "Racial Segregation and the American Foreclosure Crisis," *American Sociological Review* 75, no. 5 (2010): 637–41.

40. Jacob S. Rugh, "Double Jeopardy: Why Latinos Were Hit Hardest by the US Foreclosure Crisis," *Social Forces* 93, no. 3 (2015): 1157–61.

41. Hall et al., "Neighborhood Foreclosures," 536–39.

42. Ibid., 541–43.

43. Ann Owens, "Housing Policy and Urban Inequality: Did the Transformation of Assisted Housing Reduce Poverty Concentration?" *Social Forces* 94, no. 1 (2015): 336–40.

44. Ann Owens, "Assisted Housing and Income Segregation among Neighborhoods in U.S. Metropolitan Areas," *ANNALS of the American Academy of Political and Social Science* 660 (2015): 108–12.

45. Robert J. Sampson and Patrick Sharkey, "Neighborhood Selection and the Social Reproduction of Concentrated Racial Inequality," *Demography* 45, no. 1 (2008): 22–25.

46. Stefanie Deluca, Philip M. E. Garboden, and Peter Rosenblatt, "Segregating Shelter: How Housing Policies Shape the Residential Locations of Low-Income Minority Families," *ANNALS of the American Academy of Political and Social Science* 647 (2013): 280.

47. John Goering, Ali Kamely, and Todd Richardson, "Recent Research on Racial Segregation and Poverty Concentration in Public Housing in the United States," *Urban Affairs Review* 32, no. 5 (1997): 733–36.

48. Deluca et al., "Segregating Shelter," 276–88.

49. Eva Rosen, "Rigging the Rules of the Game: How Landlords Geographically Sort Low-Income Renters," *City & Community* 13, no. 4 (2014): 317–35.

50. Ibid.

51. Margery Austin Turner, "Beyond People Versus Place: A Place-Conscious Framework for Investing in Housing and Neighborhoods," *Housing Policy Debate* 27, no. 2 (2017): 306–14.

52. See Patrick Sharkey, *Stuck in Place: Urban Neighborhoods and the End of Progress Toward Racial Equality* (Chicago: University of Chicago Press, 2013).

53. Deluca et al., "Segregating Shelter," 288–92.

54. Ann Owens, "How Do People-Based Housing Policies Affect People (and Place)?" *Housing Policy Debate* 27, no. 2 (2017): 273.

55. Michael D. M. Bader and Maria Krysan, "Community Attraction and Avoidance in Chicago: What's Race Got to Do with It?" *ANNALS of the American Academy of Political and Social Science* 660, no. 1 (2015): 268–76; Hwang and Sampson, "Divergent Pathways of Gentrification," 744–45; Wenquan Zhang and John R. Logan, "Global Neighborhoods: Beyond the Multiethnic Metropolis," *Demography* 53, no. 6 (2016): 1943–44.

56. Ellen Ingrid Gould, *Sharing America's Neighborhoods: The Prospects for Stable Racial Integration* (Cambridge, MA: Harvard University Press, 2000).

57. Douglas S. Massey, Len Albright, Rebecca Casciano, Elizabeth Derickson, and David N. Kinsey, *Climbing Mount Laurel: The Struggle for Affordable Housing and Social Mobility in an American Suburb* (Princeton, NJ: Princeton University Press, 2013); Jonathan T. Rothwell and Douglas S. Massey, "Density Zoning and Class Segregation in U.S. Metropolitan Areas," *Social Science Quarterly* 91, no. 5 (2010): 1132–34; Rugh and Massey, "Segregation in Post–Civil Rights America," 206–7.

58. Rolf Pendall, Mark Treskon, Marisa Novara, and Amy Khare, "Three Steps to Building a Less Segregated Future," *Next City,* April 7, 2017, nextcity.org/daily/entry/cost-of -segregation-report-three-steps.

MEDIA INCLUSION, RACIAL JUSTICE, AND DIGITAL CITIZENSHIP

SRIVIDYA RAMASUBRAMANIAN

Media are a ubiquitous and integral part of everyday living in this networked, interactive, and global world. The digital revolution has dramatically changed how we experience life, what we know about ourselves,
how we spend our leisure time, how we connect with others around us,
and what we learn about the world. This rapid diffusion of new digital media technologies has led to a breaking down of divisions across
various media formats. In this convergence culture of transmedia storytelling and spreadable media, digital users are constantly creating,
sharing, and engaging with a variety of media types. Race as a social
construct has real-world implications for shaping media-related public
policy, playing a significant role in perpetuating inequalities in media
access, ownership, representation, and uses. Inclusive media policies
are needed for greater active digital citizenship and racial justice at the
individual, organization, and community levels.

MEDIA PROLIFERATION, CONVERGENCE CULTURE, AND MEDIATIZATION

Given the intense pace of personalization, convergence, and proliferation of various media platforms, understandings of "media," "audiences," and "exposure" are being constantly redefined.[1] Words such as
"prosumer" have been coined to describe how the same individual simultaneously produces, as well as consumes, digital content in most
contexts. These technological developments have implications for media access, media education, media workforce, and media ownership.
Just the sheer amount of time that people are spending with media
makes them significant sources of socialization that are important to
examine. American adults spend more than twelve of their waking

hours consuming media.[2] Thanks to media multitasking, digital convergence, and the mobile-phone revolution, half of this media exposure is devoted to digital media. Social networking sites and image-based social media such as Instagram, Snapchat, Facebook, and Twitter have fundamentally changed our understanding of media use, engagement, and production, with a predicted 1.3 trillion photos to be taken just in 2017.[3] Although the mediascape is shifting rapidly, the rates at which various communities have adopted new media technologies vary considerably, leading to what scholars refer to as the "digital divide" between "media-haves" and "have-nots."

Media are also a significant source of information, along with peers, family, acquaintances, and coworkers, in shaping attitudes and behaviors. Information gleaned from media narratives shapes individuals' dynamic cognitive representations of people, issues, and events, which are called "mental models." In turn, these models influence perceptions of social reality.[4] Individuals who rely heavily on mediated sources for information are likely to hold worldviews similar to the media world in which they immerse themselves.[5] Emotion-laden, vivid, and anecdotal media exemplars are especially likely to influence audiences' perceptions and attitudes about issues, events, and people.[6] Over the long term, constant exposure to media can have cumulative effects that can shape individuals' social reality, as well as values, attitudes, belief systems, and policy opinions.[7] Through repeated association among related thoughts, ideas, and emotions, a cognitive-affective network of nodes is created and maintained in audiences' minds.[8] Mere exposure to a media stimulus can activate associated feelings and thoughts, which can subconsciously influence viewers' evaluations and judgments in subsequent scenarios.[9] In sum, media matter because they shape mental models and cognitive structures through which individuals learn about and interact with the world.

Emphasizing the interrelationship between changing media technologies and the dynamic sociocultural environment in which we live, the mediatization perspective suggests that media have become co-constitutive in shaping almost every aspect of contemporary social life and the construction of reality.[10] Not only have several non-media activities now become mediated, there is also an increase in new media replacing traditional modes of communication. Mediated and unmediated activities have become intertwined and intermingled in everyday life. Social institutions are slowly but steadily adapting to the presence of media so that media cannot be separated from cultural processes in contemporary societies. As scholars such as Stig Hjarvard notes, "The media are at once part of the fabric of society and culture and an independent institution that stands between other cultural and social institutions and coordinates their mutual interaction."[11] Discourses about politics, health, wealth, community, education, religion, and so forth are both heavily mediated and mediatized. That is, media frame and shape the processes through which we understand these constructs and ideas.

DIGITAL DIVIDE, MEDIA ACCESS, AND MOBILE REVOLUTION

Despite the rapid diffusion of media technologies, universal access to media has not been achieved. Several factors such as race, income, age, gender, and education contribute to the "digital divide," the gap between those who have access to new media technologies and those who do not.[12] There is a long history of systemic exclusion of racial minorities from media access, ownership, representation, and policy-making in the United States. Racially minoritized groups have been historically disadvantaged, not just technologically but also economically, politically, socially, and culturally. Although there has been a steady increase in the adoption of media, racially minoritized groups continue to lag behind, as compared to the white American majority in terms of even basic media access.

According to a recent Pew Center report, African Americans are below whites by 7 percent when it comes to overall Internet use (80 percent and 87 percent respectively), 12 percent when it comes to home broadband adoption (62 percent and 75 percent respectively), and 9 percent in social media use (65 percent and 56 percent respectively).[13] Among those who do have online access, social media preferences also vary by race. Latinx Americans (34 percent) and African Americans (38 percent) are more likely to prefer the photo-sharing site Instagram, as compared to 21 percent of whites. However, African Americans and Latinx Americans with online access are equally likely to be on Twitter (25 percent) while only 21 percent of online whites are on Twitter.[14]

About 92 percent of black adults are cell phone owners, but only

56 percent of the phones are smartphones. When it comes to African Americans and Latinx Americans older than sixty-five years, these differences across racial groups become starker. More than a million black and Latinx seniors do not have access to the Internet or broadband.[15] Just 45 percent of African Americans sixty-five and older use the Internet, and only 30 percent have access to broadband from their homes. However, cell phone ownership is much more common than Internet use among older African Americans. While 77 percent of people in this demographic are cell phone owners, most of these seniors own basic cell phones, as only 18 percent are smartphone owners. Overall, 72 percent of all African Americans—and 98 percent of those between the ages of eighteen and twenty-nine—have either a broadband connection or a smartphone.[16] Racial minorities, especially those living in rural and low-income communities, have lesser access to home broadband and Internet services.[17] Although the digital divide exists, among those who do have access to online digital media, racial minorities do engage positively with digital tools. Some studies find that racial minorities are more active in online spaces in terms of creating, sharing, and posting messages.[18] Racial minorities have more positive attitudes towards technology and media than do white participants. They were also more likely to report in this study about posting in social networking sites, creating their own blogs, writing poetry and fiction online, and using their voices as citizen journalists.[19] For instance, young African American women in middle school have the highest frequency of use of mobile phones, which they use to access the Internet, search for information online, download music, and text message.[20] However, the same was not true of African American males in this study, who reported lesser time with all digital media except video games.

The intersection of various identities such as race, class, gender, age, ability, citizenship status, and incarceration status influences media access and use. For instance, African Americans are disproportionately incarcerated at almost six times the rate of whites, with African Americans comprising 37 percent of all male inmates in 2013.[21] Given that cell phone ownership is prohibited in prisons, a large number of African American men have severely restricted access to media. Similarly, Hispanic Americans, about nineteen million of whom are new immigrants from Latin America and at least a third of Hispanics in the United

States, do not speak fluent English, which is the dominant language of mainstream U.S media, business, and other social institutions.[22] And only 10 percent of tribal residents have access to home broadband.[23] The marketization of media means that most broadcasters are unwilling to serve Native Americans in rural tribal lands because it is easier for them to raise advertising monies in dense urban markets. Since racial identity often coincides with other social inequalities based on social class, citizenship status, language fluency, physical ability, and geographic location, multiple burdens fall upon racial minorities that limit media access. In turn, limited media access constrains access to other resources.

A hypothetical case study will illustrate how the digital divide further widens the gap between haves and have-nots. To drive home the point about how digital inequalities can get compounded over time, let us imagine a young Latina woman, Delicia, living in downtown Houston. She does not own a computer or a cell phone. She comes from a low-income family and lives in housing provided for such families. Although her parents have phones, they cannot afford smartphones or Internet connectivity on them. As on many other days, today her teacher has assigned homework that requires access to the Internet. Their family does not own a car. She has to take a bus to the local library to access a computer. However, the library is open only until 6:00 that evening, which is another constraint because Delicia has to work. Over time, Delicia falls behind on her academic work. Almost all communication about schoolwork is sent via email to her parents. Although she would qualify for a free lunch program, her parents have not been able to fill out the required paperwork, which is online and in English, a language that they are not familiar with at home. Delicia gets a sack lunch in school, and it is not enough to keep her from being hungry. She falls sick easily. All of her medical records have been digitized. They do not have health insurance. Delicia is keen on going to college. She is a bright kid. However, even when she is at the library computer, she does not know how to access materials relating to college applications and scholarships. She takes the preparatory exam, but does so without any preparation, unlike the white kids in her class who have gone through online mock tests and have had access to tips on testing skills from websites. She ends up not being admitted into any college. She also does not know how to look for jobs online, which restricts her career options.

As in this imaginary case study, most aspects of contemporary sociocultural institutions are mediated and mediatized, making it challenging to access key societal resources such as education, jobs, wealth, food security, health care, and housing. Absence of media access can lead to further disenfranchisement of racial minorities through discrimination in housing and employment, oppression from law enforcement officers, inadequate school and city services in their segregated neighborhoods, and economic, as well as educational, inequalities in general.

WHITE MONOPOLIZATION, MEDIA COMMODIFICATION, AND CORPORATIZATION

Historically, there has been a white monopolization of media workforce and media ownership. This is significant, as prior research has demonstrated that newspapers and television stations with more diverse journalists of color are likely to be supportive of diversity efforts and at recognizing the importance of serving communities of color.[24] After the civil rights movement, the Kerner Commission recommended that policies have to be put in place to ensure better coverage of minority issues in media and to integrate minority communities into news content.[25] The American Society of Newspaper Editors (ASNE), formed in 1978, set out to achieve greater racial balance in the news media industry. It set a goal in 1998 to reach racial parity in the news media workforce by 2000. However, this objective has not been achieved. Since only 11.85 percent of newsrooms hired journalists of color by 2000, ASNE has had to change its benchmark and set a new racial parity target by 2025. In 2015, minorities comprised only 12.8 percent of employees at daily newspapers.[26] Unless there are significant changes in how the news media industry hires and retains staff, this goal will remain impossible. TV newsrooms are much better with a 23.1 percent minority workforce, but radio has only 9.4 percent minorities on staff, and digital sites report only 11 percent minority.[27] The racial inequalities are just as striking in the film industry, with the ratio of whites to racial minorities at 3:1 among film leads, 3:1 among film directors, 5:1 among film writers, and 5:1 among broadcast scripted leads.[28] Several scholars have noted that white actors are given preferential treatment over racial minorities, which have led those from marginalized groups to be motivated to create alternative progressive cultural productions that are critical of mainstream corporate media culture.[29]

Not only is there a dominance of white employees in the media workforce, there are fewer racial minorities as one moves up the ranks. Only 13 percent of supervisors were nonwhites in newsrooms, and only 28 percent of news organizations reported having at least one racial minority member among the top three editors.[30] According to the National Association of Black Journalists, there were only eleven black top editors at daily newspapers in 2015. In 2013, minorities owned just 3 percent of full-power television stations, 6 percent of FM stations, and 11 percent of AM stations.[31] The 1996 Telecommunication Act, in the guise of promoting greater competition, ended up being detrimental in promoting racial diversity in media ownership. By eliminating limits and relaxing caps on the number of radio stations and television stations that can be owned by a single entity, it solidified white monopolization of the broadcast industry. It ushered in a new era of corporatization of media and deregulation of the media industry, which made it difficult for media stations owned by black, brown, and indigenous media owners to survive in their communities.[32] Under such neoliberal policies, media are seen as commodities, rather than as public goods that serve all members of our communities. From the late 1980s onwards, the market-based logic of neoliberal broadcast deregulation had taken over, where the emphasis was on individual and corporate rights rather than on social justice.[33] Rather than content diversity and source diversity, format or outlet diversity is emphasized in current public policies relating to telecommunication and media. Most of these policies only regulate broadcast media, not websites and online content. In other words, the policies have not necessarily been able to keep pace with the rapid changes in digital media technologies.

Apart from having to deal with a historic legacy of discrimination and racism, minority-owned media have to contend with corporatization of media and consolidation. Over the last two decades or so, the Federal Communications Commission has continued with policies that focus on deregulation and pro-competition, making it easier for megacorporations such as Comcast and Time Warner to merge and consolidate such that it is practically impossible for small media owners to compete. This marketization of media diversity wrongly assumes that simply removing restrictions on the market will automatically lead to content diversity. In fact, the opposite has happened. The rapid changes in media technologies, convergence across media formats, and digital revolution has meant that it has been challenging for start-ups and lesser-known media enterprises to successfully adapt to these changes and survive in a white-controlled industry. Such small business owned by minorities are also more vulnerable to economic downturns and bankruptcies. The transition to web-based online media content has often been hindered by financial constraints. It has also been hampered by the majority of readers that minority media cater to being less likely to have access to broadband and the Internet.

SYMBOLIC ANNIHILATION, MEDIA REPRESENTATIONS, AND WHITE-SUPREMACIST DISCOURSES

One of the consequences of marketization and commodification of media has been that, in order to sustain the twenty-four/seven news cycle, media often focus on sensationalism, including and especially at the level of local media. Driven by profits as their goal to survive in a tight and competitive market, media outlets typically focus on crime, sex, and drug dealing, portraying racial minorities in a condescending manner. Beyond convergence of media technologies and format, there is also an increase in the blurring of news, entertainment, and advertising in ways that sometimes make them indistinguishable from one another. Thus, it makes it challenging to distinguish fact from fiction, reality from fantasy, and news from propaganda. In fact, the anonymity, ease of access, and spreadability of media mean that online hate is rather rampant in media today.[34] It is estimated that, on Twitter alone, there are more than ten thousand explicit racial slurs expressed every day.[35] By using techniques such as "information laundering," extremist white-nationalist groups are attempting to get into the mainstream by creating websites that mimic mainstream media posts in form and structure. Increasingly, there is a concern about how media, especially social media, are being used to promote fake news, alternative facts, and white-supremacist rhetoric that deliberately intends to present racial minorities in extremely negative ways.

Another aspect of racial/ethnic inequalities in media has been the absence or low frequencies of representations in media, in a variety of media contexts such as prime-time television, films, advertising, and video games.[36] Scholars have used the term "symbolic annihilation" to characterize how stigmatized groups have been historically erased, trivialized, and condemned using negative unidimensional portrayals in mainstream popular culture.[37] Early Internet scholars predicted that new media technologies would lead to more inclusive and democratic online spaces, as compared to traditional media, but this projection has not come true.[38] Racial/ethnic minorities continue to be gravely underrepresented in mainstream media, including in online spaces. They are positioned as marginal characters who are incidental to the main storyline or as background characters, without allowing for full participation. Only 1.9 percent of news stories in their analysis were related to African Americans in some way, with newspapers devoting 1.5 percent, cable television 2.5 percent, talk radio 2.5 percent, and online news 1.9 percent.[39] Most of these stories painted a negative picture of the community by focusing on crime, poverty, health issues, and unemployment. Similarly, only 1.9 percent of news time was used to cover stories about the Hispanic community, according to this study.

Even when racial parity is achieved in some genres, in terms of frequency, the quality of portrayals continues to be limited.[40] Racial/ethnic minorities are often "othered" in mainstream white-owned media and are associated with negative traits such as criminality, violence, poor work ethic, and dishonesty. For instance, African Americans have been historically depicted through gendered stereotypical tropes such as buffoonish clowns, criminal gangsters, submissive Uncle Toms, sexually promiscuous Jezebels and Hottentot Venuses, and obedient mammies.[41] Racial minorities, as compared to their white counterparts, are portrayed as less intelligent, hardworking, attractive, friendly, law abiding, and reliable.[42] Latinx people are depicted as sexualized, violent, and lazy.[43] Asians are also underrepresented in media and are often assigned side or background characters, rather than those central to the story.[44] They are represented as yellow peril, perpetual foreigners, exotic, untrustworthy, and model minorities.[45]

Racial minority groups are often highly aware of how their portrayals compare with majority group members in mainstream media and are sensitive to these biased representations.[46] They often express conflicted relationships with mainstream media and challenge traditional representations of their groups. Not surprisingly, they often avoid mainstream media and instead prefer media content produced by and featuring members of their own in-group. For instance, a survey from an alliance of ethnic news media in the United States suggests that 45 percent of racial minority members prefer ethnic television, radio, and newspapers, compared to mainstream media counterparts.[47] When minority group members view media content about their group in mainstream media, especially positive portrayals, it increases their subjective assessment of their group's relative position in society in terms of power, prestige, resources, and influence, which indirectly increases collective esteem.[48] Research suggests that exposure to ethnic media, as compared to mainstream media, is associated with positive self-concept and increased self-esteem.[49] In contrast to ethnic-owned media, mainstream white-dominated media lead to negative self-images for minorities.

The negative stereotypical images of racial minorities in mainstream white-owned media not only affects how minorities view themselves, but also how majority white audiences perceive and respond to racial minorities. According to media priming perspectives, repeated associations of racial minorities with stereotypical traits and characteristics in narratives can lead to the formation of cognitive-affective networks of related thoughts and emotions.[50] Exposure to media stimuli serves as a prime that activates relevant nodes, which leads to spreading activation of other series of nodes in the network. For instance, if readers are exposed to crime stories about African Americans in the news, they prime thoughts and feelings about welfare and poverty, even if these topics are not even mentioned in the article.[51] Long-term exposure to demeaning portrayals of racial minorities in the media can lead to cumulative effects that distort viewers' perceptions of social reality, thus resulting in biased estimates of real-world experiences and related values, belief systems, and policy opinions as secondary effects.[52] For example, heavy viewers of news or crime dramas are likely to have accessible examples of African American criminals as compared to those who view educational programming or soap operas.[53]

Chronic accessibility to racialized media stereotypes makes them easily available in influencing person perceptions and social judgments of racial minorities by white audiences.[54] For instance, exposure to even dark-skinned Afro-centric facial features is sufficient to evaluate alleged criminal offenders as more guilty and assign them longer prison sentences than those with less Afro-centric features.[55] Exposure to stereotypical, rather than counter-stereotypical, African American media characters leads to greater real-world stereotypical beliefs about this racial group, negative intergroup feelings toward them, and lack of support for pro-minority policies such as affirmative action.[56] Using attribution theory, the same study also shows that exposure to stereotypical African American media characters leads white audience members to attribute failures of African Americans to internal personal deficiencies, rather than external societal factors such as discrimination or lack of access to education.[57]

DIGITAL CITIZENSHIP, CRITICAL MEDIA LITERACY, AND RACIALLY INCLUSIVE MEDIA POLICIES

Inclusive media policy-making cannot just take a myopic approach that relates to media users, industry, or messages. All of these interrelated aspects of media have to be simultaneously considered for recommendations to solve racial disparities and misrepresentations. Admittedly, solutions are hard to achieve because of several reasons, such as the dynamic and rapidly evolving media landscape and a long history of exclusion of racial minorities in media ownership, workforce, representations, and policy-making. Policy-makers are often stuck in the traditional media era and narrowly focused on conventional broadcast news media policies. They do not account for media convergence, social media, and the mobile-phone revolution in their policies, which have changed our notions of what media are, who content creators are, and how media messages are accessed, analyzed, produced, and shared by users.

In racially inclusive policy-making, media must be treated as public goods rather than as marketable commodities.[58] Universal media access for all citizens is a right of all citizens. A useful framework has been provided by Philip Napoli for examining diversity in communication policy-making by emphasizing three types of diversity: source diversity, content diversity, and exposure diversity.[59] Source diversity refers to media ownership and the workforce. Content diversity examines media messages and representations in terms of diversity of worldviews, perspectives, genres, and programming. Exposure diversity focused on whether media users expose themselves to multiple media outlets rather than relying only on a single source or few channels. These interpretations of what media diversity means are crucial to influencing regulation and policy. More often than not, diversity is problematically defined only as outlet diversity, which simply means using multiple media channels (such as television, websites, and so forth). Providing broadband access to less connected and wired areas such as tribal lands and rural areas has to be prioritized, given how mediatization and mediation of social institutions have led to media being a gateway to information about almost every aspect of living. One recommendation is to collaborate with community institutions, such as schools and libraries, in such areas in need of greater connectivity.

It is not sufficient, though, to provide access to information and media technology without educating media users about how to use, access, and engage with these tools in meaningful ways. If media technologies do not offer culturally sensitive and socially relevant content, simply bridging the digital divide by providing access is not going to lead to a significant reduction in social inequalities across racial groups. Stricter policies need to be in place to monitor and restrict online white-supremacist and white-nationalist rhetoric. It is also important to be vigilant about the ways in which hate groups are now mainstreaming their hateful messages and using slick marketing tools to do so. Such groups often use stealth and anonymity to promote their anti-minority sentiments. Even traditional mainstream-media content tends to be exclusionary and negative in its portrayals of racial minorities. One recommendation is to have journalists and other media makers become more self-aware of their implicit biases in content selection, framing, and use. Media organizations and professional associations must take the lead on implicit bias training for content creators, so that they can be more aware of what stories are being erased and silenced in a media environment that privileges whiteness. Disillusioned by mainstream corporate-media culture, several minority media producers have used low-tech and low-budget new media to create independent progressive counter-narratives. They often use the marketing strategies and formulas of mainstream media industry but leverage the power of new media technologies to create more diverse and inclusive stories and characters.[60]

Apart from media representations, another area in which policy recommendations are needed relate to the media workforce. With white-owned media outlets largely employing white workers, especially in leadership positions, topics and issues that are relevant to minority audiences are often neglected. Labor organizing and collective bargaining rights for all media workers, but especially those from racial minority groups, will play a key role in ensuring that the media workforce continues to become more equitable and inclusive. We cannot assume that media localism will automatically lead to more inclusive and diverse content.[61] There is often a gap between ideal normative media policy-making and actual decision-making practices based on a variety of community factors. Leadership institutes, mentoring networks, and microfinancing support for small minority-owned media businesses could play a central part in helping such units stay afloat and compete in a white-monopolized media market. Minority ownership of media is likely to lead to a greater commitment to catering to minority audiences and to content diversity.

Given the lack of racial inclusion in media contexts, citizens need to make a conscious effort to support alternative, community-oriented, ethnic media. A network of hyperlocal, ethnically inclusive, alternative citizens' media would facilitate sharing of resources, ideas, and support. The notion of geo-ethnic storytelling refers to the creation of culturally relevant narratives that pertain to a specific ethnic group in a particular geographic location.[62] In a politically divided and racially segregated context, there is a need now more than ever for interethnic and interfaith community conversations that can be facilitated through media, especially using social media networking sites. Community-based organizations need to support not just culturally focused programming, but also need to get involved in sociopolitical issues that can lead to greater media engagement among racial/ethnic minority group members.

Media are powerful tools that can be used to resist, redefine, and reframe what it means to be a racial minority in our society. Such alternative forms of mediated storytelling are more inclusive, racially equitable, and participatory. For example, Ramasubramanian outlines two case studies (*Question Bridge* and *East Los High*) that use community-based storytelling to challenge mainstream portrayals of racial minorities and provide an alternative space for expressing minority voices.[63] While *Question Bridge* uses real-world question-and-answer video formats to redefine black masculinity, *East Los High* engages in alternative storytelling using fictional entertainment narratives. Beyond these cases, there are several media-activist groups such as Silk Road Rising, Honor the Treaties, Media Rise, Citizens' Critics, and Dialogues on Race in Louisiana that are committed to using media, storytelling, and art for promoting meaningful media that focus on social justice and positive inclusive storytelling about stigmatized groups. There are also a few professional networks for content creators and media producers to provide mentoring support and shared resources. These organizations include Media Action Grassroots Network, National Association of Black Journalists, National Hispanic Media Council, and Media Action Network for Asian Americans, among others.

A recommended initiative that would encourage greater digital inclusion and media engagement of racial minorities could be "Citizens' Media Corp," where citizens conduct seminars, courses, and workshops about media literacy education for fellow citizens. Other scholars have similarly recommended providing financial support to create a network of college graduates to work with low-income high-risk groups through public institutions such as libraries.[64] These community-based forums should focus on media access, analysis, production, and assessment, so that community members can gauge the best media formats that would fit their needs and goals. They also learn critical media literacy skills to be able to evaluate media messages for their values, intent, objectives, and biases. They are also taught how to create their own messages actively by sharing their stories, perspectives, and voices on various topics that are relevant in their own everyday lives. Media literacy can serve as a skill of inquiry as well as a means of self-expression in the context of an increasingly digital media–saturated environment. Critical new-media literacy education should emphasize the use of digital media tools as means to foster greater support for marginalized voices, create inclusive spaces for alternative public discourses, and engage with the larger community about issues of media justice and inclusion.

It is crucial to continue advocating for more diverse and auspicious portrayals of racial minorities in the media, especially for groups such as Native Americans and Latinx Americans who are sorely underrepresented in the media. We need to be proactive as media educators, policy-makers, activists, and citizens in demanding media portrayals of racial minorities that challenge and counter existing cultural stereotypes. Although much of the research on media stereotyping has focused on news media, entertainment scholars have found that counter-stereotypical portrayals in fictional entertainment media can have positive outcomes on audiences' racial attitudes and beliefs. Specifically, exposure to counter-stereotypical media characters rather than stereotypical ones can lead to prejudice reduction and more support for pro-minority policies.[65] Taking a multifaceted approach that incorporates both media users and messages is likely to be more effective than any one single approach by itself.[66] Specifically, combining media-literacy training along with exposure to positive counter-stereotypical media exemplars is likely to lead to prejudice reduction toward racial minorities.

CONCLUSION

There are many ways in which race and policy are shaped within and by media contexts through inequalities in ownership, workforce, representation, use, and policy-making. The central role of media in our mediated digital world today and its intertwined relationship with other sociocultural institutions cannot be overemphasized. Given the increased proliferation of media types, news channels, online sites, and social media, media users live in a media-saturated world, and there is intense competition in the media market for gaining audiences' attention. The information divide continues to exist across racial groups, which means that racial minorities are put at a disadvantage not only technologically but also economically, socially, politically, and culturally. Racial minorities should be able to be active digital citizens who fully engage in and participate in society using digital technologies, through civic participation, self-expression, political engagement, and economic actualization. Racial parity has not been reached in media ownership, representation in the media itself, or in the media workforce. Achieving active digital participation by racial minorities would require sustained, multipronged, long-term, and proactive efforts that include media-activist organizing, advocacy for racial parity in the media, hiring and retention efforts in the media workforce, inclusive media policy-making, greater support for community-based alternative media initiatives, and critical media-literacy education. It will be important to consider the intersection of racial identity with other markers of difference such as age, gender, education, social class, citizenship status, ability, sexual orientation, religious identity, and place of residence as we work toward a more inclusive media world. These initiatives should take into account the multiracial, multicultural, and multilingual media context that often mark the lived everyday experiences of racial minorities.

NOTES

The author would like to thank Alexandra N. Sousa and Caitlin Miles for their research assistance on this chapter. She is grateful to the editors, Josh Grimm and Jaime Loke, and the fellow panelists at the LSU Breaux symposium for their input. Special thanks to Manship School faculty member Meghan S. Sanders for her support.

1. Henry Jenkins, *Fans, Bloggers, and Gamers: Exploring Participatory Culture* (New York: New York University Press, 2006); Henry Jenkins, Sam Ford, and Joshua Green, *Spreadable Media: Creating Value and Meaning in a Networked Culture* (New York: New York University Press, 2013).

2. "Growth in Time Spent with Media Is Slowing," *E-marketer*, June 6, 2016.

3. Stephen Heyman, "Photos, Photos Everywhere," *New York Times*, July 29, 2015.

4. Beverly Roskos-Ewoldsen, John Davies, and David R. Roskos-Ewoldsen, "Implications of the Mental Models Approach for Cultivation Theory," *Communications* 29, no. 3 (2004): 354–64.

5. Sandra J. Ball-Rokeach, "Dependency Model of Mass-Media Effects," *Communication Research* 3, no. 1 (1976): 3–19; Srividya Ramasubramanian, "Intergroup Contact, Media Exposure, and Racial Attitudes," *Journal of Intercultural Communication Research* 42, no. 1 (2013): 54–72.

6. Rick W. Busselle and L. J. Shrum, "Media Exposure and Exemplar Accessibility," *Media Psychology* 5, no. 3 (2003): 255–82; Yuki Fujioka, "Television Portrayals and African-American Stereotypes: Examination of Television Effects When Direct Contact Is Lacking," *Journalism & Mass Communication Quarterly* 76, no. 1 (1999): 52–75; Rhonda Gibson and Dolf Zillmann, "Exaggerated versus Representative Exemplification in News Reports: Perception of Issues and Personal Consequences," *Communication Research* 21, no. 5 (1994): 603–24.

7. George Gerbner, Larry Gross, Michael Morgan, Nancy Signorielli, and James Shanahan, "Growing Up with Television: Cultivation Processes" in *Media Effects: Advances*

in Theory and Research, ed. Jennings Bryant and Dolf Zillmann (Hillsdale, NJ: Lawrence Erlbaum Associates, 2002).

8. Eunkyung Jo and Leonard Berkowitz, "A Priming Effect Analysis of Media Influences: An Update" in *Media Effects,* ed. Bryant and Zillmann.

9. Roskos-Ewoldsen et al., "Implications of the Mental Models Approach for Cultivation Theory."

10. Nick Couldry and Andreas Hepp, "Conceptualizing Mediatization: Contexts, Traditions, Arguments," *Communication Theory* 23 (2013): 191–202; Knut Lundby, *Mediatization: Concept, Changes, Consequences* (New York: Peter Lang Publishing Inc., 2013).

11. Stig Hjarvard, "The Mediatization of Society," *Nordicom Review* 29, no. 2 (2008): 105–34.

12. Pippa Norris, *Digital Divide: Civic Engagement, Information Poverty, and the Internet Worldwide* (Cambridge, UK: Cambridge University Press, 2001).

13. Aaron Smith, "African Americans and Technology Use," *Pew Research Center,* January 2014; Andrew Perrin, "Social Networking Usage: 2005–2015," *Pew Research Center,* October 2015.

14. Jens Manuel Krogstad, "Social Media Preferences Vary by Race and Ethnicity," *Pew Research Center,* February 2015.

15. "Report on Ownership of Commercial Broadcast Stations," *Federal Communications Commission,* June 2014.

16. Smith, "African Americans and Technology Use."

17. Karen Mossberger, David Kaplan, and Michele A. Gilbert, "Going Online without Easy Access: A Tale of Three Cities," *Journal of Urban Affairs* 30, no. 5 (2008): 469–88.

18. Teresa Correa and Sun Ho Jeong, "Race and Online Content Creation: Why Minorities Are Actively Participating in the Web," *Information, Communication & Society,* 14, no. 5 (2011): 638–59; Eszter *Hargittai* and Gina Walejko, "The Participation Divide: Content Creation and Sharing in the Digital Age," *Information, Community and Society* 11, no. 2 (2008): 239–56; Linda A. Jackson, Yong Zhao, Anthony Kolenic III, Hiram E. Fitzgerald, Rena Harold, and Alexander Von Eye, "Race, Gender, and Information Technology Use: The New Digital Divide," *CyberPsychology & Behavior* 11, no. 4 (2008): 437–42.

19. Mossberger, Kaplan, and Gilbert, "Going Online without Easy Access"; *Hargittai* and Walejko, "The Participation Divide."

20. Jackson et al., "Race, Gender, and Information Technology Use."

21. E. Ann Carson, "Prisoners in 2013," *Bureau of Justice Statistics,* September 2014.

22. Jean Manuel Krogstad, Renee Stepler, and Mark Hugo Lopez, "English Proficiency on the Rise among Latinos," *Pew Research Center,* May 2015.

23. "Report on Ownership of Commercial Broadcast Stations."

24. Edward C. Pease, Erna Smith, and Federico Subervi, "The News and Race Models of Excellence Project: Overview Connecting Newsroom Attitudes toward Ethnicity and News Content," *The News & Race Project,* October 17, 2001.

25. "National Advisory Board on Civil Disorder," *Report of the National Advisory Commission on Civil Disorders,* 1968.

26. "ASNE Releases 2016 Diversity Survey Results," *ASNE.*

27. Ibid; Bob Papper, "RTDNA Research: Women and Minorities in Newsrooms," *Radio Television Digital News Association,* 2015.

28. Darnell Hunt, Anna-Christina Ramon, and Michael Tran, "2016 Hollywood Diversity Report: Busine$$ as Usual?" *UCLA Bunche Center,* 2016.

29. Francesca Coppa, "Women, *Star Trek,* and the Early Development of Fannish Vidding," *Transformative Works and Cultures* 1 (2008); Aymar Jean Christian, "Fandom as Industrial Response: Producing Identity in an Independent Web Series," *Transformative Works and Cultures* 8 (2011).

30. "ASNE Releases 2016 Diversity Survey Results."

31. "Report on Ownership of Commercial Broadcast Stations."

32. Mari Castañeda, Martha Fuentes-Bautista, and Felicitas Baruch, "Racial and Ethnic Inclusion in the Digital Era: Shifting Discourses in Communications Public Policy," *Journal of Social Issues* 71, no. 1 (2015): 139–54.

33. Jeffrey Layne Blevins and Karla Martinez, "A Political-Economic History of FCC Policy on Minority Broadcast Ownership," *Communication Review* 13, no. 3 (2010): 216–38.

34. Jessie Daniels, "Race and Racism in Internet Studies: A Review and Critique," *New Media & Society* 15, no. 5 (2013): 695–719; Matthew W. Hughey and Jessie Daniels, "Racist Comments at Online News Sites: A Methodological Dilemma for Discourse Analysis," *Media, Culture and Society* 35, no. 3 (2013): 332–47.

35. Abraham H. Foxman and Christopher Wolf, *Viral Hate: Containing Its Spread on the Internet* (Basingstoke, UK: Palgrave Macmillan, 2013); Lisa Nakamura, *Cybertypes: Race, Ethnicity, and Identity on the Internet* (London: Routledge, 2013).

36. Dana Mastro, Maria Knight Lapinski, Maria A. Kopacz, and Elizabeth Behm-Morawitz, "The Influence of Exposure to Depictions of Race and Crime in TV News on Viewer's Social Judgments," *Journal of Broadcasting & Electronic Media* 53, no. 4 (2009): 615–35; Nancy Signorielli, "Television's Gender Role Images and Contribution to Stereotyping" in *Handbook of Children and the Media,* ed. Dorothy G. Singer and Jerome L. Singer (Thousand Oaks, CA: Sage, 2001).

37. George Gerbner and Larry Gross, "Living with Television: The Violence Profile," *Journal of Communication* 26, no. 2 (1976): 172–94; Sherryl Brown Graves, "Psychological Effects of Black Portrayals on Television," in *Television and Social Behavior: Beyond Violence and Children* (Hillsdale, NJ: Lawrence Erlbaum Associates, Inc., 1980).

38. Norris, *Digital Divide.*

39. "Technology Trends among People of Color," *Pew Center Report,* 2010.

40. Nancy Signorielli, "Minorities Representation in Prime Time: 2000 to 2008," *Communication Research Reports* 26, no. 4 (2009): 323–36.

41. Donald Bogle, *Toms, Coons, Mulattoes, Mammies, and Bucks: An Interpretive History of Blacks in American Films,* (New York: Continuum, 2001); Travis L. Dixon and Daniel Linz, "Overrepresentation and Underrepresentation of African Americans and Latinos as Lawbreakers on Television News," *Journal of Communication* 50, no. 2 (2000): 131–54; Robert M. Entman and Andrew Rojecki, *The Black Image in the White Mind: Media and Race in America* (Chicago: University of Chicago Press, 2001).

42. Dana E. Mastro and Bradley S. Greenberg, "The Portrayal of Racial Minorities on

Prime Time Television," *Journal of Broadcasting and Electronic Media,* 44 (2000): 690–703; Mary Beth Oliver, "African American Men as "Criminal and Dangerous": Implications of Media Portrayals of Crime on the "Criminalization" of African American Men," *Journal of African American Studies* 7, no. 2 (2003): 3–18.

43. Elizabeth Behm-Morawitz and Michelle Ortiz, "Race, Ethnicity, and the Media," *The Oxford Handbook of Media Psychology* (New York: Oxford University Press, 2012); Dana Mastro and Elizabeth Behm-Morawitz, "Latino Representation on Primetime Television: A Content Analysis," *Journalism & Mass Communication Quarterly* 82 (2005): 110–30.

44. Guy Aoki and Jeffrey Scott Mio, "Stereotypes and Media Images" in *Asian American Psychology: Current Perspectives,* ed. Nita Tewari and Alvin N. Alvarez (New York: Routledge, 2009); Kent A. Ono and Vincent N. Pham, *Asian Americans and the Media* (Cambridge, UK: Polity Press, 2009).

45. Aoki and Mio, "Stereotypes and Media Images"; Amita Nijhawan, "Mindy Calling: Size, Beauty, Race in The Mindy Project," *M/C Journal* 18, no. 3 (2015): 1; Ono and Pham, *Asian Americans and the Media*; Srividya Ramasubramanian, "A Content Analysis of the Portrayal of India in Films Produced in the West," *Howard Journal of Communication,* 16, no. 4 (2005): 243–65; Srividya Ramasubramanian, "The Impact of Stereotypical versus Counter-stereotypical Media Exemplars on Racial Attitudes, Causal Attributions, and Support for Affirmative Action," *Communication Research* 38 (2011): 497–516; Srividya Ramasubramanian, Marissa Joanna Doshi, and Muniba Saleem, "Mainstream versus Ethnic Media: How They Shape Self-Esteem and Ethnic Pride among Ethnic Minorities," *International Journal of Communication,* 11 (2017): 1879–99.

46. Osei Appiah, "Black, White, Hispanic, and Asian American Adolescents' Responses to Culturally Embedded Ads," *Howard Journal of Communication* 12, no. 1 (2001): 29–48; Yuki Fujioka, "Black Media Images as a Perceived Threat to African American Ethnic Identity: Coping Responses, Perceived Public Perception, and Attitudes towards Affirmative Action," *Journal of Broadcasting & Electronic Media* 49, no. 4 (2005): 450–67.

47. "The Ethnic Media in America: The Giant Hidden in Plain Sight," *New California Media,* 2005.

48. Jessica R. Abrams, William P. Eveland, and Howard Giles, "The Effects of Television on Group Vitality: Can Television Empower Nondominant Groups?" *Communication Yearbook* 27 (2003): 193–220.

49. Richard L. Allen, *Concept of Self: A Study of Black Identity and Self-Esteem* (Detroit: Wayne State University Press, 2001); Ramasubramanian et al., "Mainstream versus Ethnic Media."

50. Jo and Berkowitz, "A Priming Effect Analysis of Media Influences."

51. Nicholas A. Valentino, "Crime News and the Priming of Racial Attitudes during Evaluations of the President," *Public Opinion Quarterly* 63, no. 3 (1999): 293–320.

52. Gerbner et al., "Growing Up with Television"; Busselle and Shrum, "Media Exposure and Exemplar Accessibility."

53. Entman and Rojecki, *The Black Image in the White Mind*; Mary Beth Oliver, "Portrayals of Crime, Race, and Aggression in 'Reality-Based' Police Shows: A Content Analysis," *Journal of Broadcasting & Electronic Media* 38, no. 2 (1994): 179–92.

54. Travis L. Dixon and Christina L. Azocar, "Priming Crime and Activating Blackness: Understanding the Psychological Impact of the Overrepresentation of Blacks as Lawbreakers on Television News," *Journal of Communication* 57, no. 2 (2007): 229–53; Thomas E. Ford, "Effects of Stereotypical Television Portrayals of African-Americans on Person Perception," *Social Psychology Quarterly* 60, no. 3 (1997): 266–75; Franklin D. Gilliam Jr. and Shanto Iyengar, "Prime Suspects: The Influence of Local Television News on the Viewing Public," *American Journal of Political Science* 44, no. 3 (2000): 560–73.

55. Dixon and Azocar, "Priming Crime and Activating Blackness"; Mary Beth Oliver, Ronald L. Jackson, Ndidi N. Moses, and Celnisha L. Dangerfield, "The Face of Crime: Viewers' Memory of Race-Related Facial Features of Individuals Pictured in the News," *Journal of Communication,* 54, no. 1 (2004): 88–104.

56. Srividya Ramasubramanian, "Television Viewing, Racial Attitudes, and Policy Preferences: Exploring the Role of Social Identity and Intergroup Emotions in Influencing Support for Affirmative Action," *Communication Monographs* 77, no. 1 (2010): 102–20; Ramasubramanian, "The Impact of Stereotypical versus Counter-Stereotypical Media."

57. Ramasubramanian, "The Impact of Stereotypical versus Counter-Stereotypical Media."

58. Castañeda et al., "Racial and Ethnic Inclusion in the Digital Era"; Philip M. Napoli, *Foundations of Communications Policy: Principles and Process in the Regulation of Electronic Media* (Cresskill, NJ: Hampton Press, 2001).

59. Napoli, *Foundations of Communication Policy.*

60. Christian, "Fandom as Industrial Response."

61. Sandra Braman, "The Ideal v. the Real in Media Localism: Regulatory Implications," *Communication Law and Policy* 12, no. 3 (2007): 231–78.

62. Yong-Chan Kim and Sandra J. Ball-Rokeach, "Civic Engagement from a Communication Infrastructure Perspective," *Communication Theory* 16, no. 2 (2006): 173–97.

63. Srividya Ramasubramanian, "Using Celebrity News to Reduce Racial/Ethnic Prejudice," *Journal of Social Issues* 71, no. 1 (2015): 123–37.

64. Castañeda et al., "Racial and Ethnic Inclusion in the Digital Era."

65. Ramasubramanian, "The Impact of Stereotypical versus Counter-Stereotypical Media"; Ramasubramanian, "Using Celebrity News to Reduce Racial/Ethnic Prejudice."

66. Srividya Ramasubramanian, "Media-Based Strategies to Reduce Racial Stereotypes Activated by News Stories," *Journalism & Mass Communication Quarterly* 84, no. 2 (2007): 249–64; Erica Scharrer and Srividya Ramasubramanian, "Intervening in the Media's Influence on Stereotypes of Race and Ethnicity: The Role of Media Literacy," *Journal of Social Issues* 71, no. 1 (2015): 171–85.

PUBLIC POLICIES DESIGNED TO INCREASE HEALTH EQUITY

HOLLEY A. WILKIN

Predominantly lower-income, ethnic-minority neighborhoods often lack health-promoting resources such as high-quality health care facilities[1] and healthy food options[2] while having an abundance of health-compromising resources such as fast-food restaurants and liquor stores.[3] Features of the built environment such as the presence or absence of parks, walking and biking trails, and public transportation can be health enhancing, while features like factories, vacant properties, conditions of available housing, and the like can be health compromising.[4] Additionally, social factors such as the amount of social cohesion, social capital, collective efficacy,[5] crime, violence, and social disorder[6] impact health outcomes. As a result, lower-income, predominantly minority neighborhoods have higher rates of asthma, mental health issues, and obesity-related diseases than higher-income communities.[7]

"Food deserts" is a term used to identify neighborhoods that lack healthy food options, like high-quality fruits and vegetables.[8] One increasingly popular solution to this problem is community gardens. However, a potential problem with this solution is that lower-income neighborhoods are also more likely to be affected by environmental pollutants.[9] These pollutants may adversely affect the quality of soil or water used to grow produce. Therefore, care must be taken in the selection of sites for community gardens and/or the types of produce grown in these spaces so as to not inadvertently increase health risks. Neighborhood-level health determinants like these contribute to health disparities.

Health disparities occur when groups of people—for example, racial/ethnic groups, age groups, genders, sexualities, religious groups, socioeconomic groups, those living in certain geographic locations—are disproportionately affected by health problems associated with economic, social, and/or environmental disadvantages.[10] For example, African Americans and Latinos are more likely than other racial/ethnic groups to suffer from chronic diseases like diabetes, hypertension, and obesity.[11] While white/Caucasian women have the highest incidence rates of breast cancer, black/African American women have the highest mortality rates of any ethnic/racial group.[12] Scholars point to other disparities—in income, insurance rates, primary health care access, rates of being screened for health issues, and so forth—as contributing toward health-outcome disparities.[13]

Health equity can be improved through policies designed to increase access to health-promoting resources (for example, primary health care, adequate health insurance, healthy foods, cleaner air and water) or by reducing factors that serve as detriments to mental and physical health (for example, social disorder, urban blight, toxic waste). In 2000, the leading causes of death in the United States were tobacco, poor diet, physical inactivity, alcohol consumption, microbial agents, and toxins.[14] Therefore, this chapter focuses on policy related to increasing access to health care (needed to reduce incidence and mortality rates), and on policies directly related to the mortality rates: reducing exposure to tobacco smoke, improving access to healthy foods, and creating healthier environments to reduce exposure to microbial agents and toxins.

INCREASING HEALTH CARE ACCESS

A primary health care home—where patients have personal physicians who oversee their medical care, track referrals, and provide continuous patient care—can lead to early detection of health issues and proper management of chronic diseases.[15] This type of care helps reduce serious health complications from illnesses, the use of emergency rooms for nonemergencies,[16] and the overall costs of health care.[17] Primary health care use has been shown to have a positive impact on the care of children with chronic diseases and other special health care needs.[18] Essentially, it can improve health equity by connecting people with the resources needed to prevent, diagnose, and manage illnesses.

The most often cited barrier to primary health care is a lack of health insurance.[19] Insurance is also necessary for patients to be able to afford medical treatment (medical laboratory exams, X-rays, prescription medicines) that may be necessary to detect and treat illnesses. For those with health insurance, copayments may be cost-prohibitive for low-income households.[20] Health care costs are one explanation for health disparities. For example, early detection is associated with higher breast-cancer survival rates.[21] African Americans, Latinos, and American Indians/Alaskan natives are more likely to be uninsured or underinsured than whites in the United States.[22] There are programs that provide low- or no-cost mammography tests, but someone who lacks insurance to help pay for treatment may opt not to be tested, which leads to later diagnoses and a lower chance of survival. This is one reason why African American women are more likely to die from breast cancer then white women, even though white women have a higher incidence rate.

The majority of racial/ethnic minority families in the United States has at least one full-time worker; however, they are more likely than whites to work in lower-income professions that do not offer health insurance.[23] This contributes to higher uninsured rates in these populations. To date, the largest health care reform effort designed to increase access to health insurance in the United States is the Patient Protection and Affordable Care Act (ACA).

Often referred to as "Obamacare," the ACA was signed into law by President Obama in 2010. It was designed to increase health equity by increasing access to health insurance through the expansion of Medicaid and tax breaks on insurance provided through health-insurance-exchange marketplaces.[24] ACA provisions include: (1) insurance companies cannot deny patients based upon preexisting health conditions, cannot charge patients more due to preexisting conditions or biological sex, cannot drop patients due to existing medical conditions, and cannot have maximum annual or lifetime coverage amounts; (2) dependents can stay on parents' or guardians' insurance plans up until age twenty-six, even if the dependent is no longer living in the parents' home or is no longer being claimed as a dependent on taxes; (3) insurance plans must cover reproductive health care (for example, contraception) for women; and (4) no copayments can be charged for preventative care such as wellness visits or health screenings like colonoscopy, mammography, sexually transmitted disease testing, and counseling.[25]

More than 20 million Americans (17.7 million nonelderly adults through open enrollment and 2.3 million young adults through the parental insurance provision) gained insurance coverage as a result of the ACA.[26] Between the start of open enrollment in 2013 to early 2016, the uninsured rate dropped from 22.4 to 10.6 percent (an increase of approximately 3 million black nonelderly adults with coverage) among black non-Hispanics; dropped from 41.8 to 30.5 percent (an increase of approximately 4 million Hispanic nonelderly adults with coverage) among Hispanics; and dropped from 14.3 to 7.0 percent (an increase of approximately 8.9 million white nonelderly adults with coverage) among white non-Hispanics.[27] Additionally, between 2010 and 2014, 3.6 million adults with preexisting conditions gained health insurance, representing a 22 percent decline in the share of adults with preexisting conditions who were uninsured.[28]

The ACA has increased access and use of mental health and substance abuse care,[29] access to primary medical care, increased diagnoses of chronic diseases, and increased medical prescription-drug adherence.[30] Individual state results vary based upon whether Medicaid expansion was adopted. Between 2014 and 2016, uninsured rates declined by 9.2 percent (representing a 49.5 percent decline of uninsured) in states that adopted Medicaid expansion and by 7.9 percent (representing a 33.8 percent decline in uninsured) in states that did not adopt Medicaid expansion.[31] Low-income adults who indicate a regular source of health care (for example, a primary health care home) increased by 7.2 percent points in states that expanded Medicaid and 1.3 percent points in those that did not.[32] Safety-net hospitals—those that treat low-income, uninsured, Medicaid enrollees, and other vulnerable populations— in states that expanded Medicaid benefited financially by seeing an increase in insured patients and a decrease in uninsured patients. Those that did not adopt the Medicaid expansion saw no change in patient type and increasing financial costs.[33]

Despite these strides toward health equity, the ACA does not completely eliminate all barriers to health care.[34] One limitation of the ACA's use of state health care exchanges to provide qualified health plans (QHPs) is "the creation of narrow networks, where insurers offer plans and policies with fewer doctors and hospitals."[35] Public criticism of this type of practice "has created the perception that exchange-based QHPs are limiting access to a greater extent than did pre-ACA policies."[36] Another ACA limitation is related to the cost of health care. The ACA requires QHPs to provide essential health benefits. The cost sharing of those benefits are offered through different plans that range from Platinum (higher monthly premiums, lower out-of-pocket costs) to Bronze (lower monthly premiums, higher out-of-pocket costs). The Bronze plan is the second most popular due to the lower monthly cost but requires the highest deductibles.[37] Higher deductibles and co-pays remain deterrents to health care seeking among lower-income individuals and families.[38]

Health care premiums are expected to increase in some state marketplaces in 2017.[39] This may affect whether people remain enrolled in insurance plans. Another factor that might affect future health-insurance rates in the United States is that, in the 2016 elections, the Republican Party took control of the House of Representatives, Senate, and Office of the President. Republican leadership has been promising to repeal and replace "Obamacare" since its conception. In March 2017, House Republicans passed the American Health Care Act. If this bill became law, it would likely reverse many of the recent gains toward health equity. For example, the House bill removes the provision that protects those with preexisting health problems from being charged higher premiums or completely denied coverage by insurance companies. It is estimated that between 23 percent (using a narrow definition) and 51 percent (using a broader definition) of Americans have preexisting health conditions.[40] The nonpartisan Congressional Budget Office (CBO) estimates that this bill would save the federal government $119 billion in costs between 2017 and 2026, but in that time, 23 million Americans would lose insurance coverage.[41]

Instead of voting on the House bill, Senate Republicans opted to write their own bill, "The Better Care Conciliation Act of 2017." This bill would not allow insurance agencies to deny coverage to those with preexisting conditions but would allow states to reduce the types of coverage provided and insurance companies to increase premiums for nonessential care, impose limits to the benefits they provide, and remove the caps for annual out-of-pocket costs.[42] States could petition to "opt out" of providing essential benefits included in the ACA (for example, mental health care, reproductive health care), which can make certain types of care cost-prohibitive.[43] The ACA's Medicaid expansion would be phased out and the Medicaid program further reduced starting in 2025.[44] The CBO estimates that "enacting this legislation would reduce the cumulative federal deficit over the 2017–2026 period by $321 billion" while increasing "the number of people who are uninsured by 22 million in 2026 relative to the number under current law. . . . By 2026, an estimated 49 million people would be uninsured, compared with 28 million who would lack insurance that year under current law."[45] A few conservative Republican senators have stated that they will not vote for the current version of the bill because it retains too many ACA provisions. Meanwhile, some moderate Republican senators oppose the cuts to Medicaid, which would adversely affect their state's elderly and rural populations and/or their ability to fight ongoing opioid epidemics. At the time of the writing of this chapter, Republican leadership delayed the vote in order to revise in ways that might acquire enough votes for the bill to pass[46] and have been unsuccessful with subsequent efforts to repeal and/or replace the ACA.[47]

REDUCING TOBACCO SMOKING AND EXPOSURE TO SECONDHAND SMOKE

According to the Centers for Disease Control and Prevention's timeline of tobacco-related policies, research linking lung cancer and other diseases to excessive cigarette smoking first started appearing in the 1940s and 1950s. Cigarette ads were banned from television and radio in 1969. The 1972 U.S. Surgeon General's Report included research indicating the dangers of secondhand smoke, or environmental tobacco smoke (ETS). Arizona was the first state to adopt policies to reduce ETS in 1973. The federal government started restricting tobacco use in the 1970s, including a ban on smoking in federal government facilities (with the exception of the White House, where it was not banned until 1993). In 1990 Congress prohibited smoking on all commercial U.S. flights. In 1994, states started suing the tobacco industry to recover Medicaid costs associated with tobacco-related illnesses. In 1998, a Master Settlement Agreement was made between the tobacco industry and forty-six states. In 1999 the U.S. tobacco industry started to remove all tobacco ads from outdoor billboards and public transportation.[48]

In 2006, the Surgeon General stated that the only way to reduce health problems associated with secondhand smoke is to completely eliminate smoking in all indoor areas.[49] Between 2000 and 2015, twenty-seven states enacted policies banning smoking in work sites, restaurants, and bars. The southeastern United States, where tobacco is grown and the production of tobacco products is often tied to the economic welfare of the individual states, lags behind on smoke-free policy adoption. There are also loopholes in the existing smoke-free laws. For instance, Las Vegas casinos are exempted from the workplace tobacco bans in Nevada.[50]

Smoking policies have contributed to a reduction in smoking rates. For example, a study found that smoking rates had declined in the United States and Canada by approximately 50 percent over the span of four decades.[51] Smoking reductions were greatest among individuals with higher education and socioeconomic status, which contributes to smoking-related disease disparities. Low-income women, particularly those who are members of racial/ethnic minorities, are more likely to be exposed to tobacco smoke in the home and workplace than higher-income women and men.[52] There are fewer bans on smoking in food-preparation and service occupations, where low-income women make up the majority of the workforce. Additionally, studies have shown that, even when smoke-free laws exist in bars, they are not always enforced when managers and patrons are predominantly male and the staff predominantly female.[53] Thus, men have benefited more from workplace smoking bans. Another common policy to reduce smoking behavior is the use of tobacco taxes. This strategy is designed to make cigarettes more cost-prohibitive. While this strategy has led to a greater decline in smoking among low-income women, higher taxes mean that that poor women who are unable to quit might forego other needs (such as food, electricity, water) to support their habit, which could lead to other health concerns.[54]

Current smoke-free policies need to be expanded and loopholes closed.[55] Future policies need to take into consideration "the intended and unintended effects of tobacco-control policies, gender and diversity related differences in the effects of smoking and of tobacco control policies, psychosocial factors underlying tobacco use and [secondhand smoke] exposure, social divisions created through smoking and/or policy, gendered relational dynamics, and the effects of denormalization on stigma related to smoking."[56]

IMPROVING ACCESS TO HEALTHY FOODS

Lower-income neighborhoods are often food deserts. They may also be "food swamps" due to higher concentrations of unhealthy food options.[57] A study of Los Angeles found lower-quality foods in grocery stores in the predominantly African American and Latino neighborhoods in South Los Angeles than in the predominantly white (and higher-income) grocery stores in West Los Angeles neighborhoods.[58] A community-based project took steps to improve access to healthy foods in South Los Angeles neighborhoods. First, they worked with the local grocery stores to increase the availability and quality of fresh produce and to rearrange the food displays to more prominently feature health-promoting items (such as fresh produce) instead of health-compromising items (for example, alcohol, tobacco). Second, community mobilization was used to obtain a ten-year moratorium on the building of fast-food restaurants in the neighborhoods.[59] This is one smaller-scale example of improving access to healthy foods. Policy at the federal level has focused on improving children's access to healthy foods through school breakfast and lunch programs.

The National School Lunch Act was signed into law in 1946 by President Truman to help provide nutritionally balanced, low-cost or free lunches to children at public and nonprofit private schools and residential childcare institutions. In 1966, based upon the recognition that poor children came to school hungry and were unable to concentrate and learn, the Child Nutrition Act was signed into law by President Johnson. It established a School Breakfast Program and Special Milk Program. In 1970, the National School Lunch Act was reformed to emphasize child nutrition. In the 1980s the USDA was criticized for discrepancies between their nutritional recommendations and the lunch program.

The 1994 Healthy Meals for Healthy Children Act required schools to update their meals to comply with the Dietary Guidelines for Americans.[60] In 1998 the programs were expanded to include snacks for children in after-school programs.[61] Most recently, stemming from First Lady Michelle Obama's "Let's Move" campaign to reduce childhood obesity, the Healthy, Hunger-Free Kids Act was signed into law in 2010.[62] The current guidelines require more fruits, vegetables, and whole grains, specific calorie limits for different age groups, and the reduction of sodium content,[63] along with regulations requiring other foods sold in schools (for example, in vending machines or à la carte lines) to uphold the nutritional standards of the National School Lunch and School Breakfast programs.[64]

The new standards have been met with some criticisms. A nutrition-based criticism points to differences in USDA caloric-intake recommendations—regarding biological sex, level of activity, and body size—and those that of the School Lunch Program that consider only age. Thus, a small, inactive teenaged girl might be getting too many calories while a tall, active teenaged boy might be getting too little in the School Lunch Program.[65] While the federal government sets the standards, local schools are responsible for deciding what foods to serve and how to prepare them, leading to variances in lunch quality and children's reactions to them.[66] There has also been politically driven criticism from Republicans and conservative media. As a result, the current administration is relaxing the guidelines. For example, the USDA, under Agriculture Secretary Sonny Perdue, announced that schools can serve non–whole grain foods, flavored 1 percent milk, and will not have to further reduce the sodium content for at least three more years.[67]

CREATING HEALTHIER ENVIRONMENTS

Environmental health risk factors (for example, noise pollution, air pollution, and lack of green space) tend to cluster together in lower-income neighborhoods.[68] Lower-income, racial-minority neighborhoods have higher exposure risk to both indoor and outdoor environmental hazards that are linked to increased rates of cancer and respiratory diseases.[69] Indoor pollutants are more prevalent in low-income housing (such as lead-based paint and pipes, the presence of cockroaches, and black mold) and contribute to disparities related to the mental and physical health problems associated with lead poisoning and respiratory illnesses associated with increased allergens.[70] Poor housing conditions may also include a lack of hot water needed to clean and sanitize dishes, which increases the spread of diseases.[71] Outdoor pollutants (the presence of factories, power plants, and highways contributing to increased air pollution and illegal dumping of environmental waste contributing to ground and water pollution) increase respiratory and cancer risk.[72] Green space—parks, trees, trails—can help reduce environmental toxins and are also important for improved mental health outcomes.[73]

"The built environment" refers to the human-made aspects of neighborhood, including commercial and residential buildings, factories, signs, roadways, parking lots, and public spaces like plazas, parks, and recreation areas. Built environment features are associated with disparities in physical health[74] and mental health.[75] For example, "walkable neighborhoods"—those with connected streets, sidewalks, and pedestrian-oriented retail—are associated with more physical activity, lower levels of obesity, and less air pollution due to few people driving on the streets.[76]

Neighborhood blight, as represented by a high percentage of unsafe and vacant properties in various stages of disrepair, contribute to poor levels of mental health.[77] A community-based participatory research project found that 42 percent of houses in southeast Atlanta were vacant. Residents participated in a survey during listening sessions and reported poor mental health at a rate 2.5 times the national average (26 percent reported fourteen or more days of poor mental health in the past thirty days). The project worked to improve access to mental health services and created the Dirty Truth Campaign (now a nonprofit organization) to address built-environmental issues affecting mental health.[78] Participants used PhotoVoice, a method that uses photos taken by members of marginalized communities to help tell their stories and influence policy.[79] The City of Atlanta agreed to policy changes enabling nonprofit organizations to acquire and renovate the vacant properties closest to schools and parks.[80] In 2016, the first of these houses went on the market with incentives for police and schoolteachers to buy and live in the neighborhoods. The long-term impact of this project is yet to be realized.

There are several larger-scale policy changes in the United States that impact indoor and outdoor environmental risks, including federal policies designed to improve air and water quality and to reduce exposure to lead. It should be noted that, at the time this chapter was written, the current administration was taking various actions to reduce environmental protection regulations.[81]

The 1970 Clean Air Act (CAA) is a federal law designed to regulate air quality by allowing the Environmental Protection Agency (EPA) to set National Ambient Air Quality Standards (NAAQS) that are in the interest of public health and wellness and to regulate hazardous air emissions. Each state was required to develop its own implementation plans that considered the unique aspects of industry and production and other sources of air pollution in the states. The CAA was amended in 1977 and 1990 to set new goals since NAAQS had not been met. The 1990 amendment (section 112) requires technology-based standards to reduce emissions from major sources of hazardous pollutants.[82] The Centers for Disease Control and Prevention (CDC) found that, while air quality has improved, "during 2006–2008, a total of 53 counties did not meet the standard for fine particulate matter and during 2007–2009, a total of 201 counties did not meet the standard for ozone. . . . Minority groups, including Asians and Hispanics, were more likely to reside in these counties in comparison with non-Hispanic whites. Pollution sources (for example, heavy traffic) and other environmental hazards often affect these areas."[83] The CDC recommends efforts at the local level in these areas to educate the public, increase public transportation options and use, and to influence state industry regulations.

The 1948 Federal Water Pollution Control Act went through major amendments in 1972 and became known as the Clean Water Act (CWA). The CWA gives the EPA authority over pollution-control programs and setting industry wastewater standards; made it illegal to dump pollutants into navigable waters without permit; established a structure to regulate pollutant discharges into U.S. waters; funded the construction of sewage-treatment plants; and maintained existing standards regarding water-surface contaminants. Revisions in 1981 and 1987 changed the structure of the treatment-plant construction programs. The latter replaced it with the State Water Pollution Control Revolving Fund, more commonly known as the Clean Water State Revolving Fund, leveraging established partnerships between states and the EPA. The 1978 Great Lakes Water Quality Agreement between the United States and Canada required the "EPA to establish water quality criteria for the Great Lakes addressing 29 toxic pollutants with maximum levels that are safe for humans, wildlife, and aquatic life. It also required EPA to help the States implement the criteria on a specific schedule."[84]

The United States has made significant gains in improving water quality and sanitation. However, the Centers for Disease Control and

Prevention still recognize areas for concern.[85] Over 13 million households obtain water from unregulated sources (such as wells, local springs, rainwater, livestock water tanks). Access to "healthy water is, or may soon be, limited by the presence of environmental pollutants in local water sources, drought and aquifer depletion that limits water availability, flooding events that overwhelm local treatment capacity, local weather changes associated with climate change, new and more stringent regulations, or failures in water-related infrastructure."[86] The Flint water crisis highlights how regulated water sources can become contaminated, despite various policies aimed to reduce lead exposure.

The 1971 Lead-Based Paint Poisoning Prevention Act (LBPPPA) and its various amendments restrict the use of lead in all residential properties, including public housing. Amendments to the LBPPPA also required the U.S. Department for Housing and Urban Development (HUD) to develop a plan for cost-effective inspection and lead-based abatement plans. The Consumer Product Safety Commission limited the amount of lead allowed in residential paint to .06 percent in 1978 and to .009 percent in 2008. In 1992, Title X made changes that shifted HUD's focus from reacting to lead-based paint poisoning to being proactive in reducing children's lead-based poisoning risks.[87] Other policies have also reduced lead-exposure risk. For example, the phasing out of leaded gasoline started in 1973, the ban on lead used in food cans in 1995, and the U.S. Environmental Protection Agency's Lead and Copper Rule requires the testing and treatment of consumer water to prevent high levels of lead or copper.

Collectively, these policies have contributed to a dramatic reduction in blood lead concentrations in children since the 1970s.[88] Between 2007 and 2010 about 2.6 percent or 535,000 U.S. children aged one to five still had blood lead levels that were too high, indicating that more work needs to be done.[89] The water crisis in Flint, Michigan, which changed from using Lake Huron water to Flint River water without adding a required anticorrosive treatment, caused lead pipes to corrode and thereby poison the drinking water. Flint is a lower-income city with a high percentage of African Americans. The Flint crisis drew attention to the existence of neighborhoods throughout the United States— often in lower-income neighborhoods with crumbling infrastructures that include lead-based pipes, industry waste, and paint—where blood lead levels in children are dangerously high. In fact, a study found three thousand areas that had rates of blood lead poisoning that were double or even as much as four times the rates found in Flint at the peak of the water crisis.[90] Various policies have drastically reduced lead poisoning in the United States, but there is still work needed in both rural and urban neighborhoods to create health equity.

CONCLUSIONS

Health inequities are caused by a number of factors, including access to health care, access to healthy foods, and the nature of people's environments. A number of different policies have been enacted over the years to reduce health disparities. For example, the Patient Protection and Affordable Care Act has reduced the numbers of Americans who are uninsured, increased the use of primary health care, and increased chronic illness diagnosis and treatment.[91] Numerous tobacco policies have been credited with reducing the rates of smoking and exposure to secondhand smoke.[92] The School Breakfast and Lunch program has provided more than 224 billion lunches since its conception, enabling access to food for children who attend public and nonprofit schools and childcare facilities. The Clean Air and Clean Water acts have significantly reduced environmental health risks, and various lead-related policies have reduced lead-based toxicity in children. Despite the relative successes of these programs, health inequities persist in the United States. In some cases, the health policies meant to reduce health disparities actually increase them as they do not benefit every socioeconomic groups evenly or at the same rate. For example, workplace tobacco bans have been shown to be less effective at reducing workplace exposure for the predominantly female, racial minorities who work in lower-income service-industry professions.[93] New policies that consider the contextual factors involved in creating health inequities are needed. Additionally, policies need to address health issues at a local level. For example, excessive lead blood levels in neighborhoods with crumbling infrastructures as well as loopholes in tobacco or clean-air policies must be tackled.

NOTES

1. Kathryn Pitkin Derose et al., "Review: Immigrants and Health Care Access, Quality, and Cost," *Medical Care Research and Review* 66 (2009): 355–408.

2. Renee E. Walker, Christopher R. Keane, and Jessica G. Burke, "Disparities and Access to Health Food in the United States: A Review of Food Deserts literature," *Health & Place* 16 (2010): 876–84.

3. David C. Sloane et al., "Assessing Resource Environments to Target Prevention Interventions in Community Chronic Disease Control," *Journal of Health Care for the Poor and Underserved* 17 (2006): 146–59.

4. Nancy Brisbon, James Plumb, Rickie Brawer, and Dalton Paxman, "The Asthma and Obesity Epidemics: The Role Played by the Built Environment—A Public Health Perspective," *Journal of Allergy and Clinical Immunology* 115 (2005): 1024–28; Gary W. Evans, "The Built Environment and Mental Health," *Journal of Urban Health* 80 (2003): 536–55; James Krieger and Donna L. Higgins, "Housing and Health: Time Again for Public Health Action," *American Journal of Public Health* 92 (2002): 758–68.

5. Ichiro Kawachi and Lisa F. Berkman, eds., *Neighborhoods and Health* (New York: Oxford University Press, 2003).

6. G. C. Richard, Iwachi Kawachi, and Bruce P. Kennedy, "Mortality, the Social Environment, Crime and Violence," *Sociology of Health & Illness* 20 (1998): 578–97.

7. Jennifer L. Black and James Macinko, "Neighborhoods and Obesity," *Nutrition Reviews* 66 (2008): 2–20; Brisbon et al., "The Asthma and Obesity Epidemics"; Evans, "The Built Environment and Mental Health," 536–55.

8. Walker et al., "Disparities and Access to Health Food."

9. Katie M. Booth, Megan M. Pinkston, and Walker S. Carlos Poston, "Obesity and the Built Environment," *Journal of the American Dietetic Association* 105 (2005): 110–17; Susan Strife and Liam Downey, "Childhood Development and Access to Nature: A New Direction for Environmental Inequality Research," *Organization and Environment* 22 (2009): 99–122.

10. U.S. Department of Health and Human Services, "The Secretary's Advisory Committee on National Health Promotion and Disease Prevention Objectives for 2020. Phase I report: Recommendations for the Framework and Format of Healthy People 2020, Section IV: Advisory Committee Findings and Recommendations," last updated January 6, 2010, accessed August 30, 2016, www.healthypeople.gov/sites/default/files/PhaseI_0.pdf.

11. Office of Minority Health, "Obesity Data/Statistics," accessed October 4, 2011, minorityhealth.hhs.gov/templates/browse.aspx?lvl=3&lvlid=537. Brian D. Smedley, Adrienne Y. Stith, and Alan R. Nelson, eds., *Unequal Treatment: Confronting Racial and Ethnic Disparities in Healthcare* (Washington, DC: Institute of Medicine, National Academies Press, 2003).

12. Centers for Disease Control and Prevention, "Breast Cancer Rates by Race and Ethnicity," last modified June 15, 2016, accessed June 1, 2017, www.cdc.gov/cancer/breast/statistics/race.htm

13. Derose et al., "Review: Immigrants and Health Care Access"; Nicole Lurie and Tamara Dubowitz, "Health Disparities and Access to Health," *JAMA* 297 (2007): 1118,

doi:10.1001/jama.297.10.1118; Richard G. Wilkinson, "Socioeconomic Determinants of Health: Health Inequalities: Relative or Absolute Standards?" *BMJ* 314 (1997), 591–95.

14. Ali Mokdad et al., "Actual Causes of Death in the United States, 2000," *JAMA* 291 (2004): 1238–45.

15. Robert Hurley, Deborah Freund, and Donald Taylor, "Emergency Room Use and Primary Care Case Management: Evidence from Four Medicaid Demonstration Programs," *American Journal of Public Health* 79 (1989): 843–47.

16. Dylan Roby et al., "Impact of Patient-Centered Medical Home Assignment on Emergency Room Visits among Uninsured Patients in a County Health System," *Medical Care Research & Review* 67 (2010): 412–30; Cheng Wang et al., "Cost and Utilization Analysis of a Pediatric Emergency Department Diversion Project," *Pediatrics* 116 (2005): 1075–79.

17. Jeff Guo et al., "School-Based Health Centers: Cost—Benefit Analysis and Impact on Health Care Disparities," *American Journal of Public Health* 100 (2010): 1617–23.

18. Judith Palfrey et al., "The Pediatric Alliance for Coordinated Care: Evaluation of a Medical Home Model," *Pediatrics* 113 (2004): 1057–1516.

19. David Himmelstein and Stephanie Woolhandler, "Care Denied: US Residents Who Are Unable to Obtain Needed Medical Services," *American Journal of Public Health* 85 (1995): 341–44; Cathy Schoen and Catherine DesRoches, "Uninsured and Unstably Insured: The Importance of Continuous Insurance Coverage," *Health Services Research* 35 (2000): 187–206.

20. Howard Freeman and Christopher Corey, "Insurance Status and Access to Health Services among Poor Persons," *Health Services Research* 28 (1993): 531–41.

21. Kenneth Chu et al., "Recent Trends in U.S. Breast Cancer Incidence, Survival, and Mortality Rates," *Journal of the National Cancer Institute* 88 (1996), 1571.

22. Kaiser Family Foundation. "Health Coverage by Race and Ethnicity: The Potential Impact of the Affordable Care Act," March 13, 2013, accessed June 1, 2017, www.kff.org /disparities-policy/issue-brief/health-coverage-by-race-and-ethnicity-the-potential -impact-of-the-affordable-care-act/.

23. Kaiser Family Foundation, "Health Coverage by Race and Ethnicity."

24. Ibid.

25. U.S. Department of Health and Human Services, "About the Affordable Care Act," last reviewed on March 16, 2017, accessed June 1, 2017, www.hhs.gov/healthcare/about -the-aca/index.html.

26. Namarata Uberoi, Kenneth Finegold, and Emily Gee, "Health Insurance Coverage and the Affordable Care Act, 2010–2016," Department of Health and Human Services ASPE Issue Brief, 2016, accessed June 1, 2017, aspe.hhs.gov/system/files/pdf/187551/ACA 2010–2016.pdf.

27. Ibid.

28. U.S. Department of Health and Human Services, "Health Insurance Coverage for Americans with Pre-existing Conditions: The Impact of the Affordable Care Act," January 5, 2017, accessed June 1, 2017, aspe.hhs.gov/system/files/pdf/255396/Pre -ExistingConditions.pdf.

29. U.S. Department of Health and Human Services, "Continuing Progress on the Opioid Epidemic: The Role of the Affordable Care Act," last reviewed on March 16, 2017, accessed June 1, 2017, aspe.hhs.gov/system/files/pdf/255456/ACAOpioid.pdf.

30. U.S. Department of Health and Human Services, "Medicaid Expansion Impacts on Insurance Coverage and Access to Care," January 18, 2017, accessed June 1, 2017, aspe.hhs.gov/system/files/pdf/255516/medicaidexpansion.pdf.

31. U.S. Department of Health and Human Services, "Medicaid Expansion Impacts on Insurance Coverage."

32. Ibid.

33. Laurie Felland et al, "Effects of the Affordable Care Act on Safety Net Hospitals," *Mathematica Policy Research Report* (2016), accessed June 1, 2017, aspe.hhs.gov/system/files/pdf/255491/SafetyNetHospital.pdf.

34. Gerald F. Kominski, Narissa J. Nonzee, and Andrea Sorensen, "The Affordable Care Act's Impacts on Access to Insurance and Health Care for Low-Income Populations," *Annual Review of Public Health* 38 (2017): 489–90.

35. Ibid., 490.

36. Ibid.

37. Ibid.

38. Freeman and Corey, "Insurance Status and Access to Health Services."

39. Cynthia Cox et al., "2017 Premium Changes and Insurance Participation in the Affordable Healthcare Act's Insurance Marketplace," Kaiser Family Foundation (2016), accessed June 1, 2017, www.kff.org/health-reform/issue-brief/2017-premium-changes-and-insurer-participation-in-the-affordable-care-acts-health-insurance-marketplaces/.

40. U.S. Department of Health and Human Services, "Health Insurance Coverage for Americans with Pre-existing Conditions."

41. Congressional Budget Office, "Congressional Budget Office Cost Estimate of H.R. 1628 American Health Care Act of 2017, as Passed by the House of Representatives on May 4, 2017," accessed June 2, 2017, www.cbo.gov/system/files/115th-congress-2017-2018/costestimate/hr1628aspassed.pdf.

42. Gisele Grayson, Alyson Hurt, and Alison Kodjak, "CHART: Who Wins, Who Loses with Senate Health Care Bill," *NPR*, June 22, 2017, accessed July 5, 2017, www.npr.org/sections/health-shots/2017/06/22/533942041/who-wins-who-loses-with-senate-health-care-bill.

43. Ibid.; Kaiser Family Foundation, "Summary of the Better Care Reconciliation Act of 2017," updated June 26, 2017, accessed July 5, 2017, files.kff.org/attachment/Summary-of-the-Better-Care-Reconciliation-Act.

44. Grayson et al., "CHART: Who Wins, Who Loses with Senate Health Care Bill."

45. Congressional Budget Office, "Congressional Budget Office Cost Estimate of H.R. 1628 Better Care Reconciliation Act of 2017."

46. Bob Bryan, "THE FLOODGATES OPEN: GOP senators Come Out in Furious Force against Healthcare Bill after Vote Delayed," *Business Insider,* June 27, 2017, accessed July 5, 2017, www.businessinsider.com/which-gop-senators-against-healthcare-bill-2017-6; Thomas Kaplan and Robert Pear, "Vote Delayed as G.O.P. Struggles to Marshall Support

for Health Care Bill," *New York Times*, June 27, 2017, accessed July 5, 2017, www.nytimes
.com/2017/06/27/us/politics/republicans-struggle-to-marshal-votes-for-health-care-bill
.html.

47. Lauren Fox, M. J. Lee, Dana Bash, Deirdre Walsh, and Phil Mattingly, "Senate Won't Vote on GOP Health Care Bill," *CNN*, September, 26, 2017, accessed June 11, 2018, www.cnn.com/2017/09/26/politics/health-care-republican-senate-vote/index.html.

48. Centers for Disease Control and Prevention, "Highlights: Tobacco Timeline," last reviewed July 21, 2015, accessed June 1, 2017, www.cdc.gov/tobacco/data_statistics/sgr /2000/highlights/historical/index.htm.

49. Michael Tynan et al., "State and Local Comprehensive Smoke-Free Laws for Worksites, Restaurants, and Bars—United States, 2015," *Weekly* 65 (2016): 623–26, accessed June 1, 2017, www.cdc.gov/mmwr/volumes/65/wr/mm6524a4.htm?s_cid=mm6524a4_w.

50. Ibid.

51. Susan Kirkland, Lorraine Greaves, and Pratima Devichand, "Gender Differences in Smoking and Self-Reported Indicators of Health," *Women's Health Surveillance Report: A Multidimensional Look at the Health of Canadian Women,* ed. Marie DesMeules et al. (Ottawa: Canadian Institute for Health Information, 2004).

52. Lorraine Greaves and Natasha Jategaonkar, "Tobacco Policies and Vulnerable Girls and Women: Toward a Framework for Gender Sensitive Policy Development," *Journal of Epidemiology and Community Health* 60 (2006): ii57–65.

53. Lorraine Greaves and Natalie Hemsing, "Women and Tobacco Control Policies: Social-Structural and Psychosocial Contributions to Tobacco Use and Exposure," *Drug and Alcohol Dependence* 104S (2009): S121–30.

54. Greaves and Jategaonkar, "Tobacco Policies and Vulnerable Girls and Women."

55. Tynan et al., "State and Local Comprehensive Smoke-Free Laws."

56. Greaves and Hemsing, "Women and Tobacco Control Policies," S129.

57. Michele Ver Ploeg et al., *Access to Affordable and Nutritious Food—Measuring and Understanding Food Deserts and Their Consequences: Report to Congress,* U.S. Department of Agriculture: Administrative Publication No. AP-036, June 2009, accessed January 4, 2011, www.ers.usda.gov/publications/pub-details/?pubid=42729

58. David C. Sloane et al., "Improving the Nutritional Resource Environment for Healthy Living through Community-Based Participatory Research," *Journal of General Internal Medicine* 18, no. 7 (2003): 568–75.

59. Patrick J. McDonnell, "Council Limits New Fast Food Outlets in South LA," *Los Angeles Times*, December 8, 2010, accessed January 4, 2011, www.latimes.com/news/la-me -1208-fast-food-m,0,3282372.story.

60. 'Lizabeth DiSiena, "Practice What You Preach: Does the National School Lunch Program Meet Nutritional Recommendations Set by Other USDA Programs?" *Journal of Law and Health* 164 (2015): 163–99.

61. Ver Ploeg et al., *Access to Affordable and Nutritious Food.*

62. DiSiena, "Practice what you preach."

63. Ver Ploeg et al., *Access to Affordable and Nutritious Food.*

64. DiSiena, "Practice What You Preach."

65. Ibid.

66. Ver Ploeg et al., *Access to Affordable and Nutritious Food.*

67. Lydia Wheeler, "Trump unwinding Michelle Obama's school lunch program rules," *The Hill*, May 1, 2017, accessed June 1, 2017, http://thehill.com/regulation/healthcare/331 400-trump-unwinding-first-ladys-school-lunch-program-rules

68. Johannes Flacke et al., "Mapping Environmental Inequalities Relevant for Health for Informing Urban Planning Interventions—A Case Study in the City of Dortmund, Germany," *International Journal of Environmental Research and Public Health* 13 (2016): 711–30.

69. Strife and Downey, "Childhood Development and Access to Nature."

70. Krieger and Higgins, "Housing and Health."

71. Ibid.

72. Brisbon et al., "The Asthma and Obesity Epidemics."

73. Strife and Downey, "Childhood Development and Access to Nature."

74. Booth et al., "Obesity and the Built Environment"; Brisbon et al., "The Asthma and Obesity Epidemics"; Penny Gordon-Larsen et al., "Inequality in the Built Environment Underlies Key Health Disparities in Physical Activity and Obesity," *Pediatrics* 177, no. 2 (February 2006).

75. MinHee Kim and Philippa Clarke, "Trajectories of Decline in Social Engagement in Vulnerable Elders: Findings from Detroit's Medicaid Home and Community-Based Waiver Population," *Research on Aging* 37 (2015): 413–35; Marshall Kreuter et al., "The Impact of Implementing Selected CBPR Strategies to Address Disparities in Urban Atlanta: A Retrospective Case Study," *Health Education Research* 27 (2012): 729–41.

76. Lawrence Frank et al., "Many Pathways from Land Use to Health; Associations between Neighborhood Walkability and Active Transportation, Body Mass Index, and Air Quality," *Journal of the American Planning Association* 72 (2006): 75–87.

77. Kreuter et al., "The Impact of Implementing Selected CBPR Strategies."

78. Ibid.

79. Yanique Redwood et al., "Social, Economic, and Political Processes that Create Built Environment Inequities: Perspectives from Urban African Americans in Atlanta," *Family and Community Health* 33 (2010): 53–67.

80. Kreuter et al., "The Impact of Implementing Selected CBPR Strategies."

81. Michael Greshko, Laura Parker, and Brian Clark Howard, "A Running List of How Trump Is Changing the Environment," *National Geographic,* June 14, 2017, accessed July 5, 2017, news.nationalgeographic.com/2017/03/how-trump-is-changing-scienc e-environment/.

82. Environmental Protection Agency, "Clean Air," accessed May 20, 2017, www.epa .gov/laws-regulations/summary-clean-air-act; "Clean Air Act," published February 24, 2004, accessed May 20, 2017, www.epw.senate.gov/envlaws/cleanair.pdf.

83. Centers for Disease Control and Prevention, "Fact Sheet: Health Disparities in Unequal Air Quality: Findings from the CDC Health Disparities and Inequalities Report—United States, 2011," accessed June 1, 2017, www.cdc.gov/minorityhealth/chdir/2011/fact sheets/airquality.pdf.

84. Environmental Protection Agency, "History of the Clean Water Act," accessed May 20, 2017, www.epa.gov/laws-regulations/history-clean-water-act.

85. Centers for Disease Control and Prevention, "Health Studies Branch—Promoting Clean Water for Health," last modified April 1, 2016, accessed June 1, 2017, www.cdc.gov /nceh/hsb/cwh/default.htm; "Clean Water Act," published November 27, 2002, accessed May 2017, www.epw.senate.gov/water.pdf.

86. Centers for Disease Control and Prevention, "Health Studies Branch—Promoting Clean Water for Health"; Centers for Disease Control and Prevention, "Clean Water Act."

87. U.S. Department of Housing and Urban Development, "Legislative History of Lead-Based Paint," published 1992, accessed June 1, 2017, portal.hud.gov/hudportal/doc uments/huddoc?id=20258_legislativehistory.pdf.

88. American Academy of Pediatrics, "Prevention of Childhood Lead Toxicity," *Pediatrics* 138 (2016): 1–15, accessed May 15, 2017, pediatrics.aappublications.org/content/138/1 /e20161493

89. Ibid.

90. M. B. Pell and Joshua Schneyer, "Thousands of U.S. Areas Affected with Lead Poisoning beyond Flint's," *Scientific American* (2017), accessed June 1, 2017, www.scientific american.com/article/thousands-of-u-s-areas-afflicted-with-lead-poisoning-beyond -flints/.

91. U.S. Department of Health and Human Services, "Medicaid Expansion Impacts on Insurance Coverage."

92. Kirkland et al., "Gender Differences in Smoking."

93. Greaves and Jategaonkar, "Tobacco Policies and Vulnerable Girls and Women."

ON THE EDGE

Multiracial Groups and Public Policies

MARY E. CAMPBELL AND SYLVIA M. EMMANUEL

Policies that explicitly address inequality between ethnic and racial groups were designed with a rather simple view of race and racism. They were generally predicated on the idea that there was a single group that had privilege (whites) and all other groups (people of color) were easy to identify, mutually exclusive, and disadvantaged across all domains. While some policies have already wrestled with exceptions to this pattern (for example, deciding whether Asian Americans are counted as an underrepresented group in certain universities for the purpose of educational equity programs), the underlying assumption of most policies has remained that groups are mutually exclusive and can be easily identified by strangers across contexts and without regard to the source of the information about an individual's racial group.[1]

Reality, however, is more complex, and the racialized experience of multiracial groups and others who straddle ethnic and racial boundaries (such as those who are perceived by strangers as belonging to a group different from the one with which they self-identify) is more difficult to adequately incorporate into these policies. The results of a recent survey of Texas residents examining perceived unfair treatment or everyday discrimination in public settings suggest how policies designed to prevent or redress discrimination could be revised to incorporate the experiences of multiracial groups, and how general principles could underpin policies for others who challenge standard conceptualizations of race, ethnicity, and minority status. Just as people who do not identify with only one racial category challenge the existing structure of policies designed to combat racial inequality in the United States, so do people whose racialized experience is not neatly aligned with mutually exclusive, static racial categories whose boundaries and content are clear and unchanging.

WOULD WE EXPECT MULTIRACIAL INDIVIDUALS TO EXPERIENCE RACIAL DISCRIMINATION?

There is good reason to expect that in the United States today individuals who identify as multiracial experience negative treatment. Multiracial individuals report encountering discrimination and microaggressive behaviors such as racial exclusion and marginalization, exoticization, invalidation of their racial identities, and racial essentialization.[2] These behaviors are in part a result of the kinds of racism that all groups of color face, and in part products of monoracism, a system which privileges single-race categories over racial mixing.[3] This system leads to the systematic exclusion and reduction of multiracial identities. For example, during much of the history of the United States, the "one-drop rule" (the idea that every person with any black ancestry was to be identified as only black) was both a social and a legal principle that was heavily enforced."[4]

Monoracism and the discriminatory and microaggressive behavior it produces continue to affect multiracial individuals today. For example, there have been numerous cases of workplace racial discrimination presented to courts by multiracial plaintiffs alleging the violation of Titles VI and VII of the Civil Rights Act of 1964.[5] A common type of microaggressive behavior found in many of the court cases was racial essentialization; individuals were assigned to a single, monoracial group by others despite their multiracial background.[6] For example, multiracial individuals with a black parent are typically described and treated as if they are solely African American.[7] Even the courts themselves generally describe multiracial people with any black ancestry as simply black. Many scholars who are supporters of the "Personal Identity Equality" approach have critiqued this pattern, arguing that the "misrecognition of one's identity" is a form of "social subordination,"[8] although it is not against the law to refuse to acknowledge the racial identity that a person claims.

* * *

We can find this reduction to a monoracial identity in cases such as *Mitchell v. Champs Sports* (1998) and *Richmond v. General Nutrition Centers (GNC), Inc.* (2012). In the *Mitchell v. Champs Sports*[9] case, plaintiff Jill E. Mitchell filed a motion against Champs Sports alleging racial discrimination in violation of Title VII of the Civil Rights Act. Mitchell is a biracial woman with a light complexion; she is the child of a mother who identifies as white and a father who identifies as black, but is often mistaken to be of Latinx and European descent.[10] After the store manager found out that part of Mitchell's heritage was black, his attitude toward her changed dramatically.[11] He became fixated on her race and began to direct negative comments about blacks toward her. Throughout the legal proceeding, despite conveying to the court that she is multiracial, the court continuously referred to Mitchell as "black."[12]

In *Richmond v. General Nutrition Centers (GNC)*,[13] four plaintiffs alleged that they were subjected to a hostile work environment and treatment due to their race and ethnic origin. One plaintiff, Marlon Hattimore, is biracial.[14] He claimed that, for the duration of his employment, there were many negative comments made about blacks by white employees and managers. However, he was partially protected from some of the harsher treatment the black employees experienced because of his biracial status.[15] His case with GNC was resolved out of court. Despite his biracial status being known by the court, he was still, in many ways, treated as solely black.[16] However, this may have been due to Hattimore claiming that he was treated poorly only because of his black ancestry.

There are several examples of cases where individuals claimed that they were discriminated against specifically because of their multiracial identity, such as *Graves v. District of Columbia* (2011) and *Nash v. Palm Beach County School District* (2010). In *Graves v. District of Columbia*,[17] Stephen Graves, who self-identified as a multiracial man of "Native American, African American and Caucasian heritage," claimed to have been exposed to a hostile work environment because of racially charged taunts made about his multiracial identity.[18] The taunts, "Yellow," "Light Brown Wanna-be White," and "Red," were usually about his light skin tone.[19]

His case was settled outside of court. Similarly, in *Nash v. Palm Beach County School District*[20] the multiracial plaintiff alleged that he had been subjected to discriminatory comments due to his identity. For example, the school principal made a remark about Nash's multiracial identity at a Thanksgiving luncheon, asking him what he would prefer: "white or dark meat because I know you are a little of both."[21] However, his claims were dismissed by the court due to lack of evidence and the insufficient severity of the accusations.

Longmire v. Wyser-Pratte (2007)[22] is another example of an individual whose multiracial identity was central to his discrimination claim. Eric Longmire was a biracial man with a "Mediterranean or Semitic" appearance.[23] He elected to keep his biracial status a heavily "guarded secret"[24] and live his life out as a white person in order "to avoid discrimination on Wall Street."[25] His boss threatened to publicly reveal his biracial status to his coworkers, who Longmire contends made negative comments about black people routinely at their workplace. The court dismissed Longmire's claims on the ground of legal insufficiency because there is no charge for the unauthorized, public disclosure of a person's race or racial background under New York law.[26]

EVIDENCE OF DISCRIMINATION IN SOCIAL RESEARCH

One key question that remains when studying these court cases alleging discrimination against multiracial people is whether multiracial Americans are experiencing systematic discrimination in public settings such as the workplace, or whether this represents an unusual set of cases. Experimental work confirms the kinds of patterns we are seeing in the court cases; for example, biracial applicants are generally stereotyped as colder and less competent than white and single-race minority applicants.[27] Assessing experiences of discrimination is especially complicated for multiracial populations for several reasons. One is that different multiracial groups have very different backgrounds, histories, and experiences. We would not expect the experiences of someone with black and white heritage to be the same as someone with Asian and white heritage, for example, because of these very different histories and racialized meanings.

Another reason it is difficult to generalize about discrimination for multiracial individuals is that multiracial groups are especially likely to experience a disconnect between their self-identification and how other people see them (their "observed" racial category) or how they believe others see them (their "reflected" racial category).[28] For example, many part-black individuals report that others perceive them as solely black, no matter what their self-identification is.[29] Part-Asian individuals, on the other hand, are perceived in a wide range of ways, and many report that their identity has been shaped in part by how other people perceive them.[30] Other single-race groups also experience this mismatch between different aspects of their racialized experience; for example, Latinx and American Indians report high rates of mismatch between their self-identification and how they are perceived.[31] Because multiracial groups often experience this, it becomes challenging to know the basis of discrimination for a given event. For example, a multiracial individual might experience discrimination because of self-chosen identity, or because the observer has classified the individual into another racial category that the observer stigmatizes, or because the observer has trouble classifying the person into any single category.

These types of racial discrimination have negative effects on multiracial individuals, just as they do on other groups of color.[32] Lisa S. Giamo and colleagues found that multiracial people who perceived more discrimination had lower life satisfaction, but those multiracial people with a strong multiracial identity were somewhat protected from these negative effects because of their sense of belonging to a collective.[33] Those who perceived themselves as similar to the average member of the group were more likely to be protected by this sense that they "fit in" a group. This racialized experience as a multiracial person affects the way an individual identifies. Since one of the types of negative treatment that multiracial people often face is the refusal of others to validate their identity,[34] it makes sense that having a strong sense of belonging to the group would offer protection from some of the negative effects of discrimination for multiracial people, as would strong social networks and embracing racial fluidity.

DATA AND RESULTS

To test the experiences of multiracial individuals in a diverse and representative sample of respondents, we use the 2015 Texas Diversity

Survey (TDS). The TDS was a phone-based survey of white, black, and Latinx individuals living in Texas. The survey was conducted in English or Spanish, and respondents were only surveyed if at least one of the racial/ethnic groups with which they identified was white, black or Latinx; thus, while this is a probability sample of multiracial people living in Texas, it does not include multiracial people who identify only with other categories (for example, someone who identified as Asian and American Indian). The survey includes a total N=1,322 respondents, with N=121 individuals who identified as multiracial.

Measuring multiracial groups. The self-identification question on the TDS asked: "What is your racial or ethnic background? Please choose ALL that apply: *Black or African American; White or European American or Anglo; Hispanic or Latino/a; Asian or Pacific Islander; American Indian or Native American; Other.*"

One significant advantage of the data is that the question that asked individuals to racially self-identify allows us to identify multiracial people who are part-Latinx. Most large surveys first ask whether the individual identifies as Latinx and then ask a separate question about racial identification. This means that it is not possible in most major surveys to tell whether individuals who identify as Latinx *and* identify with a racial category are identifying as multiracial or choosing two identifications simply because they are asked two questions. It is important to include multiracial people who identify as part-Latinx, because they are a sizeable part of the multiracial population. In the TDS sample, N=58 multiracial people named Latinx as one of their backgrounds, and N=64 multiracial people did not. Table 5.1 shows the sample sizes of the largest multiracial groups in the sample; white-Latinx individuals are (perhaps unsurprisingly) the largest of the multiracial groups in this Texas-based sample.

Measuring everyday discrimination. The measure of racial discrimination in the TDS varied across respondents. Half of the sample were asked: "In your day-to-day life, how often have any of the following things happened to you because of your race or ethnicity?" This was followed by ten examples of everyday discriminatory treatment (being treated with less courtesy than other people, receiving less respect than other people, receiving poor service, people act as if you are not smart, people act as if they are afraid of you, people act as if you're dishon-

Table 5.1. Multiracial Groups in TDS

	Number of respondents
White-Latinx	35
White–American Indian	33
Black-White	13
Black-Latinx	7
Other	33
Total	121

Source: 2015 Texas Diversity Survey.

est, people act as if they are better than you are, you are called names, you are threatened, you are followed in stores). For each item, they are asked whether it occurs almost every day, at least once a week, a few times a month, a few times a year, less than once a year, or, if they volunteer the answer, never.

The other half of the respondents were asked, with the same examples and the same options: "In your day-to-day life, how often have any of the following things have happened to you?" After they have answered for all ten examples, these respondents were asked, "What do you think was the main reason for these experiences?" They were given a series of options: ancestry or national origin or ethnicity; gender or sex; race; age; height; skin color; sexual orientation; weight; income or educational level; other. We combine responses to these two versions of the question by including everyone who said that their experiences were because of ancestry, race, or skin color (even if they also named other reasons in addition to these). Those who report negative treatment but do not mention race as one of the reasons are dropped from the sample, reducing the total number of multiracial individuals with valid discrimination data to N=76.

Table 5.2 shows that black-whites (and the catch-all "other multiracial" category) report more discrimination than white-Latinx, who report more discrimination than white–American Indians. The black-Latinx group is too small to result in reliable estimates. Tests of these patterns with a multivariate regression (available from the authors on request) show that, even after controlling for which version of

Table 5.2. Racial Discrimination for White, Black, Latinx, and Largest
Multiracial Groups (Weighted and Adjusted for Survey Design)

Race	Mean	Std. dev.	N
White	1.04	0.8	354
Black	1.79	1.3	220
Latinx	1.30	0.9	193
Black-White	1.45	0.9	11
Black-Latinx	1.96	0.8	3
White-Latinx	1.06	0.5	21
White–American Indian	0.66	.05	17
Other multiracial	1.52	1.0	24

Note: The mean frequency of reporting discrimination across ten different domains, where 5=1 experience discrimination almost every day and 0=1 never experience it. Discrimination reports constructed by combing variables measuring general discrimination and race-specific discrimination.

Source: 2015 Texas Diversity Survey.

the question the respondent received, as well as their gender, immigration status, and working hours, those who identify as white–American Indian report statistically significantly less racial discrimination than those who identify only as white, a surprising finding given that other work has found that individuals who identify as white–American Indian have significantly worse health outcomes than whites.[35] Perhaps this is explained in part by the high levels of identity fluidity that white–American Indians experience;[36] that is, those who identify as American Indian and white are especially likely to identify in multiple different ways over time. This table shows that perceived discrimination varies significantly across multiracial groups, from very low values to values greater than the average level of discrimination reported by blacks.

Table 5.3 demonstrates how the experiences of multiracial individuals correspond with their reflected racial category (that is, the racial category that the respondent believes strangers assign them to). The first three columns of numbers refer only to those individuals who identified with multiple races, while the last three include all respondents who believe they are perceived as part of that racial group. Multiracial people who believe that other people see them as white report relatively

Table 5.3. Racial Discrimination by Reflected Race (Weighted and Adjusted for Survey Design)

Reflected Race	Multiracial only	Std. dev.	N	All respondents	Std. dev.	N
White	.094	0.6	34	1.05	0.8	388
Black	1.84	0.6	12	1.80	1.0	204
Latinx	1.32	0.9	19	1.30	1.0	192
Asian	0.81	0.7	2	1.10	.08	9
American Indian	0.78	0.7	2	1.60	1.3	14
Other	1.52	1.3	7	1.40	1.2	36

Note: The mean frequency of reporting discrimination across ten different domains, where 5=1 experience discrimination almost every day and 0=1 never experience it. Discrimination reports constructed by combing variables measuring general discrimination and race-specific discrimination.

Source: 2015 Texas Diversity Survey.

low levels of discrimination, similar to what people who self-identify as white report and similar to all respondents who report they are perceived as white. Those who believe that other people see them as black report significantly higher levels, and those who believe they are seen as Latinx or "other" fall in between (with large standard deviations, making them statistically indistinguishable from either group). Only four respondents believed they were perceived as Asian or American Indian, making these estimates unreliable. Table 5.3 thus also shows significant variation within the multiracial population, reflecting the racial categories they believe are assigned to them by strangers, with patterns similar to what we see when we examine reflected racial categories for all respondents.

POLICY IMPLICATIONS

Given this reality, how can we design good public policy to combat ethnic and racial inequality in a way that fairly incorporates the experiences of multiracial people? Can we look to court cases for inspiration? Research focused on identity emphasizes the importance of rejecting essentialist racial ideologies and recognizing multiracial identities as legitimate identities with experiences that are distinct from other racial groups,[37] while courts often group such identities together with single-race people of color. However, Tanya Katerí Hernández cautions against assuming that, simply because the law often ignores these nuances, it will always lead to negative outcomes for multiracial groups. She refers to this perspective as the Personal Identity Equality approach where the "misrecognition of one's identity is social subordination."[38] For example, when scholars focused on issues of racial identity analyze court cases involving multiracial discrimination, they tend to critique the courts' reduction of the multiracial complainants' identities to a single, mono-racial category. However, Hernández argues that most of the courts are not necessarily insensitive to the existence of the complainant's multiple identities, but instead focus on one identity because the argument presented by the complainants are typically representative of a social structure that supports white supremacy and perpetuates discrimination against people of color. She argues that the courts are usually able to adequately recognize and address issues deriving from the lingering influence of white supremacy and privilege, and therefore there is no need to divert from current civil right laws; we can simply reinforce these laws to address the discrimination that multiracial groups face just as it is faced by all people of color.[39]

What about public opinion? Examining how multiracial identities are discussed within the public sphere is important to understanding how the general public may perceive such identities. By understanding their perceptions, we can better predict the support or opposition for resource allocation with regard to multiracial applicants. For example, white and black American newspapers from 1996 to 2006 can give some insight as to how individuals with multiracial heritage are perceived as well as how readers are informed about multiracial experiences.[40] Newspapers such as the *Washington Post,* the *New York Times,* and the *Oregonian* framed people of multiracial heritage as the pioneers of a new era where race is becoming unimportant and ideas like "race" hinders us from advancing as a nation; this "new era" theme appeared in 63 percent of relevant articles from 1996 to 2006.[41] Newspapers targeting black audiences such as the *Miami Times,* the *New Pittsburg Courier,* and the *Philadelphia Tribune* often questioned the legitimacy of multiracial identities, particularly in regard to multiracial individuals with black heritage. The newspapers often debated whether multiraciality should be seen as a legitimate identity or if multiracial blacks were using such a label as a way to distance themselves from blackness.[42] This "denial" theme was found in about 17 percent of relevant articles. Some newspapers dismissed multiracial identities, revealing the ongoing effects of the one-drop rule, claiming that multiracial individuals with black heritage are going to be seen as black regardless of how they personally identify.[43] Many of the articles also expressed suspicion of white support of a multiracial category, arguing that Whites only support the cause because it will somehow lead to their benefit.[44] These radically different perspectives show us the heart of the debate about designing policy that includes multiracial people: are they legitimate groups with needs of their own, or a way for individuals to distance themselves from stigmatized groups, or even groups that herald a coming era of racial equality?

By examining these groups we learn a larger lesson that extends beyond identity: self-identification may not always be the best way to capture the kinds of inequality that policies are usually designed to prevent or remedy. Instead, what we often wish to capture is one (or both) of two things. The first is how individuals are perceived by important others in their lives: strangers who are in a position to discriminate against them, as well as authority figures such as teachers, bosses, realtors, and bankers. As this research suggests and other authors have pointed out,[45] self-identification data are not always the best way to capture who is reporting the most discrimination or how they are perceived by others. Table 5.3 shows that, if the purpose of a particular policy is to address how individuals are perceived by others, asking them to answer a reflected-race question results in similar reporting of discrimination for those who are multiracial and those who are single race, if they believe they are perceived the same way. The second thing we often wish to capture is how the legacy of discrimination has shaped an individual's life experiences, because of the way both contemporary discrimination and the legacy of historical discrimination can shape experiences today. These concepts may be better captured by questions about ancestry, for example, rather than a question about how an individual self-identifies, since connections to disadvantaged communities are not always captured in self-identification.

Race-based policy interventions like affirmative action programs have always been heavily contested within both public and private spheres, because they are dealing with these tensions: they seek to remedy both past and current discriminatory patterns. The topic becomes even more heated when trying to ascertain which groups should be the beneficiaries of such policies, and this is especially true for the multiracial populations. Indeed, whether multiracial individuals should be assigned to a single racial group or assigned to their own distinct category, and who should decide multiracial individuals' race—program officials or the individuals themselves—are decidedly difficult decisions to make.[46] The same studies that show multiracial people are perceived negatively and therefore likely to experience discrimination also show that multiracial people are viewed by others as less worthy of scholarships and other programs targeted at minority groups.[47]

So, the question is then: when policies are assessing diversity, how is multiracial status considered? When addressing this question, we should remember that the racialized experience of multiracial individuals is different from their mono-racial counterparts, especially because others often find it difficult to assign them to a particular racial group. It is for this reason that multiracial people are often subject to feelings of rejection and alienation from mono-racial groups.[48] We should also be careful not to oversimplify the multiracial experience and generalize across all groups because each multiracial group presents its own distinct experience and therefore will have different claims of discrimination.[49]

There are two components involved in many policy decisions: individual input and institutional processing.[50] Individual input in the case of racial policies refers to how the applicant answers the race question. Some respondents may feel constrained to the boxes provided in the question, rather than feeling they can emphasize the parts of their identity that they feel can contribute to the diversity of the program. Kerry Ann Rockquemore and David L. Brunsma posit that biracial individuals situate their identities in four ideal types: border, singular, protean, and/or transcendent identity.[51] "Border" identities exists between both multiple racial identities. For example, black and white biracial individuals may feel as if they are not one identity over the other—not just black or white—but a blend of both races. For those with a "singular" identity, self-understanding is derived from only one of their racial identities (for example, white or black).[52] For some multiracial people, their identities exhibit more flexibility because they are defined by social context or a "protean" identity. Biracial individuals with a protean identity state that they feel simultaneously a part of multiple identities, and may feel equally comfortable in both communities or have more of an affinity for one group over the other. People with protean identities may also feel that one identity becomes more salient than the other in some situations. For example, white and Asian multiracial individuals with a protean identity may feel more Asian in some situations while more white in others. Finally, the "transcendent" identity refers to opting out of categorizations completely.[53] Border, protean, and transcendent identities are generally not adequately addressed by current policies, as they were designed for singular identities and do not address the possibility of identities that cross categories, are contextually dependent, or reject racial categories altogether.[54]

On the structural or organizational end, it is about how the policy is applied—how the institution processes the information as part of their decision.[55] Institutional members are susceptible to the same biases that all members of society can fall into, including their thoughts about multiracial identities. For example, Jacqueline M. Chen and Jasmine B. Norman say that we should consider the role of physical appearance among other factors such as socioeconomic status (SES) and ancestry in the way institutional members perceive potential recipients.[56] Danielle M. Young, Diana T. Sanchez, and Leigh S. Wilton found that, among college students, affirmative-action resources are often awarded in an experimental setting to individuals based on socioeconomic status and to those who have a prototypical minority appearance.[57] Furthermore, it is important to take into account white perceivers' or institutional members' recognition of their group privilege when trying to predict how affirmative-action resources are given. Whites who are interested in dismantling group privilege and are supporters of affirmative action are more likely to perceive applicants as multiracial and may be more critical when considering who is deserving of affirmative-action resources. Whites who do not support affirmative action are more likely to categorize multiracial applicants as minorities and thereby make them seemingly more deserving of these resources.

Many school programs reclassify multiracial students into a monoracial minority category.[58] As we can see in the results above, that can be problematic; the experiences of black-white respondents, for example, are not precisely the same as those who identify only as black, and are not the same as those who identify as black-Latinx. When deciding who is eligible for race-based interventions, we should keep in mind the sociohistorical pasts of the groups these programs seek to help, as well as their daily experiences, which might be measured by other approaches, such as asking individuals how they are perceived by others, what kinds of discrimination they experience, or what their ancestry is.

CONCLUSION

Multiracial groups provide a case study for how race-conscious policies must evolve as we come to understand the complexity of the daily experience of racialization in the United States. Even this more complex understanding of how racialized experiences shape inequality remains incomplete; for example, we have largely discussed racialization processes in the United States as a whole, with little attention to the ways in which racialized experiences actually vary across the life course or across places. For example, multiracial youth and young adults are often treated as "exotic," and there is great emphasis placed on their appearance and beauty, an emphasis that is often limited to the young. Similarly, groups are racialized differently in different regions of the country, with far more acceptance of multiracial identities in Hawaii than in the mainland United States, and with different beliefs about boundaries like the "one-drop rule" in the North than in the South. Texas is an unusual case because of its long history of a large and established Latinx community, its growing black community, and its placement at the boundary between the South and the Southwest, but these findings would undoubtedly vary across the country.

Despite its incomplete nature, however, this case study of experiences of multiracial groups in Texas points a way forward for designing new policy. If we design our race-conscious policies to incorporate multiple measures and understandings of race, rather than relying on a simple construct that assumes race is always obvious to all and falls neatly into simple, exclusive categories, we can design policies that can adequately address the variety of racialized experience today, and that are flexible enough to adapt to new experiences tomorrow. Directly asking applicants and respondents for the information we want (such as the types of discrimination they experience, for example, or how they are perceived by others) rather than assuming that self-identification maps directly and simply onto these experiences is a powerful corrective that would apply across many different types of groups, experiences, and social contexts.

NOTES

Contact the first author at *m-campbell@tamu.edu* or at 4351 TAMU, Sociology, Texas A&M University, College Station TX 77843. The authors would like to thank the Race and Ethnic Studies Institute (RESI) at Texas A&M University for their support and data collection.

1. Mary E. Campbell, Jenifer L. Bratter, and Wendy D. Roth, "Measuring the Diverging Components of Race: An Introduction," *American Behavioral Scientist* 60, no. 4 (2016): 381–89.

2. Arnold K. Ho, Steven O. Roberts, and Susan A. Gelman, "Essentialism and Racial Bias Jointly Contribute to the Categorization of Multiracial Individuals," *Psychological Science* 26, no. 10 (2015): 1639–45; Samuel D. Museus, Susan A. Lambe Sariñana, April L. Yee, Thomas E. Robinson, "A Qualitative Analysis of Multiracial Students' Experiences with Prejudice and Discrimination in College," *Journal of College Student Development* 57, no. 6 (2016): 680–97; Jessica C. Harris, "Multiracial College Students' Experiences with Multiracial Microaggressions," *Race Ethnicity and Education* 20 no. 4 (2017): 429–45.

3. Harris, "Multiracial College Students' Experiences."

4. Ibid.

5. Title VI of the Civil Rights Act prohibits discrimination based on race, color, and national origin in programs and the receiving of federal financial assistance. Title VII prohibits discrimination in any aspect of employment on the basis of race, color, and national origin (Title VI, 42 U.S.C. § 2000d; Title VII, 42 U.S.C. § 2000e).

6. Museus et al., "A Qualitative Analysis of Multiracial Students' Experiences," 331–48.

7. Tanya Katerí Hernández, "Multiracial in the Workplace: A New Kind of Discrimination?" in *Gender, Race, and Ethnicity in the Workplace: Emerging Issues and Enduring Challenges*, ed. Margaret Foegen Karsten (Santa Barbara, CA: ABC-CLIO, LLC, 2016), 3–26; Tanya Katerí Hernández, "Racially-Mixed Personal Identity Equality," *Law, Culture and the Humanities*, March 2017, doi.org/10.1177%2F1743872117699894.

8. Hernández, "Racially-Mixed Personal Identity Equality," 6.

9. *Mitchell v. Champs Sports*, 42 F. Supp. 2d 642 (E.D. Tex. 1998).

10. *Mitchell v. Champs Sports*, 42 F. Supp. 2d 642, 646 (E.D. Tex. 1998) ("At the hearing, movant testified that she is the offspring of a mixed-race marriage. Her mother is white and her father is black").

11. *Mitchell v. Champs Sports*, 42 F. Supp. 2d 642, 646 (E.D. Tex. 1998) ("after observing repeated visits to the store by movant's black friends and relatives").

12. *Mitchell v. Champs Sports*, 42 F. Supp. 2d 642, 645 (E.D. Tex. 1998) ("Champs Sports hired Mitchell, a black female").

13. *Richmond v. General Nutrition Centers (GNC)*, No. 08 Civ. 3577 (PAE) (HBP) (S.D.N.Y. 2012).

14. *Richmond v. General Nutrition Centers (GNC)*, No. 08 Civ. 3577 (PAE) (HBP) (S.D.N.Y. 2012) (Id. 7–8).

15. *Richmond v. General Nutrition Centers (GNC)*, No. 08 Civ. 3577 (PAE) (HBP) (S.D.N.Y. 2012) (Id. 7–8).

16. *Richmond v. General Nutrition Centers (GNC)*, No. 08 Civ. 3577 (PAE) (HBP) (S.D.N.Y. 2012) ("Defs. 56.1 St. 130").

17. *Graves v. District of Columbia*, No. 07-00156, 777 F. Supp. 2d 109 (2011).

18. *Graves v. District of Columbia*, 777 F. Supp. 2d 109, 5 (D.D.C. 2011) ("Compl., Docket No. [1], 6").

19. *Graves v. District of Columbia*, 777 F. Supp. 2d 109, 6 (D.D.C. 2011) (" Pl.'s Resp. 3.2").

20. *Nash v. Palm Beach County School District*, 08-80970-CIV-MARRA (S.D. Fla. Aug. 18, 2009).

21. *Nash v. Palm Beach County School District*, 08-80970-CIV-MARRA (S.D. Fla. Aug. 18, 2009) (Affidavit of Plaintiff 17).

22. *Longmire v. Wyser-Pratte*, 05 Civ. 6725 (SHS) (S.D.N.Y. Sept. 6, 2007).

23. *Id* at "Declaration of Eric Longmire dated Oct. 25, 2006 ("Longmire Decl.") 3."

24. *Longmire v. Wyser-Pratte*, 05 Civ. 6725 (SHS) (S.D.N.Y. Sept. 6, 2007) ("(Def.'s 56.1 10, 12; Pl.'s Rep. 56.1 10, 12; Longmire Decl. 4, 6)").

25. *Longmire v. Wyser-Pratte*, 05 Civ. 6725 (SHS) (S.D.N.Y. Sept. 6, 2007) ("(Pl.'s 56.1 3; Longmire Decl. 3)"); Camille Rich, "Elective Race: Recognizing Race Discrimination in the Era of Racial Self-Identification," *Georgetown Law Journal* 102 (2014): 1501–72.

26. *Longmire v. Wyser-Pratte*, 05 Civ. 6725 (SHS) (S.D.N.Y. Sept. 6, 2007) ("no federal statute expressly extends privacy protection to factual information regarding a person's race").

27. Diana T Sanchez and Courtney M. Bonam, "To Disclose or Not to Disclose Biracial Identity: The Effect of Biracial Disclosure on Perceiver Evaluations and Target Responses," *Journal of Social Issues* 65, no. 1 (2009): 129–49.

28. Campbell et al., "Measuring the Diverging Components of Race"; Wendy D. Roth, "Racial Mismatch: The Divergence Between Form and Function in Data for Monitoring Racial Discrimination of Hispanics," *Social Science Quarterly* 91, no. 5 (2010): 1288–1311; Wendy D. Roth, "The Multiple Dimensions of Race," *Ethnic and Racial Studies* 39, no. 8 (2016): 1310–38.

29. Nikki Khanna, "'If You're Half Black, You're Just Black': Reflected Appraisals and the Persistence of the One-Drop Rule," *Sociological Quarterly* 51, no. 1 (2010): 96–121.

30. Nikki Khanna, "The Role of Reflected Appraisals in Racial Identity: The Case of Multiracial Asians," *Social Psychology Quarterly* 67, no. 2 (2004): 115–31.

31. Mary E. Campbell and Lisa Troyer, "Further Data on Misclassification: A Reply to Cheng and Powell," *American Sociological Review* 76, no. 2 (2011): 356–64; Nicholas Vargas and Kevin Stainback, "Documenting Contested Racial Identities Among Self-Identified

Latina/os, Asians, Blacks, and Whites," *American Behavioral Scientist* 60, no. 4 (2015): 442–64; Nicholas Vargas, "Latina/o Whitening? Which Latina/os Self-Classify as White and Report Being Perceived as White by Other Americans?" *Du Bois Review: Social Science Research on Race* 12, no. 1 (2015): 119–36; S. R. Porter, C. A. Liebler, and J. M. Noon, "An Outside View: What Observers Say About Others Races and Hispanic Origins," *American Behavioral Scientist* 60, no. 4 (2015): 465–97.

32. Lisa S. Giamo, Michael T. Schmitt, and H. Robert Outten, "Perceived Discrimination, Group Identification, and Life Satisfaction among Multiracial People: A Test of the Rejection-Identification Model," *Cultural Diversity and Ethnic Minority Psychology* 18, no. 4 (2012): 319–28; Museus et al., "A Qualitative Analysis of Multiracial Students' Experiences."

33. Giamo et al., "Perceived Discrimination."

34. Museus et al., "A Qualitative Analysis of Multiracial Students' Experiences."

35. Jenifer L. Bratter and Bridget K Gorman, "Does Multiracial Matter? A Study of Racial Disparities in Self-Rated Health," *Demography* 48, no. (2011): 127–52.

36. Jamie Mihoko Doyle and Grace Kao, "Are Racial Identities of Multiracials Stable? Changing Self-Identification Among Single and Multiple Race Individuals," *Social Psychology Quarterly* 70, no. 4 (2007): 405–23.

37. Hernández, "Multiracial in the Workplace"; Hernández, "Racially-Mixed Personal Identity Equality"; Nancy Leong, "Multiracial Identity and Affirmative Action," *Asian Pacific American Law Journal* 12, no. 1 (2006): 1–34.

38. Hernández, "Racially-Mixed Personal Identity Equality," 6.

39. Hernández, "Multiracial in the Workplace"; Hernández, "Racially-Mixed Personal Identity Equality."

40. Michael C. Thornton, "Policing the Borderlands: White- and Black-American Newspaper Perceptions of Multiracial Heritage and the Idea of Race, 1996–2006," *Journal of Social Issues* 65, no. 1 (2009): 105–27.

41. Ibid.

42. Ibid.

43. Ibid.

44. Ibid.

45. Roth, "Racial Mismatch."

46. Leong, "Multiracial Identity and Affirmative Action."

47. Sanchez and Bonam, "To Disclose or Not to Disclose Biracial Identity"; Mary E. Campbell and Melissa R. Herman, "Politics and Policies: Attitudes toward Multiracial Americans," *Ethnic and Racial Studies* 33, no. 9 (2010): 1511–36.

48. Kimberly P. Brackett, Ann Marcus, Nelya J McKenzie, Larry C Mullins, Zongli Tang, and Annette M Allen, "The Effects of Multiracial Identification on Students' Perceptions of Racism," *Social Science Journal* 43 (January 2006): 437–44; Giamo et al., "Perceived Discrimination."

49. Leong, "Multiracial Identity and Affirmative Action."

50. Ibid.

51. Kerry Ann Rockquemore and David L. Brunsma, *Beyond Black: Biracial Identity in America*. Lanham, MD: Rowman & Littlefield, 2008.

52. Ibid.

53. Ibid.

54. Leong, "Multiracial Identity and Affirmative Action."

55. Ibid.

56. Jacqueline M. Chen and Jasmine B. Norman, "Toward a Comprehensive Understanding of the Factors Underlying Multiracial Person Perception," *Analyses of Social Issues and Public Policy* 16, no. 1 (2016): 417–20.

57. Chen and Norman, "Toward a Comprehensive Understanding of the Factors Underlying Multiracial Person Perception"; Young, Danielle M., Diana T. Sanchez, and Leigh S. Wilton, "Too Rich For Diversity: Socioeconomic Status Influences Multifaceted Person Perception of Latino Targets," *Analyses of Social Issues and Public Policy* 16, no. 1 (2016): 392–416.

58. Leong, "Multiracial Identity and Affirmative Action."

BUILD THAT WALL?

Positioning Trump's Immigration Legislation
with Previous U.S. Laws

JOSH GRIMM

The presidency of Donald Trump has seen a great deal of focus on immigration, featuring a variety of policies, speeches, and tweets centered on the idea of protecting the U.S.-Mexico border and dissuading those attempting to enter the United States. Most egregious, at least at the time of publication (a deeply unsettling reminder that the worst is likely still ahead of us), was the separation of children from their parents at the border—an intended deterrent to other immigrants and asylum-seekers hoping to cross the border. Even more overt, though, is one of Trump's signature issues on the campaign trail: his promise to "build that wall." Five days after taking office, he confirmed that this was not an empty promise, stating, "A nation without borders is not a nation." He has since proposed the wall to be solar powered, roughly nine hundred miles long, and to include transparent portions so that border agents won't be hit in the head by "large stacks of drugs" that are "tossed over from the Mexican side."[1] But while the wall has captured his (and his supporters') imagination, his strategy on immigration does not end with its construction.

Trump has launched and supported a variety of policies, many of which involve entry into the country from countries across the Atlantic rather than south of the Rio Grande. Most notably, on January 27, 2017, Trump signed an executive order that vowed to keep "radical Islamic terrorists out of the United States" by preventing everyone with nonimmigrant or immigrant visas from entering the country if they were from one of seven countries: Iraq, Iran, Libya, Somalia, Sudan, Syria, and Yemen.[2] This ban would last for 90 days, but the same order also prevented refugees from anywhere in the world entering the country for 120 days, with a special exception for Syria, whose refugees were banned from entering the United States indefinitely. Following the Ninth Circuit Court's ruling against the ban, Trump issued a second travel ban that largely mirrored the first, only this time Iraq was taken off the list. A third ban was issued in September 2018, restricting entry from Iran, North Korea, Syria, Libya, Yemen, Somalia, and Venezuela to varying degrees. In a shameful display of judicial partisanship and color-blind racism, the travel ban was upheld by the Supreme Court on June 26, 2018, under the guise of national security.

Lawsuits and appeals ensued, and the courts are where the ban currently resides, with challengers calling the travel ban illegal for targeting countries with large Muslim populations and supporters cheering a decisive action seen as protecting the nation. Social media offered sites of information and organization, with Twitter in particular serving as a launching point for coordinated airport protests. However, the general response on social media to these executive orders—apart from anger—was one of surprise, with people shocked that something like this would ever be written, let alone implemented. The travel bans and Trump's border wall can be placed into a larger context of legislation targeting individuals attempting to enter the United States. But first, as racial prejudice was one of the driving forces behind Trump's election,[3] the connection between immigration and racial attitudes should be examined.

IMMIGRATION AND RACIALIZATION

Despite the country's reputation as a "nation of immigrants," the issue of immigration has long been one of, at best, reluctant acceptance. A big reason for this is the fusion of immigration and race, and so individuals have particularly strong reactions because you have strong feelings of nationalism combining with implicit (and explicit) racial biases. The result is a strong, embedded fear about "others" coming to the country, with the racial aspect at least partially masked by language discussing national security and economic concerns. Since the creation of a poll nearly a century ago asking respondents about ideal immigration levels in the United States, only *once* (in 1953) have more than 10 percent of Americans favored an increase in legal immigration.[4]

This longstanding racialization of immigrants is rooted in nativism. John Higham, a pioneer in this area, defined nativism as "intense opposition to an internal minority on the grounds of its foreign (i.e., 'un-American') connections."[5] Brian F. Fry expanded upon this definition, explaining that nativism is "a collective attempt by self-identified natives to secure or retain prior or exclusive rights to valued resources against the challenges reputedly posed by resident or prospective populations on the basis of their perceived foreignness."[6] In other words, an us-versus-them dichotomy is established, fueling animosity toward immigrants regardless of when they arrived in the country. Historical context plays a significant role in why nativism flares up at certain points in time and the degree to which fears turn into action. Higham argued that nativism was an ideology that combined feelings of nationalism with xenophobia with "anti-Catholic, anti-radical, and Anglo-Saxon traditions."[7] As a result of its unique history, the United States developed a uniquely negative ethnocentrism that would provide the "cultural subsoil" in which nativism would flourish."[8]

The nativist movement was far from relegated to the "lunatic fringe" as it reflected "widespread sentiment [that] included among their number many leaders of business and government."[9] In the 1930s, Henry Ford pushed for Americanization of southern and eastern European immigrants working in his plants, even going to far as to create "melting pot schools" where they would learn English and "certain Anglo-Protestant values," culminating in graduation ceremonies in which "Ford's employees, at first dressed as in their home countries, walked through a big pot labeled 'melting pot' and emerged in business suits holding American flags."[10]

Despite the wide variety of immigrants arriving in the past century, nativism has remained relatively consistent. Roger Daniels found that complaints against immigrants by U.S. citizens tended to fall into at least one of the following categories: "they have bad habits, they are clannish, they don't speak English, and they are going to take over."[11] Embedded in each of these concerns is a perceived threat by immigrants, a threat on citizens' imagined communities—the idea of a political community imagined by citizens who wish to belong but have no way of meeting everyone in the larger group.[12] Andreas Wimmer agreed, arguing that the perception of competition for a limited number of goods, combined with nationalism, determines the level of nativism in a nation's citizens.[13] However, Brian F. Fry took it one step further, arguing that the perception of a threat from immigrants is at the heart of nativism,[14] but Wimmer's ideas of nationalism and resource competition were only two forms that this perceived threat could take. Fry catalogued four categories of perceived threats: nationalism, resource competition, prejudice, and group position.

Fry explained that the nationalism model assumes, much like Higham's model, that U.S. citizens are "threatened by 'un-American' ideas and practices," whereas the resource competition model "interprets nativism as an outgrowth of competition between natives and aliens."[15] The prejudice model is based around the idea that "natives cope with societal change by embracing certain prejudices and conspiracy theories," while the group position model "locates nativist hostility in a population's sense of group position."[16] While each concept overlaps a bit into the others, Fry specified that "the group position model can incorporate the above interpretations into a coherent framework, which can account for the motivations and contexts conducive to nativist attitudes and activities."[17]

At the heart of all of these is a sense of group position, based on a perceived threat from immigrants and enhanced by the addition of power as cultural, legal, and economic incentives and punishments transform nativism from a concept into something with real ramifications and consequences. Of particular interest is Fry's concept of prejudice and how it relates to group position. It deals with race as the dominant and subordinate groups place themselves in a hierarchy based on racial identification. While Fry does not mention it by name, the concept is actually called group threat theory, which posits that racial hostility occurs when the dominant group perceives a threat from a subordinate group.[18] This often occurs when a large minority population is in close proximity to the dominant group, resulting in increased levels of prejudice toward the subordinate group. Here the concept of the dominant and subordinate groups is especially important given the racial component, particularly because it does not necessarily mean immigrant numbers are increasing in a particular area. In other words, "even the perception of an increase in the population sizes of blacks, Latinos, and Asians increases the likelihood that whites will express feelings of group threat and desire lower levels of Latino and Asian immigration."[19]

In the past century, national identity has become fused with the concept of whiteness.[20] Even as attitudes become less explicit, they remain entrenched. Because Anglo whites have been so visible in U.S. society, the connection between "being American" and "being white" has been established. Given this association between race and belonging, plus the fact that "general understanding of what constitutes racism has become less clear since the 1960s, it has become increasingly difficult to distinguish nativism from racism in a time when most immigrants are non-white."[21]

A key nativist concern has been a perception of disloyalty among immigrants.[22] Language also proved to be both an indicator of nativism and a barrier against acceptance. Ana Celia Zentella points out that the "trauma of migration involves the creation of cultural spaces and pockets of remembrance" exemplified by language to "ease the struggle of adaptation."[23] However, despite the importance of speaking Spanish to Latino struggles and identity, it makes the group an easy target for nativists, who consider English to be the "crucial symbol of the ethnicity of American's dominant core culture."[24] Throughout U.S. history, by focusing on the "otherness" of the use of the Spanish language, whites in power have used it as a wedge to intensify nativist feelings. These traits are often amplified as immigrants tend to cluster around particular areas and regions. For instance, in 2010, roughly one in four individuals living in California was born in another country, and over half of all immigrants live in just California, New York, Florida, and Texas.[25]

Issues of skin color, loyalty, and language continued to intensify feelings of nativism toward Latinos, but unlike immigrant groups such as the Chinese and Japanese, no laws were passed against the Latinos because of their value to laborers.[26] The California Gold Rush in 1848 led to an increased reliance on Mexican American labor because many had mining experience which was useful to the novice whites. However, once the Mexican labor had been exploited, whites ran the Mexican Americans off and used intimidation, law enforcement, and even lynching to remove Mexican American landowners from their mining claims.[27] As history continued, race became more prominent in dictating immigration laws and attitudes. While immigration opponents deny the influence of race, research consistently shows that white attitudes "toward the impact of immigration in general" tend to be "more closely aligned with their perceptions of Hispanics, suggesting that their anti-*immigrant* feeling may largely be an anti-*Hispanic* feeling."[28]

HISTORY OF IMMIGRATION LEGISLATION

These attitudes are not native to the twentieth century. The Alien and Sedition Acts were passed in 1798 as a response to growing concern about French and Irish revolutionaries. Of the four measures passed, three of them dealt with foreigners. The Naturalization Act extended the residence requirement in the United States from five to fourteen years; the Alien Act empowered U.S. presidents to expel aliens deemed threatening; and the Alien Enemy Act allowed the president to imprison aliens viewed as enemies.[29] However, while the passage of these measures was intimidating for a brief period of time, there was no lasting effect. In 1802, the new naturalization law was repealed (and the original requirement of five years was restored), the Alien Act "lapsed by its own terms in 1800," and the Alien Enemies Act "lingered on the statute books unused and forgotten."[30]

Apart from the Alien and Sedition Acts, no federal legislation restricting immigration was passed in the United States until 1875. As numbers of immigrants arriving and working in the country continued to increase, a nativist movement grew as U.S. citizens began blaming everything from labor disputes to crime rates on these new arrivals, many of whom did not speak English well. In 1875, Congress passed "a whole host of laws barring the entry of non-U.S. citizens on the basis of qualitative characteristics such as race, national origin, physical and mental health, and political beliefs."[31] However, with an increase of visible immigrants from Asia, the U.S. government passed a slew of laws restricting immigration from certain parts of the world.

The first of these was the Page Law, passed in 1875, which prevented Chinese women from entering the country due to their "debased sexual nature."[32] This stigma was expanded to include Chinese immigrants in general.[33] Under the Chinese Exclusion Act passed in 1882, no Chinese immigrants were allowed to enter the country, and those Chinese immigrants living in the United States were not eligible for citizenship. In 1907, Congress passed the Gentlemen's Agreement, essentially ending immigration from Japan and Korea.[34] In 1917, legislation was passed preventing immigration from the "Asiatic Barred Zone," which was essentially everything in Asia east of an imaginary line drawn between the Red Sea and the Ural Mountains. In each of these laws, these particular groups of immigrants received a great deal of animosity due to their financial success, making them seem a threat to white laborers.[35] The nativist sentiment in the country prevailed as each of these bills were passed over the presidential veto.[36]

These practices would continue into the twentieth century, mostly because the nativist movement from the 1860s and 1870s never really went away. In fact, Congress repeatedly passed bills restricting immigration, only to be vetoed by presidents Grover Cleveland in 1897, William Taft in 1913, and Woodrow Wilson in 1915 and 1917.[37] Then, in 1917, the Russian Revolution launched fears of communism in the United States. In 1921, assisted by a fear of communists entering the country as immigrants, Congress passed the Quota Act (also known as the Johnson Act), allowing only a certain number of immigrants from each country to enter the United States, based on 3 percent of the 1910 census.[38] Three years later, the Johnson-Reed Act was passed, restricting the quotas even further by basing them on 2 percent of the 1890 census.[39] The Quota Act was designed to restrict immigrants from certain countries from entering, giving preference to Northern Europeans. Over time, the restrictionist legislation would prove to be an embarrassment. For instance, when Japan invaded China during World War II, China became a U.S. ally. However, the Chinese Exclusion Act was still being enforced. The ban on Chinese immigrants was immediately lifted, though this did not have much practical effect. With the quotas still in effect, only 105 Chinese immigrants were permitted entry each year.[40]

Around this time, Latino immigrants became hyper-visible.[41] Mexicans began to migrate to the United States in large numbers in 1910 with the start of the Mexican Revolution; by 1920, almost 10 percent of the Mexican population had migrated to the United States in order to escape the conflict.[42] While Chinese and Japanese immigrants had once received the brunt of animosity,[43] the fluidity of racialization had resulted in a shift, leaving the increasing Latin American immigrant population on the receiving end of an unwelcome reception, even though, as a group, they were fulfilling a labor need. By the twentieth century, Mexican Americans had carved out social spaces in the United States, but not without difficulty. From the signing of the Treaty of Guadalupe Hidalgo following the U.S.-Mexican War to the turn of the century, Mexican Americans in the United States lost most of their land.[44] By 1900, Anglos and European immigrants owned seven-eighths of all the land in California.[45] As a result, rather than relying on entrenched patterns of immigration to particular destinations, Mexican immigrants relied on family connections and group ties to survive in the United States.[46]

While there had been economic concerns from businesses before, by this point it became a significant issue. With the passage of restrictive immigration legislation, this issue manifested itself; basically, businesses needed workers. Chinese immigrants in particular had worked in agriculture, but with dwindling numbers (and the stigma having already racialized that group),[47] Mexican immigrants were necessary. They proved to be ideal employees because the group had such little social and political capital. Initially, labor striking occurred. Citrus workers achieved minor success with strikes until the citrus growers organized into clubs so that striking workers would have nowhere else to go. Because Latino immigrants were restricted to certain areas, Latino towns sprung up, creating a Mexico de Afuera—Mexico outside of Mexico. These communities were still forced to endure injustices, such as low wages and extremely poor living conditions.[48] What little wages were earned often went to the company store as Anglo business owners sought to restrict the social space of Latino/a immigrants.[49] Devra Weber tells of one immigrant who said that, because of money that went directly to the company store from his paycheck, over the course of two years he had made a total of four cents. This experience was not unique and was not solely a result of capitalistic goals. Much like in sharecropping, racial prejudices were at the heart of these types of inequalities and inconsistencies.[50]

What is particularly telling is that, in Los Angeles, Mexican immigrants in particular often had little desire to become citizens of the United States because, as Mexican citizens living in the United States, they were more likely to receive assistance from the Mexican consulate than help from the U.S. consulate had they been U.S. citizens.[51] Furthermore, a lack of dual-citizenship laws, along with a desire among immigrants to return to Mexico (especially given the country's proximity) prevented many from attempting to acquire citizenship. However, such help was limited. Latino immigrants were entering both geographic and societal areas steeped in racial oppression. In some cases, there were violent results. Lisbeth Haas told the story of Francisco Torres, a man killed at the turn of the century by a mob of whites. Torres had been arrested for allegedly murdering his boss, and many blamed his actions on his having a "high proportion of Indian blood."[52] Torres was held in Santa Ana, California, a town composed mostly of whites, and racial prejudice remained high. The danger was recognized by others; in a *San Francisco Chronicle* article about the Torres case, a subhead under the headline read, "Lynching Probable." In contrast with the English press, the Spanish-language newspapers maintained Torres's innocence and denounced the villainous stereotypes. While the courts tried to move him to a different area for the trial, it did not happen in time. Torres was lynched in the Santa Ana town square.

One of the main ways that Latino immigrants were racialized during the late nineteenth and early twentieth centuries has been through association with disease. For example, Latino immigrants entering through the U.S.-Mexico border underwent a much more rigorous process of screening than those entering through Ellis Island. Alexandra Minna Stern explained that often these immigrants were subjected to showers with watered-down kerosene and sometimes dusted with DDT in order to kill diseases they might be carrying.[53] It was assumed that Mexicans carried diseases such as tuberculosis and typhus.[54] Stern suggested that there was a "conflation of germ with gene," and the Latino immigrants were seen as coming from "bad hereditary stock."[55] One of the most telling examples of inequality came with the construction of health centers in Los Angeles shortly after World War I. At first glance, the notion that Latino immigrants would be able to be treated for diseases seems encouraging. However, vast discrepancies remained. Natalia Molina explained how, in 1919 and 1920, two health centers were constructed in Los Angeles: one was for "Mexicans Only" and the other was for "Americans Only."[56] The Belvedere Center for "Americans Only" (which meant it was restricted to whites) cost $134,000 in 1920s dollars with a grand opening ceremony attended by numerous state officials and thousands from the general public. The Marvilla Center for "Mexicans Only" cost $600 in 1920s dollars, with most of its building materials coming from razed construction sites. This type of discrimination toward the racial otherness of the Latino immigrants did not stop at the border. William Deverell explained how "Mexican-ness and being Mexican" were enough to presume sickness.[57] Deserted boxcars where Latino immigrants lived were sprayed with cyanide to kill ticks and fleas (because it was assumed the immigrants had typhus).[58] Entire sections of Los Angeles where Latin American immigrants were living were quarantined during an outbreak of "pneumonic plague" in order to keep the disease from spreading to the white portions of the city.[59]

Economic crises tend to spur nativist feelings in the Anglo population,[60] and this was all too evident during the Great Depression. With increased numbers of Latinos requesting aid and applying for relief, officials at the local, state, and national levels launched repatriation campaigns.[61] Some families were separated if the children were born into citizenship but the parents were only residents, but often the entire family was forced, urged, or coerced to leave given the volatile economic environment.[62] Estimates vary, but anywhere between 300,000 and 600,000 Mexicans and Mexican Americans were deported between 1929 and 1940,[63] with some estimates placing the number as high as 1,000,000.[64] Add to this that "a depressed country was hardly a magnet, and those who wanted to move were likely to be too poor to do so, emigrating from a country hit just as hard,"[65] and overall net migration to the United States in this era was negative.

Even after the economy began to recover, the general unease remained, which was reflected in a number of ways. Public policy is far more than a simple piece of legislation or governmental order. How a problem, real or otherwise, is perceived affects the population and has a ripple effect in terms of how it's internalized. Those shock waves can shape a region—and a country—for decades to come. Following World War II, there remained an ongoing ambivalence, demonstrated by the *New York Times* frequently speaking out against notions that immigrants were in some way biologically inferior, but at the same time strongly opposing an increase in the numbers of immigrants.[66]

Despite the growing concerns about the Soviet Union and the start of the Cold War, immigration still troubled residents of the United

States, particularly Anglos. The reception during this era was reflected in popular culture. Movies such as *Double Indemnity* (1954) and *The Maltese Falcon* (1941) launched the *film noir* era, casting the inner city in darkness that represented both the racial makeup and the danger.[67] With the 1950s came science-fiction classics such as *Them!* (1954), which featured giant, mutated ants that multiplied at alarming rates. Both *film noir* and this brand of monster movies represented a way of racializing the otherness of immigrants, of addressing the very fears that were helping to construct the suburban white identity.[68] This was reinforced through domestic structural developments, such as the creation of interstate highways. As freeways were constructed, the city of Los Angeles was sliced up into racial portions, with the thruways serving as a "Berlin Wall" separating Latino neighborhoods from white neighborhoods.[69] Furthermore, these freeways offered an edited view of the urban landscape, allowing whites to ignore the racial inequalities present in the city.

It was not necessarily that discrimination dropped off following the Great Depression, but rather it simply had difficulty manifesting itself, particularly not in the violent way seen in previous years of hardship; for the most part, open racial turmoil toward Latin American immigrants was not as present as the previous era. However, isolated but pronounced incidents showed that dangerous attitudes had not disappeared; they were merely lurking below the surface. On May 31, 1943, U.S. servicemen training in Los Angeles fought with Latino teens in a scuffle that soon escalated into the Zoot Suit Riots, which lasted, off and on, for eight days.[70] Mike Davis suggested that the discrimination did not disappear, but rather simply went into hiding in the suburbs, which formed "White walls" around the inner city.[71] Businesses and attractions followed; California saw the construction of Disneyland, a "touristic fantasy built for mass consumption" that was segregated by the design of Walt Disney (whose decision was aided by corporate sponsors), providing a separate, privileged space.[72] However, as the country's immigrant population grew, the next era witnessed a backlash against immigrants, particularly those from Latin America.

The Bracero Program was launched in 1941 initially to make up for World War II labor shortages, given the high enlistment numbers of Latinos and the forced relocation of the Japanese population. The program was not the first of its kind. With the passage of the Immigration Act of 1917, Congress had included provisions that allowed laborers who would otherwise not be allowed into the United States to enter for temporary employment.[73] This program was enacted in 1918 to help compensate for labor shortages associated with World War I and lasted through 1922. However, the Bracero Program's scope and influence on shaping understandings of immigrant labor, the border, and undocumented immigration were far more influential than anything that came before it and continues to inform attitudes and prejudices even today.[74] The Bracero Program called for a set number of Mexican immigrants to enter the country for specific jobs. With many U.S. males overseas fighting, the program essentially allowed immigrants to come across the border into the United States, work, and, when the time was finished, return home. Businesses benefited tremendously from this arrangement, and the U.S. government went to extraordinary lengths to keep the businesses benefiting from the program content.[75]

As with so many narrowly tailored policy decisions, there is an increased opportunity for complications. One of the most contradictory examples emerged in Texas, a state that Mexico had initially and explicitly forbade to participate in the Bracero Program due to concerns about how the workers would be treated.[76] An amendment to Public Law 78, which authorized importing labor for agricultural needs, was called the Texas Proviso (named after the Texas growers who fought for its inclusion). The Texas Proviso "stipulated that for the purposes of this section, employment . . . shall not be deemed to constitute harboring."[77] In other words, through this "quirk of immigration law," for nearly thirty years it was legal to "hire unauthorized workers (for example, to employ them to take care of your lawn) but illegal to harbor them (for example, to invite them into your home for a drink of water)."[78] Purportedly, this was to protect growers who had unknowingly hired undocumented immigrants from prosecution. However, while its supporters insisted that it was not a loophole, a proposed amendment stating that employers who *knowingly* hired undocumented immigrants would be prosecuted was soundly rejected by Congress.[79]

This hiring of undocumented workers became an issue as a growing number of Mexicans[80] learned of the Bracero Program and headed north to find work. More and more legalizations, referred to as "drying out the wetbacks" or a "dehydration process" began occurring as growers granted instant legalization to those illegal immigrants already in the United States in order to save on transportation costs.[81] This actually increased the amount of illegal immigration as legalizations increased. Word spread that the best way to get a bracero contract was to be in the United States, and so unauthorized border crossings increased dramatically. Meanwhile, growers continued to insist that braceros were necessary despite falling wages, which is unusual in times of labor shortages, and the reduced number of workers actually needed on farms due to mechanization.[82] Agricultural output was at an all-time high, and domestic employment was low. Between 1950 and 1960, the total number of farm workers would drop by 41 percent.[83]

The start of the Korean War in 1950 prompted more negotiations with Mexico over the Bracero Program, with Mexican officials demanding reestablishment of government sponsorship of the contracts. The United States acquiesced to numerous stipulations, including guarantees by the U.S. secretary of labor that there be a demonstrated labor shortage before braceros were brought in to be hired, a prevailing wage for the braceros, and no adverse effect on other farm workers.[84] However, no guidelines were offered defining "labor shortage" or "prevailing wage," and no system of fines or punishments was established should employers not meet these guidelines.[85]

In the meantime, Congress passed more immigration legislation.[86] A number of restrictive immigration laws were still on the books and, by 1950, views had begun to change. During the Great Depression, U.S. citizens were worried about their jobs (in three years the unemployment rate in the United States went from 3.2 percent to 23.6 percent), but by 1942 the employment rate had recovered and was booming by 1950.[87] In the meantime, attitudes about the U.S. stance toward immigration were beginning to change. A number of countries were important allies during World War II, and so it seemed hypocritical not to allow immigrants from those countries to enter the United States. Furthermore, the Cold War had begun, causing "some to argue that an internationalist superpower could not tolerate a xenophobic society."[88] As a result, the McCarran-Walter Act was passed in 1952 and, while still somewhat restrictionist, it did lift the ban on Asian immigration and introduced a preference system that was based on reuniting families and professional skill sets.

In 1953, the President's Commission on Migratory Labor reported on the dangers of increased undocumented immigration, claiming that the increased "wetback traffic" exasperated problems of "infant mortality, disease, and housing conditions" while continuing to depress wages.[89] The news media, led by the *New York Times,* launched a series of exposés on illegal immigration, echoing the commission's concerns. Coupled with a fear of unions and the McCarthyism climate, fears of unrestricted undocumented immigration escalated, which resulted in governmental action.[90]

Responding to the fears about so-called illegal immigration, on June 9, 1954, the U.S. attorney general launched "Operation Wetback," a sweeping move by law enforcement to track down Latinos who had crossed the border in order to find work without going through the proper legal channels established by the Bracero Program.[91] It lasted seven months, during which time more than one million "illegals" were captured and returned to Mexico. Operation Wetback was also designed to reduce the number of "skips," which occurred when the laborers would leave to find other work (or to return to Mexico), especially when working conditions turned particularly brutal. For instance, during a three-day period in June 1962, more than five hundred braceros returned to Mexico after temperatures reached 117 degrees.[92]

While it seemed that the sweeping measure would threaten growers by eliminating a cheap source of labor, the operation actually received a great deal of support. Undocumented immigrants had the possibility of being acquired more cheaply than the braceros, but were also less reliable and could leave at any time for a chance at a better offer. Braceros were required by contract to stay until the work was completed and, with INS agents stepping up apprehensions, were less likely to skip. This "provided an important element of predictability, stability, and—above all—control, in what was otherwise an unpredictable production process."[93] With the sharp influx of braceros, increasing from 67,500 in 1950 to 445,000 in 1956, the wages of the agricultural workers plummeted "from 65 percent of the average manufacturing worker in 1948 to 47 percent in 1959."[94] Eventually, opposition to the Bracero Program by religious groups and organized labor, coupled with the mechanization of cotton harvesting (the sector of agriculture that employed the most braceros) led to the end of the program in 1964.[95]

Initially, the 1965 era looked as though it would mark a turning point in U.S. policy toward immigrants. After Lyndon Johnson picked up John F. Kennedy's 1964 statement that the United States is a "nation of immigrants," he helped pass the Immigration and Nationality Act of 1965.[96] This lifted the quota system based on individual countries and continued the McCarran-Walter Act's approach of favoring immigrants with specific job skills and who had relatives in the United States, along with changing the racial composition of so-called legal immigrants. This era also witnessed the passage of legislation allowing for refugees to request asylum and enter the country. With the legislation's passage, immigration numbers increased dramatically and remained high through the turn of the century. Between 1891 and 1920, 18.2 million immigrants legally entered the country; from 1971 to 2000, 19.9 million immigrants legally entered the United States.[97] However, despite a pleasant facade, the country's immigration concerns were lurking underneath the surface.

One indicator of these concerns appeared with the large number of refugees arriving in the United States beginning in 1975.[98] Following the Vietnam War, large numbers of refugees came from Southeast Asia and were initially welcomed, but the more refugees who arrived in the United States, the more animosity began to be expressed.[99] These refugees were arriving in the midst of an economic recession, a high point in unemployment, and a time when the country was still divided over the Vietnam War. A Harris poll in April 1975 found that 54 percent of Americans felt that Indochinese refugees should not be allowed to enter the United States.[100] Yet, despite negative attitudes toward the refugees, in many cases they had little choice but to emigrate to the country that had in some cases exacerbated their nations' problems. It took decades for the U.S. government to allow large numbers of refugees to enter the United States from these countries that had suffered as a result of intervention. In 1948, Congress had passed the Displaced Persons Act, which initially allowed for 205,000 people to enter as refugees from communist countries every year.

In October 1986, Congress passed the Immigration Reform and Control Act in response to the growing concerns about undocumented immigration. The legislation allocated more funds to expand the Border Patrol, imposed sanctions on business employers who knowingly hired undocumented immigrants, and provided amnesty for immigrants who had lived in the United States since 1982.[101] Initially, the act provided a respite for criticism against the government for allowing the so-called illegal immigration problem, but only briefly. Only four years later the government passed the Immigration Act of 1990, which capped the overall immigration numbers at 675,000 and shrank the number of immigrants allowed in based on preference categories (family, employment, and diversity), thereby curbing the number of Latin American and Asian immigrants.[102] By the late 1980s, immigrants were arriving overwhelmingly from Asia and Latin America, with 22 percent of legal immigrants arriving from Asian and 63 percent from Latin America.[103] Capping immigration numbers restricted these two regions in the number of immigrants that could be legally admitted.

Since the September 11 attacks, legislation has passed focused on security measures monitoring wide swaths of the population rather than targeting a specific race, religion, or foreign country. When comprehensive immigration reform was attempted, it fell short in Congress multiple times under the Bush administration. By the time Bush pushed for reform, it was late in his presidency, and his low approval numbers prevented any real influence in negotiations with Congressional allies.[104] While Obama touted the importance of immigration, his attention was focused on the historic recession and health care reform, after which most attempts at legislation were stymied due to unprecedented obstruction by conservatives.

BUILD THAT WALL?

Trump's fascination with building a wall and, stunningly, believing his southern neighbor would foot the bill—even though former Mexican President Vincente Fox said, "Mexico is not going to pay for that f——g wall"—is one with a long history of a desire to protect a physical border, though the resources to do so were not always in place. The passage of the Johnson-Reed Act in 1924 also saw the creation of a small department designed to assist with immigration enforcement. Days after its passage, the Department of Labor allocated one million dollars for the creation of the U.S. Border Patrol, though until Prohibition was repealed in 1933, the Border Patrol's primary concern was preventing the smuggling of alcohol into the United States.[105] Despite increases in immigrant apprehensions between 1960 and 1978, budget restrictions ensured the Border Patrol was still relatively ineffectual, able to patrol less than 10 percent of the two-thousand-mile border.[106] As a result, the border was less about deterring immigrants and more about maintaining the appearance of order for the sake of performance.[107] In 1980, the Border Patrol's budget was less than the Baltimore police budget and half of Philadelphia's.[108] President Reagan was among the first U.S. presidents to begin increasing funding in order to shore up the U.S.-Mexico border.[109] He was primarily concerned with "floods of refugees" flocking to the United States, though his "fearful scenario became a self-fulfilling prophecy of sorts when his militaristic foreign policy in Central America led to a significant refugee exodus northward from the region into the United States."[110] Funding was dramatically increased to the Border Patrol to help curb border crossings.[111]

Between passage of the Immigration Reform and Control Act in 1986 and the Illegal Immigration Reform and Immigrant Responsibility Act in 1996, the Border Patrol was "transformed from a backwater agency . . . to a large and powerful organization with more officers licensed to carry weapons than any other branch of the federal government save the military."[112] In 2000, the Border Patrol launched a series of highly publicized showings of force where massive numbers of agents would line the border in a particular area in the hopes of deterring unauthorized crossings. These strategies were given names like "Operation Gatekeeper," "Operation Blockade," and "Operation Hold-the-Line" and received widespread support among the U.S. population.[113]

In the past ten to fifteen years, protecting the border has gained traction among restrictionists. In 2005, Larry Gilchrist created the Minuteman Project, in which volunteers from across the United States meet along the Mexico border and set up patrols to capture undocumented immigrants. Some of these Minutemen even brought guns and contemplated putting alligators in the Rio Grande to stop the immigrants.[114] John McCain has been an advocate for a barrier between Arizona and Mexico, advocating in a campaign ad to "complete the danged fence."

Yet the majority of Americans do not care about building a wall. The number of people expressing support for building a wall is at an all-time high—at 36 percent. All of this is complicated by the rather complicated views on immigration held by many Americans. For instance, while the country has become more liberal about immigration since 2012 and does not support mass deportations, a majority of Americans also oppose "sanctuary cities," and the country was split on Trump's travel bans.[115] This ambivalence toward immigration is best captured in a 2017 annual survey of Texans. Surveying one thousand residents of the state (in English and Spanish), the April survey asked about a variety of immigration issues, with the responses revealing "stark differences between the heated rhetoric around immigration and the policies lawmakers want to use to address it."[116] Results showed 27 percent of Texans stating that immigration was the state's most important problem—more than health care or the economy—but while 72 percent stated they were "extremely or somewhat concerned about illegal immigration," 61 percent opposed Trump's plan to build a wall. A majority (62 percent) said immigration helps more than it hurts, but a slight majority of respondents (within the margin of error) opposed sanctuary cities. This disconnect between attitudes toward immigration and the disapproval of policies to address those attitudes remains entrenched.

Immigration is one of those issues that has no short-term answers, and even the long-term proposals are daunting. It's a complex issue, but a big part of Trump's appeal (beyond coded appeals) is his simple, straightforward message. This is why, despite other policy proposals, he keeps coming back to the wall. Even though funding seems unlikely and few in Congress, apart from the usual outspoken representatives, seem willing to back the idea. The wall is, in its heart, the most primal response to a fear of outsiders (suggesting an idea of who does and does not belong) inextricably fused with a nativist racial mindset (ignoring the border with Canada). In some form, Trump's other policies reflect this baser instinct morphed into a message, but this is ultimately at the core of what he proposes. However, his other pieces of legislation (and the discourse surrounding them), capture other important influences from previous laws.

"TERRORIST SAFE HAVENS"

National security was the stated impetus for Trump's executive order decreeing his second travel ban (after the first was struck down in the courts) from six countries. The White House titled its order, "Executive Order Protecting the Nation from Foreign Terrorist Entry into the United States," and specifically listed the countries whose nationals posed a risk as "supporting various terrorist groups" (Iran), unable to secure its borders (Libya), providing "terrorist safe havens" (Somalia), a "designated state sponsor of terrorism (Sudan and Syria), and being "supportive of, but has not been able to cooperate fully with" U.S. counterterrorism efforts (Yemen). The Trump travel ban represents a distinct shift from past pieces of immigrant legislation because it was the president, and not Congress, that captured the nativist undercurrent of the country's populace. This is a startling departure from past practices, such as Woodrow Wilson's veto being overridden by a zealous Congress to restrict who is allowed to enter the country.

National security has been an undercurrent for immigration concerns, particularly during wartime. The response to the September 11 attacks ratcheted up the rhetoric among those favoring tighter border restrictions. The most notorious of these was H.R. 4437 (also known as the Border Protection, Antiterrorism, and Illegal Immigration Control Act of 2005), which sought to prevent undocumented immigrants from having access to public services, such as education and health care, along with punishing anyone who aided an undocumented immigrant in any way. The bill also proposed a seven-hundred-mile stretch of border fence. H.R. 4437 prompted a number of heated protests across the United States, culminating in massive protest marches in cities across the country at the end of March 2006, and the bill died in committee shortly afterward.[117]

Trump shows no hesitancy in invoking terrorism when discussing immigration, using language implying a level of deviousness and malice that casts doubt on every immigrant crossing the borders: "We will continue to fight to take all necessary and legal action to keep terrorists, radicals and dangerous extremists from ever entering our country. We will not allow our general system of immigration to be turned against us as a tool for terrorism and truly bad people."[118] What's particularly noteworthy is that, unlike past pieces of legislation, or aforementioned discussions of the wall, this language deals directly with immigrants who are attempting to *legally* enter the country. This is a significant departure from legislation that targets undocumented immigrants, a group that has historically received little support from Americans. However, while Trump does equate immigration with threatening national security—similar to the Alien and Sedition Acts—other rhetoric from past legislation is surprisingly absent from his agenda.

DISEASE

The association of immigrants with disease has also been a mainstay of anti-immigrant rhetoric, something that continues to this day. Again, leading up to the 2016 election, the far-right populist press littered its pages, feeds, and walls with stories warning of outbreaks brought in by outsiders. Echoing fears in 1920s Los Angeles, the *Conservative Tribune* headline warned that "Obama lifts ban on diseases refugees . . . here's who he's dumping into your town." The *Drudge Report* headline announced, "More than one-third of refugees in Vermont test positive for tuberculosis." And a *World Net Daily* "exclusive" trumpeted the headline, "Doctors rip Obama for opening border to exotic STDs." These headlines—and ensuing talking points—are repeated endlessly online, particularly on social media. However, despite some columnists positing that Trump might decide to publicly link immigrants and disease[119]—thereby reinforcing the populist right-wing press headlines—as of the present time, he has not done that.

CRIME

Unfortunately, associating immigrants with crime was a common practice, one that only grew more so over time. Study after study reveals that immigrants commit crimes at a lower rate than people born in the United States, a finding that includes undocumented immigrants.[120] However, it's a popular tactic for proponents of restrictionist immigration policy to activate prejudices. Leading up to the 2016 election, right-wing populist media outlets prominently displayed news stories about crimes committed by immigrants, emphasizing violent murder and rape. One of the most notorious of these cases came from *Breitbart News,* which gave extensive coverage to a case alleging that a five-year-old girl in Idaho was raped at knifepoint by three Syrian refugee boys who recorded the act and then showed the video to a parent (who celebrated the act). Reports also noted that the police could not investigate the crime because of the language barrier. Months later, the courts found that there were three boys involved (ages seven, ten, and fourteen), they were not Syrian, and as for the crime itself, "The youngest boy was alleged to have touched the girl. The older boys were accused of using a cell phone to record a video of the incident."[121]

The misinformation got so bad that the prosecutor and investigators on the case had to issue a series of strongly worded statements trying to set the record straight, with the county prosecutor saying, "There is a small group of people in Twin Falls County whose life goal is to eliminate refugees, and thus far they have not been constrained by the truth."[122] However, months and months after the assault, the misinformation surrounding this case remains embedded in anti-immigrant psyches. In emphasizing rape and sexual assault, a connection is made between refugees/immigrants and sexuality, similar to what we saw with the Page Law.

Trump himself has played a role in calling attention to immigrants committing crimes: "Trump—a known germophobe—is not a natural hugger. But every time he meets 'angel moms,' whose children have been killed by illegal immigrants, they expect to receive an embrace from the president. They have become the emotional touchstone of his immigration crusade." He has used this strategy to push two bills through the House of Representatives. The first, the "No Sanctuary for Criminals Act," increased "the pool of money that cities could lose for not cooperating with federal immigration officials"[123]—a direct shot at sanctuary cities. The second—"Kate's Law"—establishes harsher penalties for immigrants who reenter the United States (named for Kathryn Steinle, who was murdered by a Mexican immigrant who had been deported multiple times before).

Given that Trump began his campaign with his infamous allegation that Mexican immigrants were rapists and criminals, it cannot be terribly surprising that he would continue to evoke that image. The far-right populist press does the same, touting problematic headlines, all of which, again, are shared on social media and echoed in arguments online. What's unique here is that, apart from the Idaho case, there simply aren't that many salacious crime stories about refugees and immigrants; often deaths by undocumented immigrants occur in car wrecks—absolutely tragic, but difficult to capture the public's attention. This is why the right-wing press features headlines from Europe: "Syrian 'Refugee' Machetes Pregnant Woman to Death, Injures Two More in Germany," "Leaked German Report Reveals 200,000 Refugee Crimes," "Germany: Afghan 'Refugee' Injures Four Train Passengers in Axe Attack." Again, we see the reference to individuals who have gone through the formal process of entering the country, and that process is questioned through the use of delegitimizing quotation marks around the word "refugee," as if to imply they tricked their way through the system in order to wreak havoc and destroy the country from within.

These strategies—a focus on the border, invoking national security, raising concerns about crime—are well-established methods of gaining support for anti-immigration legislation. What's surprising here is that the United States is not in a recession, the country has not suffered a recent terrorist attack, and there is no crime wave sweeping the nation. It's possible this is part of the reason that such policy proposals have met with limited success. Yet it's important to note how these messages echo similar themes from immigration laws in U.S. history. It's possible that things might change—much like Reagan's surprising (given the circumstances) 1986 legislation. Trump has softened his stance on prosecuting children whose parents brought them into the country illegally. However, given the pattern, it's more likely that Trump will continue to invoke nativist ideals and ideas, turning racial cues and outdated falsities into policy.

NOTES

1. Ashley Parker, David Nakamura, and Philip Rucker, "Trump's Wall: The Inside Story of How the President Crafts Immigration Policy," *Washington Post,* July 19, 2017, www.washingtonpost.com/politics/trumps-wall-the-inside-story-of-how-the-president -crafts-immigration-policy/2017/07/19/b11b8b94-68da-11e7-8eb5-cbccc2e7bfbf_story .html?utm_term=.2fe03c8b0403.

2. Meredith McGraw, Adam Kelsey, and Meghan Keneally, "A Timeline of Trump's Immigration Executive Order and Legal Challenges," *ABC News,* June 29, 2017, abcnews .go.com/Politics/timeline-president-trumps-immigration-executive-order-legal-chal lenges/story?id=45332741.

3. Thomas Wood, "Racism Motivated Trump Voters More Than Authoritarianism," *Washington Post,* April 17, 2017, www.washingtonpost.com/news/monkey-cage/wp

/2017/04/17/racism-motivated-trump-voters-more-than-authoritarianism-or-income
-inequality/?utm_term=.c33d3464bba6.

4. Rita James Simon and Susan H. Alexander, *The Ambivalent Welcome: Print Media, Public Opinion, and Immigration* (Westport, CT: Praeger Publishers, 1993).

5. John Higham, *Strangers in the Land: Patterns of American Nativism, 1860–1925* (New Brunswick, NJ: Rutgers University Press, 2002), 4.

6. Brian F. Fry, *Nativism and Immigration: Regulating the American Dream* (New York: LFB Scholarly Publishers, 2007).

7. Ibid., 11.

8. Ibid., 24.

9. Jerome R. Adams, *Greasers and Gringos: The Historical Roots of Anglo-Hispanic Prejudice* (Jefferson, NC: McFarland, 2006), 166.

10. Joe R. Feagin and Vera Hernan, *White Racism: The Basics* (New York: Routledge, 2000), 26.

11. Roger Daniels, *Guarding the Golden Door: American Immigration Policy and Immigrants Since 1882* (New York: Hill and Wang, 2005), 8.

12. Benedict Anderson, *Imagined Communities: Reflections on the Origin and Spread of Nationalism* (Brooklyn, NY: Verso Books, 2006).

13. Andreas Wimmer, "Who Owns the State? Understanding Ethnic Conflict in Post-Colonial Societies," *Nations and Nationalism* 3, no. 4 (1997): 631–66.

14. Fry, *Nativism and Immigration*.

15. Ibid., 25.

16. Ibid.

17. Ibid.

18. Justin Allen Berg, "Core Networks and Whites' Attitudes Toward Immigrants and Immigration Policy, *Public Opinion Quarterly* 73, no. 1 (2009): 7–31; Jeffrey C. Dixon, "The Ties That Bind and Those That Don't: Toward Reconciling Group Threat and Contact Theories of Prejudice," *Social Forces* 84, no. 4 (2006): 2179–2204; Lincoln Quillian, "Group Threat and Regional Change in Attitudes Toward African-Americans," *American Journal of Sociology* 102, no. 3 (1996): 816–60.

19. Berg, "Core Networks and Whites' Attitudes"; Richard Alba, Ruben G. Rumbaut, and Karen Marotz, "A Distorted Nation: Perceptions of Racial/Ethnic Group Sizes and Attitudes toward Immigrants and Other Minorities," *Social Forces* 84, no. 2 (2005): 901–19.

20. Tomas Almaguer, *Racial Fault Lines: The Historical Origins of White Supremacy in California* (Los Angeles: University of California Press, 2008); Fry, *Nativism and Immigration*; Lisbeth Haas, *Conquests and Historical Identities in California, 1769–1936* (Los Angeles: University of California Press, 1995).

21. Fry, *Nativism and Immigration*, 29.

22. Higham, *Strangers in the Land*.

23. Ana Celia Zentella, "Latin@ Languages and Identities," in *Latinos: Remaking America*, ed. Marcelo Suarez-Orozco and Mariela Paez (Los Angeles: University of California Press, 2002), 321–38.

24. Juan F. Perea, "American Languages, Cultural Pluralism, and Official English." *The Latino/a Condition* (1998): 566–73.

25. Nazli Kibria, Cara Bowman, and Megan O'Leary, *Race and Immigration* (Malden, MA: Polity, 2013).

26. Gilbert Paul Carrasco, "Latinos in the United States: Invitation and Exile," in *Immigrants Out! The New Nativism and Anti-Immigrant Impulse in the United States*, ed. J. F. Perea (New York: New York University Press, 1997), 190–204; Natalia Molina, *Fit to Be Citizens? Public Health and Race in Los Angeles, 1879–1939* (Los Angeles: University of California Press, 2006).

27. David G. Gutiérrez, *Walls and Mirrors: Mexican Americans, Mexican Immigrants, and the Politics of Ethnicity* (Los Angeles: University of California Press, 1995).

28. Wayne A. Cornelius, "Ambivalent Reception," in *Latinos: Remaking America*, ed. Suarez-Orozco and Paez, 174, *emphasis in original*.

29. George Brown Tindall and David E. Shi, *America: A Narrative History* (New York: W. W. Norton & Co., 2016).

30. Higham, *Strangers in the Land*, 97.

31. Joseph Nevins, *Operation Gatekeeper: The Rise of the "Illegal Alien" and the Making of the US-Mexico Boundary* (New York: Routledge, 2002), 26.

32. Paul Spickard, *Almost All Aliens: Immigration, Race, and Colonialism in American History and Identity* (New York: Routledge, 2009), 238.

33. Ibid.

34. Russell O. Wright, *Chronology of Immigration in the United States* (Jefferson, NC: McFarland, 2008).

35. Molina, *Fit to Be Citizens?*

36. Erika Lee, "A Nation of Immigrants and a Gatekeeping Nation: American Immigration Law and Policy," in *A Companion to American Immigration*, ed. Reed Ueda (Hoboken, NJ: Wiley-Blackwell, 2006), 3–35.

37. Tindall and Shi, *America: A Narrative History*.

38. Michael J. Heale, *American Anti-Communism: Combating the Enemy Within, 1830–1970* (Baltimore: John Hopkins University Press, 1990).

39. Lee, "A Nation of Immigrants."

40. Ibid.

41. Kevin Johnson, "The New Nativism: Something Old, Something New, Something Borrowed, Something Blue," in *Immigrants Out*, ed. Perea, 165–89.

42. Manuel G. Gonzales, *Mexicanos: A History of Mexicans in the United States* (Bloomington: Indiana University Press, 2009).

43. Almaguer, *Racial Fault Lines*; Molina, *Fit to Be Citizens?*

44. Gonzales, *Mexicanos*.

45. Haas, *Conquests and Historical Identities*.

46. Douglas Monroy, *Rebirth: Mexican Los Angeles from the Great Migration to the Great Depression* (Los Angeles: University of California Press, 1999).

47. Molina, *Fit to Be Citizens?*

48. Matt Garcia, *A World of Its Own: Race, Labor, and Citrus in the Making of Greater Los Angeles, 1900–1970* (Chapel Hill: University of North Carolina Press, 2001); Gonzales, *Mexicanos*; Monroy, *Rebirth*; Stephen J. Pitti, *The Devil in Silicon Valley: Northern California, Race, and Mexican Americans* (New Brunswick, NJ: Princeton University Press, 2003);

Devra Weber, *Dark Sweat, White Gold: California Farm Workers, Cotton, and the New Deal* (Los Angeles: University of California Press, 1994).

49. Pitti, *The Devil in Silicon Valley.*

50. Garcia, *A World of Its Own;* Weber, *Dark Sweat, White Gold.*

51. Monroy, *Rebirth.*

52. Haas, *Conquests and Historical Identities,* 169.

53. Alexandra Minna Stern, *Eugenic Nation: Faults and Frontiers of Better Breeding in Modern America* (Los Angeles: University of California Press, 2015).

54. William Deverell, *Whitewashed Adobe: The Rise of Los Angeles and the Remaking of its Mexican Past* (Los Angeles: University of California Press, 2004).

55. Stern, *Eugenic Nation,* 68.

56. Molina, *Fit to be Citizens?*

57. Deverell, *Whitewashed Adobe,* 202.

58. Deverell, *Whitewashed Adobe.*

59. Molina, *Fit to Be Citizens?* 84.

60. Leo R. Chavez, *Covering Immigration: Popular Images and the Politics of the Nation* (Los Angeles: University of California Press, 2001); Simon and Alexander, *The Ambivalent Welcome.*

61. Lee, "A Nation of Immigrants."

62. Carrasco, "Latinos in the United States."

63. Ibid.; Jeffrey Melnick, "Immigration and Race Relations," in *A Companion to American Immigration,* ed. Ueda, 255–73.

64. Lee, "A Nation of Immigrants."

65. Cheryl Lynne Shanks, *Immigration and the Politics of American Sovereignty, 1890–1990* (Ann Arbor: University of Michigan Press, 2001), 100.

66. Simon and Alexander, *The Ambivalent Welcome.*

67. Eric Avila, *Popular Culture in the Age of White Flight: Fear and Fantasy in Suburban Los Angeles* (Los Angeles: University of California Press, 2004).

68. Ibid.

69. Mike Davis, *City of Quartz: Excavating the Future in Los Angeles* (Brooklyn, NY: Verso Books, 2006), 230.

70. Eduardo Obregón Pagán, *Murder at the Sleepy Lagoon: Zoot Suits, Race, and Riot in Wartime LA* (Chapel Hill: University of North Carolina Press, 2003).

71. Davis, *City of Quartz,* 161.

72. Avila, *Popular Culture,* 24.

73. Carrasco, "Latinos in the United States."

74. Kitty Calavita, *Inside the State: The Bracero Program, Immigration, and the INS* (New Orleans: ZQuid Pro Books, 2010.

75. Douglas S. Massey, Jorge Durand, and Nolan J. Malone. *Beyond Smoke and Mirrors: Mexican Immigration in an Era of Economic Integration* (New York: Russell Sage Foundation, 2002).

76. Nevins, *Operation Gatekeeper.*

77. Calavita, *Inside the State,* 68.

78. Frank Bean and B. Lindsay Lowell, "Unauthorized Migration," In *The New Amer-*

icans: A Guide to Immigration Since 1965, ed. Mary C. Waters, Reed Ueda, and Helen B. Marrow (Cambridge, MA: Harvard University Press, 2006), 72.

79. Calavita, *Inside the State*.

80. Technically, the Bracero Program only dealt with Mexican laborers, at least as far as the U.S. government was concerned. However, it's likely that immigrants from other Central American countries migrated through Mexico to participate in the program.

81. Michael A. Olivas, "My Grandfather's Stories and Immigration Law," in *A Critical Reader: The Latina/o Condition*, ed. Richard Delgado and Jean Stefancic (New York: New York University Press, 2010), 257.

82. Massey et al., *Beyond Smoke and Mirrors*.

83. Calavita, *Inside the State*.

84. Ibid.

85. Nevins, *Operation Gatekeeper*.

86. Ibid.

87. Shanks, *Immigration and the Politics of American Sovereignty*.

88. Ibid., 125.

89. Calavita, *Inside the State*, 47.

90. Peter Andreas, *Border Games: Policing the U.S.-Mexico Divide* (Ithaca, NY: Cornell University Press, 2012).

91. Gonzales, *Mexicanos*, 175.

92. Calavita, *Inside the State*.

93. Ibid., 58.

94. John Trumpbour, and Elaine Bernard. "Unions and Latinos, Mutual Transformations," in *Latinos: Remaking America*, ed. Suarez-Orozco and Paez, 129.

95. Nevins, *Operation Gatekeeper*.

96. Feagin and Hernan, *White Racism*, 14.

97. Waters, Ueda, and Marrow, eds., *The New Americans*, 2.

98. Wright, *Chronology of Immigration*.

99. Chavez, *Covering Immigration*.

100. Lee, "A Nation of Immigrants."

101. Massey et al., *Beyond Smoke and Mirrors*.

102. Shanks, *Immigration and the Politics of American Sovereignty*.

103. Massey et al., *Beyond Smoke and Mirrors*.

104. Marc R. Rosenblum, "U.S. Immigration Policy Since 9/11: Understanding the Stalemate over Comprehensive Immigration Reform," Migration Policy Institute, 2011, www.migrationpolicy.org/research/RMSG-us-immigration-policy-cir-stalemate.

105. Nevins, *Operation Gatekeeper*.

106. Andreas, *Border Games*.

107. Ibid.

108. Nevins, *Operation Gatekeeper*.

109. Brad Plumer, "Congress tried to fix immigration back in 1986. Why did it fail?" *Washington Post*, January 30, 2013, www.washingtonpost.com/news/wonk/wp/2013/01/30/in-1986-congress-tried-to-solve-immigration-why-didnt-it-work/?utm_term=.09ed53be5102.

110. Nevins, *Operation Gatekeeper*, 69.

111. Andreas, *Border Games*.

112. Massey et al., *Beyond Smoke and Mirrors*, 96.

113. Nevins, *Operation Gatekeeper*.

114. Aasif Mandvi, "Borderline Cops," *The Daily Show with Jon Stewart*, Comedy Central, March 30, 2009.

115. Ben Casselman and Perry Bacon Jr., "How Trump's New Plan Affects the 11 Million Undocumented Immigrants in the U.S.," *FiveThirtyEight*, February 22, 2017, fivethirtyeight.com/features/how-trumps-new-plan-affects-the-11-million-undocumented-immigrants-in-the-u-s/.

116. James Barragan, "Poll: Texans Oppose Border Wall and Sanctuary Cities, Think Immigrants Help More than They Hurt," *Dallas Morning News*, April 18, 2017, www.dallasnews.com/news/immigration/2017/04/18/poll-texans-oppose-border-wall-sanctuary-citiesthink-immigrants-help-hurt.

117. Leo R. Chavez, *The Latino Threat: Constructing Immigrants, Citizens, and the Nation* (Stanford, CA: Stanford University Press, 2008).

118. Anna Giaritelli, "Trump Talks Up Economic Issues after Difficult Third Week," *Washington Examiner*, July 2, 2017, www.washingtonexaminer.com/trump-talks-up-economic-issues-after-difficult-third-week/article/2614561.

119. Arthur L. Caplan, "Ah-CHOO! Trump Could Invoke Microbes to Close America's Borders." *Chicago Tribune*, February 13, 2017, www.chicagotribune.com/news/opinion/commentary/ct-trump-border-zika-ebola-immigrants-infectious-diseases-perspec-0214-jm-20170213-story.html.

120. Richard Pérez-Peña, "Contrary to Trump's Claims, Immigrants Are Less Likely to Commit Crimes," *New York Times*, January 26, 2017, www.nytimes.com/2017/01/26/us/trump-illegal-immigrants-crime.html.

121. Ruth Brown, "Boys Accused of Sexual Assault of Twin Falls 5-Year-Old Plead Guilty," *Idaho Statesman*, April 4, 2017, www.idahostatesman.com/news/state/idaho/article142687194.html.

122. Alex Riggins, Nathan Brown, and Julie Wootton, "UPDATED: Story of Syrian Refugees Raping Idaho Girl Is Wrong, Prosecutor Says, *Idaho Statesman*, June 20, 2016, www.idahostatesman.com/news/state/idaho/article84829787.html.

123. Emmarie Huetteman and Nicholas Kulish, "House Passes 2 Strict Immigration Bills, at Trump's Urging," *New York Times*, June 29, 2017, www.nytimes.com/2017/06/29/us/politics/house-passes-strict-immigration-bills-at-trumps-urging.html.

RACE, WEALTH, AND HOMESTEADING REVISITED

How Public Policies Destroy(ed) Black Wealth and
Created the Wealth Feedback Loop

LORI LATRICE MARTIN

Racial differences in the types and levels of assets owned have endured despite structural and economic changes in the economy over the past few decades and despite the passage of legislation aimed at reducing unequal treatment based upon physical differences between racial minority groups and whites, particularly between white and black people. Public policies have played, and continue to play, important roles in creating and exacerbating racial wealth inequality and black asset poverty. Public policies, whether directly related to asset ownership or not, typically privilege *the haves* at the expense of *the have-nots.*

In the case of race in America, the haves owe much of their wealth to the labor, exploitation, and in the case of Native Americans, the genocide of the have-nots. The legacy and reign of terror fueled by an insatiable desire for materialism and the protection of whiteness are best captured in historic and contemporary differences in indicators such as overall net worth, homeownership, landownership, and asset poverty. Few measures capture the enduring legacy of the American racialized social system like racial wealth inequality and black asset poverty. Contemporary efforts to address the racial wealth gap are often shortsighted and result in the monitoring of the racial wealth gap and black asset poverty and do little to move the nation in the direction of eliminating the racial wealth gap and black asset poverty.

Dating back to the 1600s, public policies created black/white wealth inequality and perpetuate racial wealth inequality and black asset poverty in the twenty-first century. I call upon scholars to take seriously the historical roles of race and racism in maintaining racial wealth inequality and black asset poverty, historically and in recent years. Such a consideration requires not only recounting historical events but also restitution.

These policies range from homesteading in the 1860s to discriminatory and predatory lending today. Homesteading for the twenty-first century involves the creation of public policies that (1) prevent large segments of the black population from acquiring valued assets, (2) keep black people who are able to acquire assets in economic bondage through a number of exploitative practices, (3) insure limited returns on investment to prevent black people from reaching portfolio parity with white people, (4) define and redefine whiteness, and (5) protect the sanctity of white privilege.

Monetary compensation for historic and contemporary discriminatory acts suffered by black people at the hands of the dominant racial group in America, particularly discriminatory public policies, which by design kept black people, and continue to keep black people, out of the wealth-building process, must be part of any good-faith effort to narrow or eliminate racial wealth inequality. Compensation is one of the few effective ways to address what some scholars refer to as the wealth feedback loop—overlapping and cumulative effects of the barriers to asset accumulation for generations of people of color, especially people of African ancestry in America.[1]

The origins of the black/white wealth gap and creation of black asset poverty date back to early 1600s. Specific public policies that facilitated asset accumulation for whites and prohibited, or severely hindered, asset accumulation for blacks, include the Homestead Act of 1862, the Southern Homestead Act of 1866, the revocation of Special Field Order #15, the oppressive systems of sharecropping, and the convict leasing system. Black workers were also excluded from New Deal programs.

Housing policies play a role in continuing the racial wealth gap and the overrepresentation of black people among the asset poor. For example, the Federal Housing Administration (FHA) instituted discriminatory policies that favored white Americans. The present state of racial economic disparities can best be understood as a form of homesteading for the twenty-first century. Although some popular public policies have been aimed at generating assets for the poor, many of these policies have failed. What the United States should do if the nation is serious about closing the racial wealth gap and ending black asset poverty involves *radical redress*.

ORIGINS OF THE BLACK/WHITE WEALTH GAP AND THE CREATION OF BLACK ASSET POVERTY

Racial differences in the types and levels of assets owned exist in American society. A recent report from the Pew Research Center shows that white households have about thirteen times the wealth of black households, and the gap has grown over the past few years.[2] The report also shows that, in 2013, the average net worth of a black household headed by someone with at least a bachelor's degree was about $26,000. The average net worth of a white household headed by someone with at least a bachelor's degree, during the same year, was more than $300,000.[3] Education did not serve as the great equalizer that some Americans claim. Black and white people with similar levels of education had very different levels of net worth.

Home equity represents the largest single component of the average American's portfolio.[4] Racial differences on the likelihood of homeownership and on housing values impact racial differences on overall net worth. White households are not only more likely to own homes compared with black households, but also white households are more likely to own houses with higher values than homes owned by black householders.[5] Moreover, racial differences in homeownership persists even among blacks and whites with relatively high incomes and education. According to the Pew Research Center, "The homeownership rate of upper-income blacks (68%) is significantly lower than the rate of the upper-income whites (84%). The same is true among the highly educated—58% of black householders with a college degree own their home, compared with 76% of whites."[6]

How do scholars explain differences in the types and levels of assets owned or the persistence of black asset poverty? Do disparities in educational achievement, family structure, or cultural and moral deficiencies explain variations in wealth and asset poverty by race? Decades of research show this is simply not the case. In fact, a recent report from Demos and the Institute for Assets and Social Policy at Brandeis University's Heller School for Social Policy and Management found that education, family structure, full- or part-time employment, even personal consumption patterns cannot adequately explain racial wealth disparity and black asset poverty.[7]

Additionally, white people who attended college had 7.2 times the wealth of black people who attended college. Moreover, on average, a single white parent had 2.2 times more wealth than a black two-parent household.[8] White households with a full-time worker had 7.6 times more wealth than a black household with a full-time worker.[9] Cyril Josh Barker, the author of the study from the Demos and Institute for Assets and Social Policy Study, concludes that changing behavior in any of the areas identified previously would not reverse the economic harm of structural racism.[10]

Racism accounts for at least some of the variations in overall net worth of black and white households. To be clear, racism is not merely a belief or an attitude about an entire group of people. Racism can best be understood as a multilevel and multidimensional system of oppression where the dominant group scapegoats subordinate groups.[11] This system of oppression has its origins, in the American context, in the 1600s, when the first group of black people were brought against their will and settled in Jamestown, Virginia.[12] From that point on, what would become the United States set out on a long pathway toward creating policies aimed at controlling every aspect of black life, including whether black people were to be considered as human beings or as chattel property. The nation enacted policies that determined to whom the offspring of enslaved black people rightfully belonged. Other policies dictated whether black people could even own land and control their own economic destinies.[13]

Although wealth includes far more than land and homeownership, much of the literature on race and wealth inequality and black asset poverty tends to focus either on net worth or on home ownership.[14] Studies about black businesses are also prevalent, but are often not discussed within the context of narrowing the racial wealth gap and curbing asset poverty.[15] Given that the home is the largest asset in the average American's portfolio, it is understandable how much scholarly attention is devoted to housing tenure and land ownership.[16] We shift our attention now to a period when many Americans, mostly white Americans, benefited from public policies that contributed to their overall net worth.

THE GREAT LAND GRAB: THE HOMESTEADING ACT OF 1862

White wealth is a direct consequence of many public policies. These policies include the removal of indigenous people. For example, the 1830 Indian Removal Act forced indigenous people east of the Mississippi River, such as the Cherokee, westward.[17] Four decades earlier, the 1790 Naturalization Act prohibited nonwhites from becoming naturalized citizens, and only citizens were entitled to certain rights, including land ownership.[18] Similarly, Alien Land acts in many states built up barriers for nonwhites to own or lease land because they were not eligible for citizenship.[19] Some public policies created wealth for some, while keeping it at bay for others, like the Homestead Act of 1862. The act gave "away millions of acres-for free-of what had been Indian Territory west of the Mississippi. Ultimately, 270 million acres, or 10% of the total land area of the United States, was converted to private hands, overwhelmingly white, under Homestead Act provisions."[20] How the act created a land grab for whites is outlined in the text of the act, which was issued on May 20, 1862.

Years before black people were granted citizenship and protections under the Fourteenth Amendment, the U.S. government undertook an effort to practically give away "a quarter-section or a less quantity of unappropriated public lands" to "any person who is the head of the a family, or who has arrived at the age of twenty-one, and is a citizen of the United States, or who shall have filed his declaration of intention to become such, as required by the naturalization laws of the United States, and who has never borne arms against the United States Government or given aid and comfort to its enemies."[21] Homesteaders were required to pay a small fee, eighteen dollars, and make a commitment to live on the land for at least five years.[22]

Dr. Tim Wise describes the Homestead Act of 1862 as a textbook example of whiteness shaping public policy and perceptions about public policy as it relates to race. I would argue that the Homestead Act of 1862, as a public policy, also shaped whiteness. Whiteness meant citizenship. Whiteness meant access to land. According to Wise, while whites were the greatest beneficiaries of the act, the policy was viewed as an important mechanism for nation building and not a form of "welfare" for whites in the same way that contemporary safety net programs, such as affirmative action policies, are often viewed as "entitlement" programs for undeserving people of color, especially black people.[23]

Blacks, immigrants, and single women eventually gained access to land laws such as the Southern Homestead Act of 1866, which included language prohibiting discrimination on the basis of race.[24] Just like the Homestead Act of 1862, for the land grab in the West, individuals received title to the land after five years of residency and evidence of improvements. Within a decade, Congress repealed the Southern Homestead Act. The act was considered a failure, due in large part to "the overall poor quality of land available for homesteading; white resistance to black landownership; fraud; mismanagement by government officials; and homesteaders' lack of adequate farm implements, other capital, and access to credit."[25] Indeed, Neil Canaday and his colleagues were able to show, empirically, that more whites than blacks were homesteaders in places like Louisiana.[26]

Natural disasters, like the devastating floods in 1866 and 1867 in Louisiana did not help a system already fraught with challenges. The challenges facing the administration of the Southern Homestead Act of 1866 throughout the South, especially in Louisiana, included understaffed and closed land offices and general "chaos and confusion."[27] Claude Oubre argued that the white Democrats felt threatened by the very notion that ex-slaves might receive parcels of land that formerly belonged to former Rebels.[28] Oubre also observed that, when homesteading conflicted with the party and economic interests of southern whites, even sympathetic whites sided with railroad companies and abandoned efforts to secure land for ex-slaves.[29] Oubre concluded that, while homesteading was not a success for whites or blacks, "the failure of the black masses to acquire land is the tragedy of Reconstruction in Louisiana."[30] While ex-slaves enjoyed some political and civil rights for a relatively short period of time, "without the economic security provided by land ownership these gains proved to be transitory."[31]

The new nation thrived on the unpaid labor of people of African ancestry for generations. A conservative estimate places the value of slave labor in America at $1 trillion.[32] In antebellum America, free people of color were also restricted in their ability to acquire and accumulate wealth, and barriers to asset ownership endured. Efforts to address the unequal treatment of black people in America were often short-lived. Special Field Order #15 is just one example. Special Field Order #15 was a military directive issued on January 16, 1865, by Major General William Tecumseh Sherman, designed to allocate abandoned rice fields along a thirty-mile stretch from Charleston, South Carolina, to St. Johns River, Florida. Within this area, black households were to receive forty acres of land and the right to manage their own affairs.[33]

Special Field Order #15, despite its short existence, was an important document with a very interesting history. Few people living outside of Savannah, Georgia, are familiar with the city's role in creation of the order. A historical marker commemorating the order, which resulted from a meeting between Sherman and a group of black clergy, is a reminder to residents and tourists of Savannah's role in attempting to address the economic futures of newly freed men and women.[34]

The special order was unique for a number of reasons. In particular, it focused on both income and assets. Income plays a role in meeting basic needs, while wealth plays a role in giving future generations economic security and providing an individual or household with a safety net in the case of an unforeseen life event. Many people today, as was the case in the 1860s, are income rich and asset poor.

The order called for former slaves to earn a living in areas where they labored during slavery, as domestic servants, blacksmiths, mechanics, carpenters, and so forth, and to exercise the freedom to choose where they would live. The order also included resources for ex-slaves to work the newly acquired land. In placing the experiences of the former slaves in an appropriate context, providing ex-slaves with the tools they needed to be successful should not have been considered an extraordinary act, then or now; rather, it was really *the least* the nation could do for a people who suffered so much at the hands of individuals and the state.[35]

The order outlined the specifications for subdividing the abandoned land. Three "respectable" heads of family were permitted to settle the land and "establish a peaceable settlement." The three households were to divide the land, so that each family would have a maximum of forty acres. According to the special order, captured steamers were also to be made available "to afford the settlers the opportunity to supply their necessary wants, and to see the products of their land and labor."[36]

Sherman, like many leaders before and after him, did not act primarily because of a firmly held belief in the humanity of black people, but out of necessity. Seeking solutions to what was perceived as a growing problem, Sherman met with black clergy in the home of Charles Green. Garrison Frazier, Ulysses Houston, and William Campbell were among the black ministers at the historic meeting in Savannah. Sherman was trying to decide what would become of thousands of ex-slaves who fled inland plantations. These newly freed individuals were following Sherman to the coast. When Sherman asked how the sojourners could best care for themselves, Frazier remarked, "to have land."[37] Additionally, "the clergy, represented by Frazier, did not merely negotiate or discuss wages and contracts, but they lobbied for asset ownership and for land because they knew that with wealth one could truly have a stake in American society and one could truly be free.[38]

As is often the case in the history of Africans in America, the promise of the dawning of a new economic day went unrealized.[39] Anyone receiving land under Special Field Order #15 was forced to give up the land when President Andrew Johnson ordered the land returned to the white owners who occupied the land prior to the war.[40] The United States missed a golden opportunity to pay some of the debt it owned to black people and acted in such as way as to maintain the racial status quo, keeping the racialized social system firmly intact. President Johnson acted to protect whiteness and clearly sided with former Rebels and against black people. Efforts to maintain vestiges of slavery remained long after Johnson's presidency. The period following the Reconstruction era provides an example.

SHARECROPPING AND ECONOMIC BONDAGE

Although Reconstruction brought with it many promising initiatives for black people in the United States, it was in the end a failure, requiring a Second Reconstruction some one hundred years later.[41] The abolition of slavery, along with universal black male suffrage, citizenship, and due process were all Reconstruction era amendments, which led to the election of black people to governmental positions throughout the South and the establishment of financial institutions where former slaves could save their resources, as they were able to accumulate them.[42] Sadly, Reconstruction also saw an increase in overt antiblack violence, the mismanagement of institutions such as the Freedman's Savings Bank, and a general lack of funding and resources to make the idea of Reconstruction a reality.[43] The compromise that ended Reconstruction helped usher in a period characterized by race riots, land takings, lynchings, second-class citizenship, and economic bondage.[44]

Sharecropping was particularly destructive where black wealth was concerned.[45] The practice kept former slaves and their families saddled in debt and tied to land owned by former planters with the full faith and backing of the federal government.[46] Sadly, many historians are overly sympathetic about the plight of former planters, citing an overall economic recovery problem throughout the South resulting from the Civil War. The abolition of slavery created a quandary of sorts for former slave owners. They were forced to create a wage system and abandon their feudal plantation system of which unpaid black slave labor was the lynchpin. Former slave owners did not have access to a viable banking system, which presented a number of other problems, and land could no longer be used as collateral.[47] To be clear, these issues pale in comparison to the impact of slavery, not only on black wealth and black asset poverty, but also on a host of other issues, including the disruption of black families and isolation of indigenous religious orientations and culture, to name only two.

Furthermore, white people believed, just as they had before the Civil War, that it was their obligation to continually monitor and oversee black people as they labored.[48] To ensure that black people, who played a critical role in the economic foundation, vitality, and development of the nation over time, continued to work without the terror of the plantation system looming over them, whites sought to "restore gang labor, centralized plantations, and the close supervision of the work and social lives of their new laborers, which, to their mind, were central to the economics of plantation slavery."[49]

Sharecropping functioned a lot like physical slavery. It limited black people's access to credit for much-needed supplies.[50] Black sharecroppers had to use future crops to finance loans, which indebted them to white merchants.[51] The need to pay back loans forced sharecroppers to grow crops such as cotton almost exclusively, which led to the absence of adequate food production, resulting in the sharecroppers' need to borrow even more money for survival. This vicious cycle of debt and dependency trapped sharecroppers in a form of economic bondage.[52]

Laws in Tennessee, for example, allowed the landowner to provide loans to sharecroppers, thereby exacerbating the problems. It was not only the law that led to the disastrous outcomes of sharecropping, but also provisions within the contracts black sharecroppers entered into with landowners. Landowners could arbitrarily add or increase fees for noncompliance with the terms of a contract.[53] In the event of sickness or accident, the landowner, under some contract provisions, could hire someone else to do the necessary work and then charge the ailing black sharecropper for the labor expenses.[54]

CONVICT LEASING AND WEALTH ACCUMULATION IN THE SOUTH

Public policies have not only limited the ability of black people to accumulate wealth and relegated far too many to the ranks of the asset poor but, as shown in the case of slavery, Reconstruction, and sharecropping, public policies also enriched the wealth profiles of members of the dominant group at the expense and often on the backs of black people. The case of convict leasing is no exception. The system, which involved leasing inmates out to corporations, was another form of slavery. Blacks went from physical slavery to "slaves to the companies they were leased to."[55]

The importance of the Thirteenth Amendment to the convict leasing system cannot be overstated.[56] Devon Douglas-Bowers acknowledged that slavery remains totally legal as long as it is used for the punishment of a crime for which a person was convicted, and that many elected officials have been more concerned about white laborers than about slaves when debating the historic amendment.[57]

Many had a vested interest in convict leasing, including the judicial system in the South and elites in the North and South.[58] Convict leasing thrived in the South even before the Civil War, but increased at the conclusion of the conflict. With the newly freed slaves, corporations had unprecedented access to labor that was as close to free as possible.

Douglas-Bowers attributed the popularity of convict leasing to people like John Milner. Milner was a member of the elite and hailed from Alabama. He was part of a vanguard of industrial forced labor.[59] As was the case in antebellum America, and in the oppressive system of sharecropping, Milner was of the opinion that monitoring black people was the responsibility of white people; more specifically, he believed that a black person in the South could work as well in a factory as a white person in the North if there was someone from the South with experience in overseeing black people.[60]

Local governmental agencies were often complicit in the economic and physical bondage of black people through convict leasing. Power was centralized at the local level, and local sheriffs wielded a great deal of power and influence over the leasing system. Local sheriffs could lease black inmates to contractors, farmers, and corporations. Sheriffs had an economic incentive to incarcerate as many free black people as they could for their own benefit. Laws were passed to feed the physical slavery-to-prison pipeline. The purpose of these laws, commonly referred to as Black Codes, was to criminalize the life of black people.[61]

In some cases, agriculturalists and industrialists had difficulties paying workers until harvest time, and they found that creating vagrancy laws was an effective strategy for tapping into free or low-wage labor.[62] Anyone who was unemployed or refused to work was considered a vagrant and subject to arrest. A payment could be offered to avoid jail time, but in the event a person could not pay, he or she would be fined and/or imprisoned. Vagrancy laws were so vague as to place black people at risk for arrest.[63]

Calvin Ledbetter, writing about convict leasing in Arkansas, observed that both the economic conditions in the South as a result of the Civil War and the growth of the prison population contributed to an increasing reliance on convict leasing.[64] Arkansas charged a fee for the use of convicts. The relative invisibility of inmates in Arkansas and beyond kept the effects of convict leasing hidden from many residents. Moreover, tracking inmates was often difficult as contractors themselves often contracted out inmate labor. Convict leasing officially ended in 1913, but it is notable in the history of racial wealth inequality and black asset poverty because it was "one of the greatest single sources of personal wealth to some of the South's leading businessmen and politicians."[65] Even today, corporations and governments use inmates for everything from manufacturing goods to responding to natural disasters.

RACE, HOUSING, HOMESTEADING, AND PUBLIC POLICIES IN THE 1930S AND BEYOND

Just as homesteading provided opportunities for mostly white Anglo-Saxon Protestants to acquire land and accumulate wealth, public policies in the 1930s and the 1940s also provided an opportunity to whites, including white ethnic groups, to engage in one of the largest mass accumulations of wealth in the modern era in the United States. Prior to the 1930s, only the truly rich could afford to own homes. The terms of homeownership were simply out of reach for average Americans. Half of the value of the house was required at the time of sale, and the prospective buyer had a relatively short amount of time to pay off the remaining cost.

Along came the Federal Housing Administration (FHA). According to the U.S. Department of Housing and Urban Development (HUD), FHA was created in 1934 and became part of HUD in 1965. When the FHA was created, not only was homeownership out of reach for most Americans, but also millions of constructions workers were losing their jobs, and only 40 percent of Americans owned homes. HUD notes that, during the 1940s, FHA programs assisted military veterans in purchasing homes. HUD does not observe the role of the FHA in the institutionalization of discriminatory practices, such as redlining, which originated with administration and kept blacks, including black veterans, out of the home-buying process. Of the millions of dollars that went to underwrite home loans in the 1940s and 1950s, more than 80 percent of the funds went to whites. Homeownership and suburbanization were financed racially.

Even the historic New Deal was described as a Raw Deal for black people, who were largely excluded from the social programs aimed at pulling Americans out of the economic ditch caused by the Great Depression.[66] Black people worked as domestic and agricultural workers, and President Franklin D. Roosevelt excluded these occupations from the original New Deal in the 1930s.[67] Urban renewal in the 1940s and 1950s led to the destruction of black neighborhoods and the loss of black wealth as black homes were literally demolished to make way for a federal highway system to take whites through black neighborhoods to good jobs, new homes, good schools, and other amenities.[68]

The resources dedicated to the War on Poverty as a policy of Lyndon B. Johnson's administration is linked not to a narrowing of the racial wealth gap or the alleviation of black income or asset poverty but to increases in violence in inner cities and the Community Development Block Grants of the Nixon, Reagan, and George Herbert Walker Bush administrations, which focused on community development and not asset accumulation.[69]

Likewise, the Clinton administration's signature Empowerment Zone/Enterprise Community program also focused more on community development than on individual and/or household net worth and may have set the stage for the gentrification that is pushing black people out of communities where their families have lived for generations and replacing them with more affluent nonblack people.[70] The Clinton Administrations policies related to criminal justice also helped facilitate the trend of mass incarceration, which had it origins in the 1970s and the War on Drugs, which literally left hundreds of thousands of black men out of the wealth accumulation process as they were locked away as part of the prison industrial complex.[71]

President George W. Bush's record on addressing the racial wealth gap and black asset poverty involved turning over part of the responsibilities of government to selected faith-based institutions. It also involved cuts to community development programs.[72] The decades that followed further included public policies aimed at protecting wealthy elites and in instances where opportunities were opened to black people, such as in the case of home ownership in the 1990s and 2000s, it was in the subprime sector. Many cite the aforementioned phenomenon as one of the contributing factors to the bursting of the housing bubble and the onset of the Great Recession.[73] While the Great Recession was said to have impacted people of all racial and economic backgrounds from Main Street to Wall Street, black people and other people of color were hit hardest in large part because of their over-representation among the asset poor, and because their economic status, even in the middle class, was both tenuous and fragile relative to similar whites.[74]

One critique of the Obama administration was that its policies aimed at addressing the nation's economic crisis disproportionately benefited corporations and did far less for average Americans, including African Americans.[75] Indirectly, the Affordable Care Act had the potential to help Americans not only become insured, but also to protect them from the indebtedness that comes with unexpected health costs.[76] Efforts to do away with the Affordable Care Act played an important role in the triumph of Donald J. Trump's first-ever political campaign. President Trump's efforts, successes, and failures remain to be seen, but if his campaign is any indication of how he plans to govern over the next four to eight years, it is unlikely that the pendulum on the racial wealth gap or on black asset poverty will shift towards greater parity.[77]

The significance of the wealth gap in continuing inequality cannot be overstated. The head start that whites receive due to unmerited cumulative advantage accounts for the finding that it would take black people hundreds of years to close the gap.[78] The historic structural advantages afforded to whites, and the historic structural disadvantages experienced by black people, are directly responsible for what Amy Traub and colleagues call the *wealth feedback loop.*[79] The feedback loop holds that the opportunities denied people of color "reverberate" in the lives of future generations, or said another way, disadvantages of one generation serve as predictors of disadvantages for subsequent generations, such that children are unable to break with tradition may fare far worse than their parents.[80]

POPULAR POLICY RECOMMENDATIONS FOR NARROWING THE WEALTH GAP AND ELIMINATING BLACK ASSET POVERTY

Popular policy recommendations claiming to address racial wealth inequality and asset poverty do little to narrow the racial wealth gap and eliminate black asset poverty because historic and contemporary public policies fail to deal with the cumulative, material, and tangible disadvantages that contribute to—and perpetuate—racial wealth inequality and black asset poverty. The consequences of such public policies extend beyond any one person's lifespan. Contemporary public polices, many of which are highlighted as policies related to wealth and asset poverty by the Corporation for Enterprise Development (CFED), illustrate how public polices concerning asset ownership, directly or indirectly, explicitly or implicitly, intentionally or unintentionally, well meaning or with malicious intent, accomplish the following: (1) prevent large segments of the black population from acquiring valued assets by erecting barriers that place them at a disadvantage, (2) keep black people who are able to acquire assets in economic bondage through a number of exploitative and predatory practices, (3) insure limited returns on investment to prevent black people from reaching portfolio parity with white people, and as intended or unintended consequences, define and redefine whiteness and protect the sanctity of white privilege.

URBAN HOMESTEADING

Recommendations to narrow the racial wealth gap and to end black asset poverty have included a number of policy recommendations. The mid-1980s saw the call for an expansion of urban homesteading, which involved federal assistance for purchasing vacant real property that was also tax-delinquent for homesteading. However, urban homesteading did not succeed in converting vacant properties to homeownership, and it did not target those most in need.[81]

HOUSING FORECLOSURE LAWS

CFED offers a number of policy recommendations for narrowing the racial wealth gap and addressing black asset poverty. CFED identified the need for public policies aimed at controlling foreclosure at the state level. In 2012, all but one state attorneys general and the federal government reached an agreement with several of the largest loan services and implemented reforms to address fraud, increase opportunities for loan modifications, and create standards for communicating about foreclosure prevention. Black people were disproportionately affected by the foreclosure crisis, and much of that was due to racial discrimination.[82]

SOFT SECOND MORTGAGES

Soft second mortgages are also a policy recommendation made by CFED. These mortgages are subsidized for forgivable loans that enhance equity. CFED also calls for states to fund homeownership education and counseling for current and prospective buyers. Barriers to homeownership for prospective black buyers remain, including discrimination in mortgage lending and at every stage in the home-buying process. Cuts to funding for community-interest programs also limit the availability of homeownership education and counseling.

MICROBUSINESSES

While many of the public policies regarding racial wealth gaps and black asset poverty focus on homeownership, there are other forms of assets, such as business ownership. CFED calls upon states to dedicate more support to microbusinesses and recognize entrepreneurship as a legitimate form of training or participation activity, even for individuals receiving Temporary Aid to Needy Families (TANF). Black businesses continue to face a number of barriers to securing capital due to racial discrimination, including innovations such as crowdfunding, which may or may not eliminate what scholars call the entrepreneur gap.[83]

PREDATORY LENDING

Predatory lending traps many black people in a dangerous debt cycle. According to CFED, predatory lending is "wealth-stripping," especially payday loans, car-title loans, and installment loans. CFED calls upon states to ban the loans and cap the annual rates. These practices ensnare blacks in debt over successive generations.

INDIVIDUALS' AND CHILDREN'S DEVELOPMENT ACCOUNTS

Individuals' and children's development accounts provide opportunities for government to provide incentives, such as matching grants to individuals, to encourage saving. CFED calls for more partnerships between states and nongovernmental agencies to increase incentives for individuals to save. Black people are still viewed by many as undeserving. Consequently, the political will to allocate scarce or limited resources to support development savings account is virtually nonexistent.

SHARED EQUITY HOMEOWNERSHIP

Shared equity homeownership is an innovative housing strategy in which government or a nonprofit serves as a coinvestor for new home buyers. Buyers may earn less equity than if they were to go it alone, but there are a number of benefits for the buyer. CFED calls for better management of the programs and the removal of barriers to long-term affordability. Racial discrimination at every phase of the home-buying process hinders the ability of black people to purchase homes in general and to purchase homes in particular areas. The markets open to black buyers often result in lower equity over time, as evidenced in racial differences in housing values.[84]

LENDING AND MORTGAGE INTEREST REDUCTION

Laura Sullivan and colleagues, leaders in research on racial wealth inequality and black asset poverty, call for stricter enforcement of housing antidiscrimination laws, the authorization of Fannie Mae and Freddie Mac to reduce mortgage principal for loan modifications, and lowering the cap on the mortgage interest tax deduction. Racial discrimination in mortgage lending persists.[85]

EDUCATION AND LABOR

Public policies aimed at providing high-quality universal preschool education are recommended for narrowing the racial wealth gap and for addressing black asset poverty.[86] Making K-12 more equitable is also recommended, along with recommitment to racially integrated schools. Additionally, because some scholars imagine a link between employment and wealth, public policy recommendations regarding labor include the creation of a direct federal job-creation program, raising the minimum wage, and making it easier for workers to unionize.[87] Such policy recommendations, however, ignore the continued segregation of American schools. The schools black children attend are disproportionately labeled as failing, and black people, even those with no criminal past, face greater discrimination in securing employment than white people with a criminal past.[88]

REPARATIONS

Dalton Conley and William Darity are representative of the scholars recommending reparations or payment for the unpaid labor of the enslaved population in America. Both understand the concerns expressed by scholars, public policy makers, laypersons, and others with respect to reparations.[89] Conley cites concerns about who would qualify and how much each person or household would receive. He acknowledges that white people arriving in the 1600s and yesterday benefit from the unpaid labor of slaves daily.[90] Taxes and group preferences may lie at the core of reparations and are politically unpopular, but Conley says it is important to imagine how life for black people would be different with reparations.[91] Darity expresses similar concerns and recommends using "forty acres and a mule" as a standard for measuring reparations.[92] Reparations are a perceived threat to white privilege and the sanctity of whiteness. Taking responsibility and being held accountable for the racial wealth inequality and black asset poverty that exists and persists undermines the myth of whiteness as exclusively virtuous, righteous, and of the ultimate importance in American society.

CONCLUSION: TOWARD RADICAL REDRESS

Public policies facilitated wealth accumulation for members of the dominant racial group in the United States dating back centuries. Contemporary public policies do little to narrow the racial wealth gap or to reduce black asset poverty. In fact, public polices have been shown to make the racial wealth gap and black asset poverty worse. New ideas are needed to address the enduring racial wealth divide. However, new approaches to addressing racial and wealth inequality cannot simply involve the creation of public policies for the sake of creating public policies. New approaches also cannot simply monitor racial wealth inequality and black asset poverty and offer nothing meaningful to address their root causes and long-lasting consequences.

For instance, the Institute for Assets and Social Policy at Brandeis University's Heller School for Social Policy and Management—a leader on racial wealth inequality and asset poverty—developed the *Racial Wealth Audit*. The audit is described as a framework to evaluate public policy proposals to reduce the wealth gap, but it does little more than simply monitor racial wealth inequality and asset poverty.

The Racial Wealth Audit™ uses the predicted changes in household wealth to measure the racial wealth gap between white households, African American households, and Latino households at the 50th percentile. The analysis provides a measure of change in relative wealth before and after policy implementation, and delivers a concrete comparison of policy options. Any policy audit could include multiple iterations of analysis in order to investigate shifting components (such as thresholds for program inclusion) that may produce different results on the racial wage gap. The new focus on wealth disparities adds significant insights regarding the context and material consequences of adopting a policy.[93]

The audit is a tool for assessing how much potential harm a particular public policy may or may not do. *Do no more potential harm* is not an effective strategy for narrowing the racial wealth gap or eliminating black asset poverty. The audit, like many public policies, does not address structural issues. Public policies tend to focus on community development or individual behavior modifications. Cyril Baker reminds us that changing behavior is not enough to reverse the effects of hundreds of years of structural racism. Monitoring the situation will not fix the problem, either.[94]

Evidence of the negative impact of public policies on racial wealth inequality and black asset poverty is well documented. As a society, we must recognize how deeply entrenched race and racism are in the very structure of society and how both race and racism function in our social institutions and beyond. Race and racism are so foundational that the power of public policies is no match for either and certainly not for both. The viewpoint set forth here may seem pessimistic or realistic, depending on your perspective, but the evidence shows that public policies have worsened racial wealth inequality and black asset poverty. However, this is not to suggest that public policies have no place in addressing these issues. History and contemporary experiences show the dangers of ignoring the interconnectedness between public policy, race, and racism in causing and maintaining the racial wealth gap and black asset poverty. Time and time again, public policies that are created without mechanisms in place to address the fundamental issues underpinning the persistent racial divide on wealth inequality and asset poverty are doomed to fail from the start.

After centuries of public policies that have privileged white people, while simultaneously disadvantaging black people, America is not much closer to narrowing the wealth gap and eliminating black asset poverty today than in the year the Civil War ended. In 1865, black people had 0.5 percent of the national wealth, compared to 1 percent in 1990, and 2.6 percent in 2015.[95]

What is required is *radical redress*. The term *radical* evokes the idea that the solution is likely not found within the existing structure but beyond it and calls for envisioning a structure that adequately addresses and compensates black people for slavery, the Jim Crow era, and contemporary discrimination. Radical redress considers the roles of race and racism in determining the types and levels of assets owned not as insignificant or as byproducts of class processes, for example, but as foundational. Radical redress calls for a redistribution of wealth. It demands an expansion of the circle of racial groups included in the proverbial pie, and there is precedence for this. In the past, the pie has been divided, and subdivided, in such a way as to include additional groups through various iterations of homestead-esque policies. The same can be accomplished today—minus the terror that maintained slavery and the genocide of indigenous peoples—that created the conditions that made the original Homestead Act of 1862 possible.

Compensation for the unequal treatment black people have faced (and continue to face) in the United States is not a popular topic for a number of reasons. There are those who wish to reimagine horrific periods in America history, like slavery and the Jim Crow era, in a way that honors the oppressor, blames the victim, or portrays the oppressed as content and better for the experience. Far too many people are concerned with romanticizing America's past and far too few people are concerned about writing wrongs.

Reparations—or financial redress for past and current wrongs—are not unheard of in the United States. The descendants of Japanese Americans received compensation for the internment of their ancestors following the bombing of Pearl Harbor. The amount each person received was symbolic, to say the least, and did not adequately compensate the Japanese people for the billions of dollars lost, but it was a recognition of that the United States was wrong to incarcerate people based simply upon their ancestry. It was also an acknowledgment that there were not only psychological and political costs to Japanese Americans, but financial consequences as well.

The United States should move beyond mere apologies and symbolic financial gestures and in good faith work toward making amends for past and current wrongs. To do so, at the very least, the United States must make it easier (not harder) to prove racial discrimination in court. Additional resources must be provided to investigate and prosecute individuals, organizations, and even state agencies that violate the civil and human rights of black people and other people of color. The idea that it is easier to "indict a ham sandwich" than to prosecute law enforcement agents for killing an unarmed American citizen of color must change, and the surviving relatives should receive justice and more than pennies on the dollar for their pain.

Race-based programs should be part of any efforts to narrow the racial wealth gap. The idea that race-specific programs represent reverse racism is absurd. Efforts to characterize race-specific programs as discriminatory toward the dominant group should be immediately rebuked. The author is unaware of any instances in which the United States (or another other nation-state) has provided redress to groups who suffered as a result of state-sanctioned public policies that have resulted in a significant narrowing of racial wealth gaps or racial disparities on any other meaningful sociological outcome. Ideally, radial redress would result in parity between blacks and whites.

So long as the dominant group maintains its position in the racial social order, it is unlikely that radical redress will take place in the United States. It is simply not enough to say, as some have suggested, that black people have been compensated because of their participation in social programs, such as Temporary Aid to Needy Families (TANF); such claims are rooted in longstanding stereotypes about black people as an inherently lazy and inferior group always wanting something for nothing. It is also rooted in the unwillingness on the part of members of the dominant group to acknowledge the many ways in which they have benefited (and continue to benefit) from the criminalization and exploitation of black people throughout U.S. history and in contemporary times.

Again, radical redress must include financial compensation to people of African ancestry and government- and corporate-sponsored financial backing for race-specific programs aimed at narrowing racial gaps in homeownership, housing values, business ownership, business income, savings, stock ownership, and ownership of real estate beyond the primary residence. Corporations, including colleges and universities, that benefited from slavery, the Jim Crow era, and at other periods of time at the expense of black people must be included in the responsible parties. Just because the concept of radical redress seems hard does not mean it is not worth doing. Once American society confronts the ugly reality that is its history of race relations in an open and honest way, then, and only then, will the United States understand that racial wealth inequality and black asset poverty are about much more than mere dollars and cents. They are about who and what matter, and historically, white lives matter.

NOTES

1. Amy Traub, Laura Sullivan, Tatjana Meschede, and Thomas Shapiro, "The Asset Value of Whiteness: Understanding the Racial Wealth Gap," 2017, www.demos.org/publication/asset-value-whiteness-understanding-racial-wealth-gap.

2. Pew Research Center, "On Views of Race and Inequality, Blacks and Whites Are Worlds Apart," *Numbers, Facts and Trends Shaping the World*, 2016, www.pewsocialtrends.org/2016/06/27/1-demographic-trends-and-economic-well-being/ (accessed June 16, 2017).

3. Ibid.

4. Lori Latrice Martin, *Black Asset Poverty and the Enduring Racial Divide* (Boulder, CO: First Forum Press, 2013).

5. Ibid.

6. Pew Research Center, "On Views of Race and Inequality, Blacks and Whites Are Worlds Apart."

7. Cyril Barker, "Report: Racial Wealth Gap Fueled by Public Policy," *New York Amsterdam News,* 2017, amsterdamnews.com/news/2017/feb/10/report-racial-wealth-gap-fueled-public-policy/.

8. Ibid.

9. Ibid.

10. Ibid.

11. Hayward Derrick Horton and Lori Latrice Sykes, "Critical Demography and the Measurement of Racism: A Reproduction of Wealth, Status, and Power," in *White Logic, White Methods: Racism and Methodology,* ed. Tukufu Zuberi and Eduardo Bonilla-Silva (Lanham, MD: Roman and Littlefield, 2008), 239–50.

12. Darlene Clark Hine, Stanley Harrold, and William Hine, *African American Odyssey* (New York: Pearson, 2010).

13. A. Leon Higginbotham, *In the Matter of Color* (New York: Oxford University Press, 1980).

14. Lori Latrice Martin, *Income Rich, Asset Poor* (Dubuque, IA: Kendall/Hall Publishers, 2009).

15. Ibid.

16. Dalton Conley, *Being Black, Living in the Red: Race, Wealth and Social Policy in America* (Berkeley: University of California Press, 2009).

17. Hine, Harrold, and Hine, *African American Odyssey.*

18. Ibid.

19. Edwin E. Ferguson, "The California Alien Land Law and the Fourteenth Amendment." 35 Cal. L. Rev. 61. 1947, scholarship.law.berkeley.edu/californialawreview/vol35/iss1/4.

20. "RACE—The Power of an Illusion: Background Readings," 2003, www.pbs.org/race/000_About/002_04-background-03-02.htm.

21. Galusha A. Grow, "Homestead Act of 1862," *Social Policy: Essential Primary Sources,* ed. K. Lee Lerner et al. (Detroit: Thomson Gale, 2006), 94–96. *U.S. History in Context,* link.galegroup.com/apps/doc/CX2687400048/UHIC?u=leag48212&xid=630f5fe3.

22. Grow, Homestead Act.

23. Tim Wise, Homestead Act of 1862, 2012, race2012pbs.org/timeline-list/1862-the-homestead-act/.

24. Neil Canaday, Charles Reback, and Kristin Stowe, "Race and Local Knowledge: New Evidence from the Southern Homestead Act," *Review of the Black Political Economy* 42 (2015): 399–413.

25. Ibid., 400.

26. Ibid.

27. Claude Oubre, "Forty Acres and a Mule: Louisiana and the Southern Homestead Act," *Louisiana History* 17, no. 2 (1976): 147.

28. Ibid.

29. Ibid.

30. Ibid., 157.

31. Ibid.

32. "RACE—The Power of an Illusion: Background Readings."

33. Hine, Harrold, and Hine, *African American Odyssey.* Martin, *Black Asset Poverty and the Enduring Racial Divide.*

34. "Historical Marker Unveiled Commemorating Special Field Order 15," 2011, *Savannah Tribune,* www.savannahtribune.com/articles/historical-marker-unveiled-commemorating-special-field-order-15/.

35. Martin, *Black Asset Poverty and the Enduring Racial Divide.*

36. Ira Berlin, "Middle and East Tennessee and North Alabama," in *Wartime Genesis of Free Labor,* ed. Ian Berlin, Steven Miller, Joseph Reidy, and Leslie Rowland (New York: Cambridge University Press, 1993), 339.

37. Martin, *Black Asset Poverty and the Enduring Racial Divide,* 49.

38. Ibid.

39. Hine, Harrold, and Hine, *African American Odyssey.*

40. Ibid.

41. Ibid.

42. Ibid.

43. Martin, *Black Asset Poverty and the Enduring Racial Divide.*

44. Hine, Harrold, and Hine, *African American Odyssey.*

45. Susan A. Mann, "Slavery, Sharecropping, and Sexual Inequality," *Signs* 14, no. 4 (1989): 774–98.

46. Ibid.

47. Martin, *Black Asset Poverty and the Enduring Racial Divide.*

48. Ibid.

49. Devon Douglas-Bowers, "Slavery by Another Name: The Convict Lease System," 2013, www.hamptoninstitution.org/convictleasesystem.html#.WOmX1yMrI1I.

50. Avishay Braverman and T. N. Srinivasan, "Credit and Sharecropping in Agrarian Societies." *Journal of Development Economics* 9 (1981): 289–312.

51. Ibid.

52. Ibid.

53. Hine, Harrold, and Hine, *African American Odyssey.*

54. Ibid.

55. Lori Latrice Martin, Kenneth Fasching-Varner, and Nicolas Hartlep, *Pay to Play: Race and the Perils of the College Sports Industrial Complex* (Santa Barbara, CA: Praeger, 2017), 71.

56. Ryan S. Marion, "Prisons for Sale," *William and Mary Bill of Rights Journal* 18 (2009): 213–23.

57. Ibid.

58. Martin et al., *Pay to Play.*

59. John Inscoe, *Appalachians and Race: The Mountain South from Slavery to Segregation* (Lexington: University Press of Kentucky, 2001).

60. Ibid.

61. Marcus Bell, "Criminalization of Blackness: Systemic Racism and the Reproduction of Racial Inequality in the U.S. Criminal Justice System," in *Systemic Racism,* ed. Ruth Thompson-Miller and Kimberley Ducey (New York: Palgrave Macmillan, 2017).

62. Christopher Adamson, "Punishment After Slavery: Southern State Penal Systems, 1865–1890," *Social Problems* 30 (1983): 555–69.

63. Ibid.

64. Calvin Ledbetter, "The Long Struggle to End Convict Leasing in Arkansas," *Arkansas Historical Quarterly* 52 (1993): 1–27.

65. Douglas-Bowers, "Slavery by Another Name."

66. Gary Green and Ann Haines, *Asset Building and Community Development* (Los Angeles: Sage, 2016).

67. Ibid.

68. Ibid.

69. Ibid.

70. Ibid.

71. Martin, *Black Asset Poverty and the Enduring Racial Divide.*

72. Green and Haines, *Asset Building and Community Development.*

73. Martin, *Black Asset Poverty and the Enduring Racial Divide.*

74. Rakesh Kochhar and Richard Fry, "Wealth Inequality Has Widened Along Racial, Ethnic Lines Since End of Great Recession," Pew Research, 2014, www.pewresearch.org /fact-tank/2014/12/12/racial-wealth-gaps-great-recession/.

75. William Darity, "How Barack Obama Failed Black Americans," *The Atlantic*, 2016, www.theatlantic.com/politics/archive/2016/12/how-barack-obama-failed-black -americans/511358/.

76. Kasey Wiedrich, Jennifer Brooks, Holden Weisman, Lebaron Sims Jr., and Solana Rice, "The Steep Climb to Economic Opportunity for Vulnerable Families," 2016, www.issue lab.org/resource/the-2016-assets-and-opportunity-scorecard-the-steep-climb-to-econom ic-opportunity-for-vulnerable-families.html.

77. Gabriel Gatehouse, "Blacks in Trump's America," *BBC News*, 2017, www.youtube. com/watch?v=5EIusxoiMNw.

78. Joshua Holland, "The Average Black Family Would Need 228 years to Build the Wealth of a White Family Today," *The Nation*, August 8, 2016, www.thenation.com/article /the-average-black-family-would-need-228-years-to-build-the-wealth-of-a-white-family -today/.

79. Traub et al., "The Asset Value of Whiteness."

80. Ibid., 5.

81. William Rohe, "Expanding Urban Homesteading," *Journal of the American Planning Association* 91, no. 57 (1991): 444–56.

82. Ari Shapiro, "For the Black Middle Class, Housing Crisis and History Collide to Dash Dreams," *NPR*, 2016, www.npr.org/2016/09/02/492251653/for-the-black-middle-class -housing-crisis-and-history-collude-to-dash-dreams.

83. Kathleen Lanza, "Crowdfunding Sites for Black and Female Entrepreneurs Expand," www.businessopportunity.com/Blog/new-crowdfunding-sites-for-black-and -female-entrepreneurs/.

84. Laura Shin, "The Racial Wealth Gap: Why a Typical White Household has 16 Times the Wealth of a Black One," *Forbes*, 2015, www.forbes.com/sites/laurashin/2015/03/26/the -racial-wealth-gap-why-a-typical-white-household-has-16-times-the-wealth-of-a-black -one/#2ae525861f45.

85. Laura Sullivan, Tatjana Meschede, Lars Dietrich, and Thomas Shapiro, "The Racial Wealth Gap: Why Public Policy Matters," 2015, www.demos.org/sites/default/files/publi cations/RacialWealthGap_1.pdf. Kathryn Vasel, "Bank to Pay $33 Million for Discrimina-tory Mortgage Lending," *CNN Money*, 2015, money.cnn.com/2015/09/24/real_estate/cfpb -hudson-city-savings-bank-order/.

86. Sullivan et al., "The Racial Wealth Gap: Why Public Policy Matters."

87. Ibid.

88. Lori Latrice Martin, *Big Box Schools* (Lathan, MD: Lexington Books, 2015). Devah Praeger, Bruce Western, and Bart Bonikowski, "Discrimination in a Low-Wage Market," *American Sociological Review* 74, no. 5 (2009): 777–99.

89. Dalton Conley, "Forty Acres and a Mule: What if America Pays Reparations," *Contexts* 1, no. 3 (2002): 13–20. William Darity, "Forty Acres and a Mule in the 21st Century," *Social Science Quarterly* 89, no. 3 (2008): 656–64.

90. Conley, "Forty Acres and a Mule," 13–20.

91. Ibid.

92. Darity, "Forty Acres and a Mule in the 21st Century," 656–64.

93. Thomas Shapiro, Tatjaman Meschede, and Laura Sullivan, "The Racial Wealth Audit: Measuring How Policies Shape the Racial Wealth Gap," 2015, iasp.brandeis.edu/pdfs/2014/RWA.pdf.

94. Barker, "Report: Racial Wealth Gap Fueled by Public Policy."

95. Antonio Moore, "America's Financial Divide: The Racial Breakdown of U.S. Wealth in Black and White." *Huffington Post*, 2015, www.huffingtonpost.com/antonio-moore/americas-financial-divide_b_7013330.html.

POLITICAL INFORMATION IN BLACK AND WHITE

The Effect of Attention to Black Political Discourse
on Black Opinion Formation

ISMAIL K. WHITE, CHRYL N. LAIRD,
ERNEST B. MCGOWEN III, AND
JARED K. CLEMONS

INTRODUCTION

That racial segregation remains a pervasive feature of life in the United States is well documented. Black and white individuals still have very little day-to-day contact with one another. They live in different neighborhoods, attend different schools and churches, and work at different jobs.[1] The dramatic dissimilarities in the life experiences of these groups resulting from racial isolation have been found to be a powerful predictor of many forms of racial inequality in society. Racial segregation in American public schools persists and has been cited not only by scholars, but also by the U.S. Supreme Court in the *Brown v. Board of Education* decision as one of the contributing factors to racial disparities in educational attainment.[2] Researchers also continue to find evidence of the impact of residential segregation in a range of racial disparities, including income and wealth, crime victimization, and physical and mental health.[3] The persistence of racial inequality—along with the ways in which Americans perceive its existence—has profound effects on the political arena, especially as it pertains to public policy. More specifically, the ways in which this information is *communicated* to the American public have broad implications for both political behavior among voters and the policies that result from the actions of these voters.

Despite these advancements in our understanding of how race is lived in America, one consequence of racial segregation has been left virtually unexplored: the ways in which race structures exposure to political information. While both blacks and whites have access (albeit at times unequal) to at least some mainstream sources of political information—such as national television network news and daily newspapers—the average white individual has relatively little contact with the types of social and political institutions or networks that mobilize and provide political information to many in the black community.[4] That is, the racial segregation of American social, religious, media, and political institutions has generated a set of essentially black spaces, through which the political discourse of black elites is channeled.[5] This variation in exposure to black and mainstream political discourse has consequences for how blacks formulate their opinions about politics. By exposing black citizens to a distinct set of cues about the meaning and importance of political issues and events, black elite discourse plays an important role in guiding black Americans' interpretations of and positions on public affairs in directions often quite different from those suggested by the messages of mainstream political elites. Differences in the distribution of political predispositions among black individuals are important, too; black political elites' incentive to define issues in terms that are distinct from those invoked by mainstream political elites derives from those differences. Yet without black political elites, black citizens would lack the information necessary to connect those predispositions to particular events and issues systematically. More specifically, blacks would lack the wherewithal to display a distinctive racial pattern in opinion formation, particularly on issues that have no obvious racial content.

To evaluate this argument, we examine black support for the U.S. Central Intelligence Agency (CIA) in 1996. There were rather stark differences in the content of black and mainstream elite discussions of the CIA at this time, in both the tone and the racial content of elite depictions of the agency. While mainstream discussions of the agency focused mainly on the successes and failures of CIA operations outside of the United States, discussions of the CIA within black elite discourse centered on allegations that the agency was complicit in the trafficking of drugs to largely black inner-city communities. Variation in attention to these black and/or mainstream messages also resulted in intragroup differences in black opinion of the CIA. Because of the racial content within discussion of the CIA in black sources and the lack of racial discussion in mainstream sources, blacks who paid more attention to black elite discourse were not only less likely to express support for the CIA, but were also able to connect their racial identity to their opinions about this ostensibly nonracial agency. These results contribute to existing theoretical accounts of both the role that attention to political communication plays in shaping American public opinion and the formation of black opinion.

THEORIES OF ELITE OPINION LEADERSHIP

Theories of mass opinion formation have found that attention to elite discourse is essential to understanding opinion formation for many political issues. Perhaps the most comprehensive explanation of how elites matter to opinion formation can be found in the work of John Zaller in his 1992 book *The Nature and Origins of Mass Opinion*. Zaller posits a theory of mass opinion formation, the Receive Accept Sample (RAS) model, that places exposure to elite communication at the beginning of the causal stream of mass opinion formation. In Zaller's model, the influence of political elites' messages depends upon both the extent of elite agreement and the level of the individual's awareness of the political environment. He makes the case that, when elites are in agreement on political issues, those who are the most politically attentive tend to adopt the elite position; awareness simply causes the structure of individuals' opinions to mirror that of political leaders. When elites are in disagreement, however, high levels of political awareness enable individuals to grasp and follow the cues of only like-minded elites; when elites diverge, so do citizens, but only to the extent that they have heard the disagreement, and only in the directions that their political predispositions would send them. Applying his theory to the dynamics of opinion change on a number of issues, Zaller finds, in fact, that changes in elite messages frequently precede changes in mass opinion and that diverging elites produce public disagreement, especially among those he classifies as politically aware.

While Zaller's work offers a useful framework for thinking about the interaction of elite messages and individuals' levels of political information in shaping their political opinions, the RAS theory's application to racial minority group opinion is not straightforward. In particular, careful attention must be paid to the definitions of the two main moving parts of the model: elite messages and political information. For Zaller, political information or awareness is effectively captured by general or mainstream measures of political information instead of domain, issue, or group-specific measures of political information. That is, as he states, "political information is a relatively general trait that can be effectively measured with a general purpose information scale."[6] This assumption holds, however, only to the extent that information about relevant elite messages can be found in a "general" information environment. But if the messages of leaders within racial minority communities only appear in segregated information environments—indigenous institutions— and not in mainstream information channels, then imposing singular importance on the "general" or mainstream environment assumes away any significant consequence of attention paid to alternative, racial-group elite discourse.[7] It also may lead to a mischaracterization of the extent of elite consensus or disagreement on political issues, if disagreement is coming only from those outside the mainstream.

Indeed, political elites rely on quite a number of institutions to reach the American public, and they funnel these messages through networks of social organizations, religious institutions, professional and trade associations, interest-group memberships, and media outlets. However, missing from Zaller's framework is the idea that different institutions more readily reach some Americans rather than others, and different institutions are more open venues for some elites rather than others. This very simple observation, however, has consequences for how blacks might come to understand politics. Specifically, blacks are privy to the messages that flow through black institutions and social networks—a range of organizations with few white members—at the same time that black elites find it difficult to be fully incorporated into mainstream political elite discourse.[8] Through these institutions, then, blacks hear a set of interpretations of American politics that white Americans—and blacks not privy to these spaces—do not, fostering significant differences in the meaning and evaluation of policies.

BLACK ELITES AND BLACK SPACES

One of the more consistent findings in the study of black political behavior is that individual connections to black social and political institutions matter. Researchers have found strong evidence to suggest that
membership in black social and political organizations, membership
in a black church, and the use of black media[9] are strongly associated
with, among other things, engagement in certain forms of political behavior.[10] More specifically, membership in black political organizations,
such as the National Association for the Advancement of Colored People and the Southern Christian Leadership Conference, has been shown
to be related to a range of black political behaviors, ranging from participating in a protest to black campaign activism and voter turnout.[11]
Black church membership, it is argued, influences blacks' understanding
of black political symbols, such as the idea of black power, black political awareness, voter registration, campaign activism, and black voter
turnout.[12]

While black institutions seem to be associated with a broad range of
black political attitudes and behavior, explanations of exactly how this
contact results in changes in behavior are few. Here we seek to clarify
the role of black institutions by arguing that these institutions also play
an especially important role as conduits of black political information.
Whether heard coming from the pulpit, over the radio, read in a black
newspaper/website, or conveyed as secondhand accounts via conversations at the barbershop or over social media, contact with black institutions affords blacks the opportunity to be exposed to the "black"
perspective of politics.[13] Similar to how attention to mainstream news
media shapes the general public's knowledge of politics, knowledge of
the goings-on within black politics and the "black" interpretation of political issues is obtained through the institutions and social networks
that black elites use to communicate with the black public. In other
words, by acting as channels of black elite discourse, black political institutions expose those who enter these domains with alternative elite
interpretations of political issues, helping individuals connect their ideologies and other predispositions to evaluations of politics.

* * *

RACIAL ELITES AND BLACK OPINION

Despite the connection of black institutions to black political behavior, we still know very little about exactly how these institutions inspire changes in attitudes and behavior. Furthermore, accounts of elite influence on opinion must include explanations of how society structures this information, as well as how exposure to different types of information has different consequences for opinion. Thus, in an attempt to advance their own interests, ideas, and ideologies among their respective racial constituencies, black elites—including black elected officials, journalists, and religious and organizational leaders—and mainstream elites (those elites who are able to dominate mainstream discourse)—frame political issues, even issues with no apparent racial content, in substantively different ways. In particular, black elites regularly offer interpretations of political events and issues intended to resonate with black group interests and identification while mainstream elites seek to mobilize a broader, more diverse, constituency whose beliefs and values are often quite different from those in the black community. This distinctive framing of public affairs implies that those blacks who attend closely to the political discourse of black elites should understand political issues in noticeably different ways from other blacks whose political information comes largely from mainstream sources. It is, in part, exposure to black elite messages that induces blacks to employ their racial attitudes in evaluating political issues, even those issues that on their face appear to have little racial relevance. This, in turn, leads blacks to have what appear to be liberal positions on a wide range of issues.

Our explanation of black opinion, therefore, rests on two central arguments. The first is that black elites funnel a distinct set of political messages—messages that can and often do differ markedly from those of even liberal mainstream elites—through black institutions. The second contention is that blacks who are exposed to this information recognize and choose to follow where black elites lead, even when mainstream partisan elites are carrying on in another direction. These arguments imply that there is a significant segment of the black community that experiences a somewhat different political information environment than do whites, and that this asymmetry in exposure to the information provided by black political elites is one of the essential elements of the black experience that accounts for variation in black opinion.

METHODS AND PROCEDURES

To evaluate this theoretical proposition we turn to understanding black support for the CIA in 1996. The CIA represents an ostensibly nonracial agency whose primary mission has not been a racial one. While there are many issues for which black and mainstream elites disagree, most of these issues already have either explicit racial meaning, as with race-targeted issues, or have some previously coded or implicit racial meaning, such as issues like welfare and crime. Since race was not an essential defining feature of the CIA before 1996, we would expect that blacks' racial attitudes and their support for the agency would not be chronically accessible; thus, blacks' interpretations of the agency *should* be susceptible to racial cueing. If black or mainstream elites see fit to racialize the agency, then we should be able to observe changes in black opinion resulting from this exposure. As expected, significant variation does indeed exist in the content of racial discourse surrounding the agency in 1996.

While there are many issues for which black and mainstream elites disagree, support for the CIA in 1996 is one of the few that also appears in a large-N public-opinion dataset of blacks that includes both measures of support for CIA and measures of black and mainstream awareness of political communication. Discussions of the agency in black and mainstream newspapers and magazines from March 1, 1996, to December 31, 1996, reveal differences in the tone and the racial content of black and mainstream elite depictions of the agency.[14] Most importantly, this time period captures the August 1996 publication of a series of stories in the *San Jose Mercury News* entitled "Dark Alliance," which outlined the CIA's involvement in trafficking drugs into black communities in southern California. While many mainstream leaders and many within the mainstream media establishment were largely silent or dismissive of the allegations offered in the "Dark Alliance" series, black elites and those in the black media expressed outrage and were pushing for a governmental investigation into the charges.[15] Identifying the differences in black and mainstream political discourse allows us to lay out a set of clear empirical expectations for how exposure to black and mainstream political discourse on the CIA will shape black opinion about the agency. In particular, we are interested in how blacks with high levels of black and/or mainstream political information differ from other blacks who have little or no exposure to black elite discourse.

Our analysis reviews articles dealing with the CIA written between May 1, 1996, and December 31, 1996. A total of 138 articles were taken from the black press, while 72 articles were taken from the mainstream press. Included in the analysis are 10 mainstream periodicals and 30 black periodicals. Articles are coded as dealing with the CIA's role in drug trafficking if they explicitly described the CIA and its connection to Nicaragua and/or the Contras and its involvement or assistance in the illegal sale, distribution, or shipment of drugs into/within the United States. Articles are coded as dealing with black group interest if and only if they explicitly mention blacks in the same discussion as the CIA. An article is coded as quoting a black person if the individual in the article was both discussing the CIA and was identifiably black.

We test our expectations about the effects of this discourse on opinion using data from the 1996 National Black Election Study (NBES). Conducted in the fall of 1996, the NBES was in the field only a few months after the "Dark Alliance" publication and right around the time that black elites began actively forwarding the allegations and pushing for a governmental investigation into the charges. Given the timing of the NBES survey, the effect of these differences on the way black and mainstream political elites discussed—or failed to discuss— drug-trafficking allegations against the CIA can be evaluated by looking into the ways blacks' awareness of black and mainstream politics shaped their assessment of the CIA. Variation in blacks' attention to black and mainstream politics, we argue, will not only determine the ingredients that go into blacks' opinions about the CIA, but will also influence their general approval of the agency. In particular, because of the racialized nature of the discussion of the agency within in black political discourse, we expect that blacks who were attentive to black politics will use their racial predispositions to help determine their attitudes about the CIA, while blacks who are attentive mainly to mainstream politics will demonstrate little or no relationship between their attitudes about the CIA and their racial predispositions; consequently, they will be more supportive of the agency.

THE CIA, THE DRUG TRADE, AND THE BLACK COMMUNITY

Discussion of the link between the CIA and illicit drugs in black communities began after the *San Jose Mercury News* ran a series of articles by journalist Gary Webb reporting evidence that suggested the CIA, in their efforts to support the Nicaraguan *contras* in the 1980s, was complicit the in sale of tons of crack cocaine largely to black street gangs in Los Angeles. Black and mainstream news media outlets reacted very differently to these allegations. In the black media, discussion of the allegations and coverage of black organizational leaders' demands for a full investigation became a regular part of the news agenda. They were reflecting, in other words, a real engagement of the issue by black political leaders—including, but not limited to, leaders from the NAACP and the Southern Christian Leadership Conference (SCLC), pastors of black churches, and members of the Congressional Black Caucus (CBC)—who were forwarding messages that the CIA posed a threat to black communities. The messages of these black leaders sought to excite black Americans through the use of frames that invoked racial group interest, with the ultimate aim of demanding political accountability for the CIA's alleged actions. For example, SCLC board member Dick Gregory— who was arrested for protesting on the issue in front of the central offices of the U.S. Drug Enforcement Agency—promised the mobilization of his organization, framing the experiences of the inner-city of Los Angeles as linked to a general black group interest: "This is where the SCLC is important, because we can use that network. . . . If we don't get the hearing, we'll penalize the business community. We'll call for boycotts at Christmas, Thanksgiving, and take it right to the money. . . . Our neighborhoods, our families, our image has been penalized across the world."[16]

An analysis of the black press's coverage of the allegations reflected the importance of the issue to the agendas of black leaders. The charges outlined in Webb's investigative series sparked outrage among black leaders, inciting members of the CBC to call for a special investigation of the agency at their annual legislative conference in early September.

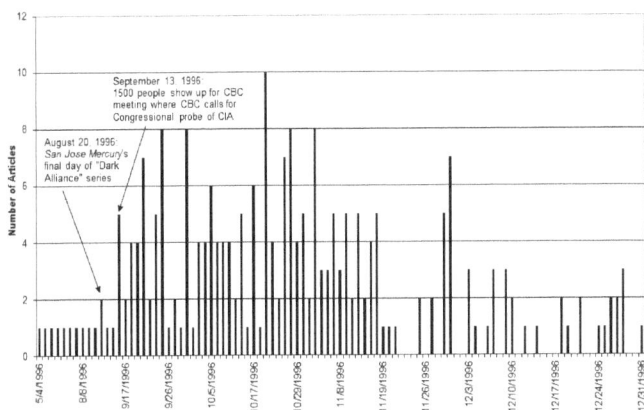

Figure 8.1. Number of articles in the black press about the CIA from May to December 1996.

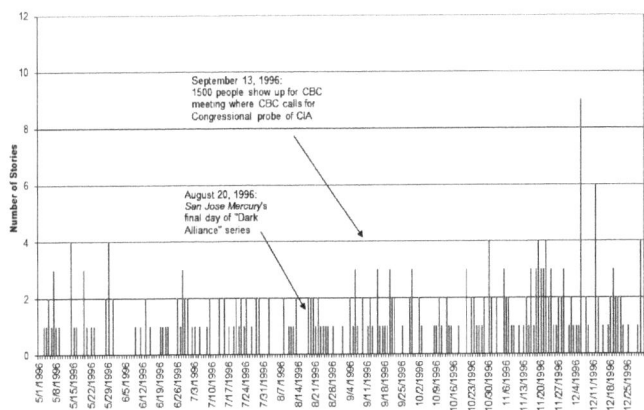

Figure 8.2. Number of articles in the mainstream press about the CIA from May to December 1996.

Immediately after the CBC issued their demand for a full government inquiry, the number and frequency of articles about the CIA in black press sources rose significantly, as depicted in figure 8.1, which displays the total number of articles about the CIA in the black press sources employed in a content analysis of the controversy. While coverage of the agency in the black press was sparse before the CBC voiced its concern over CIA involvement in the trafficking of drugs into inner-city Los Angeles, after the legislators' pronouncement, the CIA became a featured item on the black press's news agenda. A similar pattern of coverage did not exist in the mainstream press. The results presented in figure 8.2 show that, although year-over-year coverage of the agency did increase, this was largely due to a sharp rise in coverage during the month of December. Also, mainstream discussions of the agency had a much broader focus—unlike the black press, which focused almost exclusively on the CIA drug-trafficking allegations.

Although the story was first broken in a mainstream newspaper in Silicon Valley, the allegations of CIA complicity in channeling crack cocaine into the inner-city neighborhoods of Los Angeles were generally met with skepticism and dismissal by both the mainstream media and partisan leaders—Democrats and Republicans alike. Attorney General Janet Reno, in fact, denied the allegations before conducting a full investigation. And despite calls from black leaders for presidential contenders Bill Clinton and Bob Dole to respond to the issue, the allegations were not on the agenda of either candidate's campaign.[17] In fact, many questioned the placement of the "Dark Alliance" series—which appeared between the Republican and Democratic national conventions—arguing that its release in the middle of a presidential campaign might have actually drowned out what little coverage the series could have likely received.[18] When the series did get covered by mainstream media outlets, however, it was often discussed without any mention of race or the black community, despite the activism and messages of black leaders. Also common in the limited mainstream coverage were insinuations that the allegations amounted to no more than a dismissible conspiracy theory—a characterization that only furthered racialized arguments among black elites, who referenced connections to other black experiences that engendered distrust in government institutions.

In a 1997 article published in the *Columbia Journalism Review,* Peter Kornbluh described the mainstream media reaction to Webb's story: "The original reporting—on the links between a gang of Nicaraguan drug dealers, CIA-backed counterrevolutionaries, and the spread of crack in California—has drawn unparalleled criticism from the *Washington Post,* the *New York Times,* and the *Los Angeles Times.* Their editorial decision to assault, rather than advance, the *Mercury News* story has, in turn, sparked critical commentary on the priorities of those pillars of

Table 8.1. Frames Used to Describe the CIA in the Black and Mainstream Press

	Black press	Mainstream pres	Difference
CIA and African Americans	80.53	16.28	64.25*
	153	14	
Drug-trafficking allegations	82.11	16.28	65.83*
	156	14	
Foreign policy affairs unrelated	8.42	77.91	-69.49*
to *contras* and drug trafficking	16	67	
N	190	86	

* Denotes p<.05 for two-tailed test of difference.

the mainstream press." Yet in spite of the mainstream media, the allegations generated by the *Mercury News* continue to swirl, particularly through communities of color.

Content analysis of black and mainstream coverage of the CIA from August through December 1996 clearly describes the priorities of black and mainstream media when it comes to covering the agency. As we can see in table 8.1, the vast majority of the coverage of the CIA within the black media at this time focused on the drug-trafficking allegations (80 percent of stories) and how the agency's actions related to blacks (82 percent of stories). Given their tendency to dismiss the drug-trafficking allegations, the mainstream press devoted the vast majority of its coverage of the CIA to stories which focused more generally on the agency's involvement in overseas foreign affairs.

To say that mainstream media and politicians largely dismissed the story of CIA culpability in the importation of crack cocaine into the inner-city black communities of Los Angeles is not to say that mainstream discussions of the intelligence agency during this period were particularly positive or scandal-free. A number of other CIA scandals that surfaced in the fall of 1996 did manage to generate significant consideration by mainstream elites. Allegations of a CIA cover-up of information about American troops' exposure to chemical weapons during the Persian Gulf War attracted significant attention from the mainstream media. Also reported was the story of Harold Nicholson, a

Table 8.2. Percentage of Articles Discussing the CIA in the Black and Mainstream Media That Offer a Critical Evaluation of the Agency

	Black press	Mainstream pres	Difference
All stories	72.02	55.81	16.21*
	139	48	

* Denotes p<.05 for two-tailed test of difference.

CIA agent accused of selling classified information to the Russian government. Even another story of CIA involvement in the shipment of cocaine into the United States merited coverage; in this case the CIA admitted to allowing a shipment to enter from Colombia through Miami as part of an operation of intelligence gathering about a Colombian drug cartel, and then losing track of the shipment. The content-analysis results presented in table 8.2 support the idea that mainstream coverage of the agency was somewhat mixed in its criticism. The results show that mainstream discussions of the CIA at this time were just slightly negative in tone, as 55 percent of the stories in the mainstream press offered some sort of criticism of the agency. Black press discussions of the agency were, however, decidedly more negative with 72 percent of stories in the black press offering some sort of criticism of the agency. Again, the vast majority of these criticisms focused on the agency's involvement in drug trafficking.

VARIATION IN MEANING—REFLECTIONS OF ELITE DISCOURSE
Given the distinctly racialized messages about the CIA present in black elite discourse and the near absence of those messages from mainstream information environments, the fielding of the 1996 NBES—from November 8, 1996, to the first part of January 1997—provides a unique opportunity to investigate the role of black elites in defining the meaning of a political subject without obvious racial content for black citizens. Knowing the specific nature of the distinct messages that blacks attentive to black politics would have been receiving about the CIA in the time frame that the survey was conducted, we can capture the role of black elite messages in shaping black opinion by looking to the relationship between black political awareness and attitudes about

the CIA. Evidence of the influence of black elites on black public opinion would lie in the extent to which the relationship between black political awareness and blacks' assessments of the CIA is different from the relationship between mainstream political awareness and opinion.

Again, in the fall of 1996 the greatest divergence between the black and mainstream elite discourse about the CIA was in the *terms* of their discussions about the intelligence agency's performance. Black political leaders, stressing the single story of the CIA's alleged role in facilitating the channeling of crack cocaine into black communities in Los Angeles, were urging blacks to see the issue as one with repercussions for blacks regardless of where they lived. Strong criticisms were being offered about the agency, and concerted attempts were being made to mobilize blacks around the issue through the activation of racial group interest. Thus, blacks who were attentive to black politics ought to have incorporated racial group interest into their evaluations of the CIA. Yet, while the concerns of black elites were not integrated into mainstream political discussions of the CIA, neither was the mainstream discourse pushing for a necessarily positive evaluation of the agency. Hence, while blacks who attended to mainstream politics—and not black politics— would *not* have been provided with the link between their racial attitudes and the CIA, mainstream messages may have offered another set of reasons for evaluating the agency. These reasons, in turn, should have activated concerns among those predisposed to question the credibility of government agencies or concerns about defense spending given the quasi-military status of the agency.

Hypotheses

H1: Given the negative depictions of the CIA present in black elite discourse (in particular those focusing on the importation of drugs into inner-city Los Angeles neighborhoods), blacks who were attentive to black elite discourse should express more negative evaluations of the CIA.

H2: Given the somewhat mixed depictions of the agency in mainstream elite discourse, blacks who were particularly attentive to mainstream elite discourse should express neutral to perhaps negative evaluations of the CIA.

H3: Because black political discourse about the CIA focused so heavily on discussions of the agency's suspected involvement in the importation of drugs into inner-city Los Angeles neighborhoods, blacks who are attentive to black politics should use their racial identification to evaluate the agency.

H4: Given the absence of racial frames in mainstream discussions of the CIA and a focus on espionage and cover-up controversies involving the agency, blacks attentive to mainstream politics should use nonracial considerations in their evaluations of the agency.

MEASUREMENT IN THE 1996 NBES

Measuring evaluations of the CIA, awareness of black and mainstream politics, and the other relevant predispositions in the NBES is fairly straightforward. Evaluations of the CIA are captured by respondents' placement of the agency on a standard zero to one-hundred point feeling thermometer. Predispositions regarding government trust are captured by a question that asked respondents, "How much of the time do you trust the government in Washington to do what is right?" The responses were coded from zero to one, with those most trustful of the federal government at zero and those least trustful at one, yielding a scale measure of *dis*trust in the government. Other possible factors in the shaping of blacks' opinions of the CIA were also added to the analysis. In particular, given the CIA's status as a national security agency, with a focus on foreign affairs and apparent quasi-military powers, citizens might connect their general attitudes about national defense to their evaluations of the agency. To account for this influence, a control measure was added that measures the respondent's willingness to support increased federal spending on defense; this measure was coded with those who favored increased spending on defense at one, and those who favored decreased spending on defense at zero.[19] In an attempt to capture attention to mainstream elites, a measure of liberal/ conservative ideology was included.

To assess whether respondents view the CIA through a racial lens, we examine if there exists a connection between respondents' attitudes about the CIA and their sense of black racial group identification. Here, black racial group identification is measured by a scale of five variables each designed to capture, in different ways, the connectedness blacks have to their racial group. Similar to the concept of linked fate, the measures we use were generally designed to get at the respondent's acceptance of the idea that what happens to black people in this country has something to do with what happens to them.

Consistent with previous research, awareness of political discourse is captured with a measure of political knowledge. However, unlike previous research, we devise two measures of political awareness: one that captures awareness of mainstream politics and another that seeks to capture awareness of black politics. The mainstream political awareness index used here is very similar to the index used in previous studies assessing the effects of general political awareness, which consists of questions about the names and party identification of the respondent's congressperson and senators, as well as identification of the majority party in both chambers. Additionally, respondents were asked nine relevant thermometer-score items that allowed them to indicate that they did not know the individual referenced in the question. These individuals were: Richard Lamm, Newt Gingrich, and Ross Perot.[20] If an individual indicated they did not know the individual, they were coded as zero; otherwise, they were coded as one.

Black political awareness is measured by an index of questions from the NBES that assess knowledge specific to blacks in the United States. The first set of items was questions that asked the respondents to recall specific pieces of information that those attentive to black political discourse would be more likely to report correctly: the percentage of blacks in the United States, the race of their own representative in Congress, the percentage of blacks in Congress, and whether blacks in the United States were better or worse off financially than whites. Although the survey did not contain items that asked respondents to specifically identify black leaders, it did contain five relevant thermometer-score items that allowed respondents to indicate that they did not know the subject of the question. Respondents seemed quite comfortable indicating when they did not know the political figure they were being asked to evaluate; just under 60 percent of the respondents, for instance, informed interviewers that they did not know who Kweisi Mfume— then president of the NAACP—was. Similarly, just over half of the respondents indicated that they did not know Carol Moseley Braun, the then-sitting junior senator from Illinois who was the first black woman to serve in the U.S. Senate. A smaller but still notable number of respondents failed to recognize Nation of Islam leader Louis Farrakhan.[21] While information about all of these items certainly could have come from mainstream political information sources, the more likely sources are black institutions, considering the relative absence of racial discussions and obvious racial sources found in the mainstream news media.[22]

Using all of these measures, we can develop a model that assesses how support for the CIA varies and is conditional on black and mainstream political information (only mainstream in the case of whites), as well as how levels of black and mainstream political information moderate the relationship between group identification (or negative attitudes about blacks in the case of whites) and support for the CIA.

RESULTS

We begin our attempt to disentangle the effects of attention to black and/or mainstream political discourse on blacks' attitudes about the CIA in 1996 by first examining the effects of attention to black and mainstream discussions of the CIA on blacks' overall evaluation of the agency. Again, our expectation is that—given the negative depictions of the CIA present in black elite discourse—blacks who were attentive to black elite discourse should express more negative evaluations of the CIA. Moreover, given the somewhat mixed depictions of the agency present in mainstream elite discourse, blacks who were particularly attentive to mainstream elite discourse should express neutral to negative evaluations of the agency. To test these expectations, we begin by simply looking at the independent effects of black and mainstream awareness on blacks' support for the CIA. The results of this analysis are presented in table 8.3. In the first two columns of the table we see that increases in either black or mainstream awareness appear to be associated with negative feelings about the CIA among black respondents. This result is not totally surprising considering that both black and mainstream sources were at times critical of the agency; however, we certainly expected attention to black discourse to be *more* negative. By simply eyeballing the relative size of the black and mainstream coefficients (which can be found in columns one and two), there is some

Table 8.3. Black Support for the CIA by Black and Mainstream Political Awareness

	1	2	3
Mainstream political awareness	-14.70	-	-5.28
	(5.76)	-	(6.50)
Black political awareness	-	-25.68*	-23.17*
	-	(6.20)	(7.09)
Constant	47.56*	54.80*	55.84*
	(4.55)	(4.97)	(5.12)
N	7.39	739	736
Adj-R²	0.05	0.06	0.07

Notes: Entries are OLS coefficients. Each model includes controls for southern residence, urban residence, ideology, party identification, education, and gender (not shown).

*Denotes p<.05 for two-tailed test of the relationship between that variable and feelings of warmth with the CIA.

sense that attention to black discourse may in fact lead to *more* negative evaluations of the CIA. The coefficient on the black awareness variable is roughly nine points larger than the coefficient on the mainstream awareness variable. To test if the effect of black awareness is in fact different from that of mainstream awareness, we include both black and mainstream awareness in the same model of support for the CIA. This analysis is presented in column three of table 8.3. The results presented in column three show that, once we control for the effect of black awareness, we observe a significant reduction in the size of the mainstream awareness coefficient. The rather large and statistically significant negative coefficient on the black awareness measure and the smallish, now indistinguishable from zero (p=.416), coefficient on the mainstream awareness measure confirms our initial expectations that attention to black discourse seems to be a more systematic predictor of blacks' negative attitudes about the agency.[23]

To comprehend more fully the meaning of these results, we calculated the predicted CIA feeling thermometer scores at various levels (high and low) of black and mainstream awareness along with the 95 percent confidence intervals. What we see in figure 8.3 is essentially the unique effect of black awareness on support for the CIA. While blacks

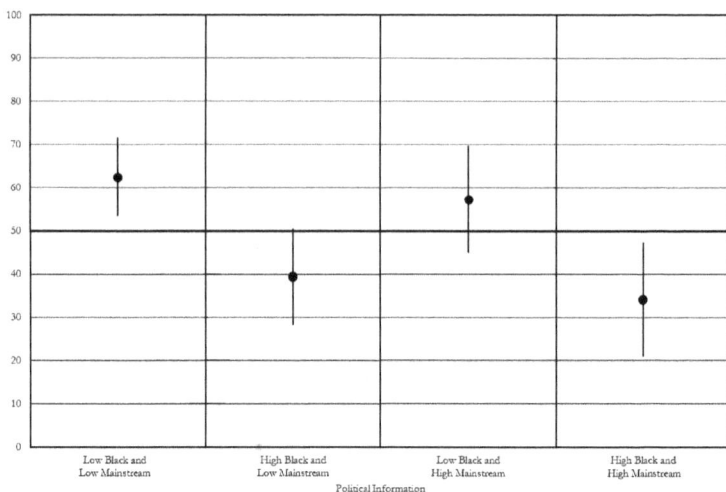

Figure 8.3. Effect of black awareness on support for the CIA.

who are low in *both* black and mainstream political awareness or who are only high in mainstream awareness give the agency a somewhat warm rating (around 60 on a 100-point scale), blacks who either only have high black political awareness or who have high black and high mainstream awareness rate the CIA well below 50 at around 40 on the 100-point scale.

THE INGREDIENTS OF OPINION ABOUT THE CIA

Increased attention to black political discourse as measured by black political awareness does indeed appear to be related to more negative feelings towards the CIA. Our second set of expectations deals with how increased attention to black political discourse might affect the mix of ingredients that go into blacks' opinions about the CIA. In the case of black elites, in particular, their primary motivation was to mobilize blacks to political action. More specifically, black elites wanted to encourage political participation that would pressure acquiescence to the demand for an investigation into the specific issue of CIA involvement in drug trafficking; convincing blacks that their group interest was important and relevant to their evaluations of the CIA was a necessary part of this mobilization effort. Thus, because black political discourse about the CIA focused so heavily on discussions of the agency's suspected involvement in the importation of drugs into inner-city Los Angeles neighborhoods, blacks who were particularly attentive to this discourse should see their racial in-group identification becoming important to their evaluations of the agency. And because of the absence of racial frames in mainstream discussions of the CIA and a focus on espionage and cover-up controversies involving the agency, blacks who are particularly attentive to mainstream politics should use nonracial considerations in their evaluations of the agency.

We test these expectations by examining the effects of liberal/ conservative ideology, black in-group identification, trust in government, and support for increased defense spending on support for the CIA across the four levels of black and mainstream political awareness shown in figure 8.3: (1) *low black awareness and low mainstream awareness,* (2) *low black awareness and high mainstream awareness,* (3) *high black awareness and low mainstream awareness,* and (4) *high black awareness and high mainstream awareness.* Each of the independent variables is fairly evenly distributed across the political awareness groups. Although those in the *low black awareness and low mainstream awareness* group appear to be somewhat more conservative than those in the *high black awareness and high mainstream awareness* group, very few other differences exist. This relative balance in the distribution of these independent variables across these groups gives us added confidence that the differences we might observe across the groups are likely due to the type of information these individuals were exposed to and not necessary the result of, for example, highly racially identified blacks selecting into black information environments.[24]

Table 8.4 presents the results of our test of the effects of these independent variables on black support for the CIA. Beginning with the results for the low black, low mainstream group presented in column one, we see, not surprisingly, very little evidence of any systematic thinking about the CIA. The effect of black in-group identification on support for the CIA among these individuals is small and fails to reach the conventional level of statistical significance. This result is not surprising considering that in the absence of information that actually racializes the CIA it is not clear how these individuals would link their racial in-group identity to their support of the agency. The only measure that offers any suggestive meaning to explaining support for the agency among these individuals is distrust in government. Among low awareness individuals, those who distrust government were somewhat more likely to offer negative evaluations of the CIA; however, this result is only marginally significant.

Having demonstrated that racial in-group identification plays, at best, only a minor role in explaining attitudes about the CIA among low awareness blacks, we turn our attention to understanding how the importance of racial in-group identification varies across groups of blacks with different levels of black and mainstream awareness. Using the *low black and low mainstream* group as a comparison group, we can now test how the importance of each of our predictors changes across the different types of awareness. In the second row of table 8.4 we can see that, consistent with our expectations, the only group for which racial in-group identification is related to attitudes about the CIA is for those blacks with low mainstream awareness but high black awareness. The coefficient on racial in-group identification in this group is more than four times the size of the racial in-group identification coefficient in the baseline group *(low mainstream and low black awareness)*.

Having seen how the different ingredients of opinion changed relative to the baseline, we may also want to compare changes across the *low black and high mainstream* and the *high black and low mainstream* groups. This test gives us a more direct comparison of the effects of attention black and mainstream communications on support for the CIA. The results of this test look very much like the previous analyses, with the only statistically significant difference in the coefficients across the two models being from racial group identification. The difference in the size of the racial group identification coefficients between the *high black, low mainstream,* group and the *low black, high mainstream,* group is even larger than the differences between the baseline *(low black, low mainstream)* group and the *high black, low mainstream,* group. The coefficient on black in-group identification in the *low black, high mainstream,* group is essentially zero compared to the 31-point decrease in support for the agency observed in the *high black, low mainstream,* group (moving from low to high levels of black in-group identification). Thus, not only were racial considerations more important to high black awareness blacks relative to those who pay little attention to politics, but it was

Table 8.4. Predictors of Blacks' Feelings toward the CIA by Level of Black and Mainstream Political Awareness

	Low black and low mainstream awareness (baseline)	Low black and high mainstream awareness	High black and low mainstream awareness	High black and high mainstream awareness
Ideology (liberal)	2.81	-7.24	2.07	-7.18*
	(4.52)	(5.68)	(6.15)	(3.69)
Black in-group identification	-5.13	-8.14	-31.63*	-16.52*
	(5.19)	(7.83)	(10.65)	(5.03)
Distrust in federal government	-18.29*	-39.60*	-24.36+	-30.33*
	(8.28)	(12.99)	(14.10)	(7.88)
Support for increased spending on defense	6.82	10.31	2.32	9.46*
	(5.10)	(6.65)	(7.78)	(4.17)
Constant	49.32*	51.32*	81.61*	53.86
	(9.54)	(14.44)	(16.80)	(9.90)
N	233	109	105	273
Adj-R^2	0.04	0.16	0.11	0.15

Notes: Entries are OLS coefficients from simultaneously estimated models. Each model includes controls for southern residence, urban residence, ideology, party identification, education and gender (not shown).

*Denotes p<.05 and +denotes p<.1 for two-tailed test of the relationship between that variable and feelings of warmth with the CIA within that condition.

also more important relative to those who attend primarily to mainstream politics.

Lastly, nonracial considerations also play a part in explaining blacks' attitudes about the CIA, but their role is largely isolated to the high mainstream awareness groups. For example, we see that the role of trust in government increases significantly relative to the baseline group for both the *low black, high mainstream,* group (p<.1) and the *high black, high mainstream,* groups (p<.05). Similarly, we see that the effect of liberal/ conservative ideology also increases relative to the baseline group for the *high black, high mainstream,* groups (p<.1). These results are consistent with our expectations that, given the absence of racial frames in mainstream discussions of the CIA, blacks attentive to mainstream politics should use nonracial considerations in their evaluations of the agency.

CONCLUSION

The United States has made significant advancements in trying to repair the damage of Jim Crow segregation on black life, but vestiges of this institution remain. On a daily basis, most blacks still have minimal interaction with whites. In modern-day America, the spaces that were created by blacks to cope with the oppressive nature of segregation continue to influence and shape their opinions on politics. Within these spaces—and particularly as it relates to the media—blacks are exposed to discourse about issues and problems facing the black community that differs from mainstream political communication. The ways in which Americans—black, white, or otherwise—receive information has a profound effect on the formulation of individual opinion. This finding relates to the study of voting behavior and political participation, both of which can have direct and indirect effects on public policy and elite behavior.

This analysis makes two important points. The first is a substantive point about the importance of alternative elite discussions of politics. We make the case for considering the effects that indigenous political elites have on structuring the opinions of blacks. Those blacks who are not privy to black elite discourse have a very different understanding of politics than those blacks who get their information primarily from attention to black elite discourse. Black individuals with high levels of black awareness were more likely to be exposed to negative depictions of the CIA and were more likely to express negative feelings toward the agency. Racialized frames utilized in black political communication increased the relevance of racial considerations when blacks evaluated the CIA. These racialized frames that discussed the suspected involvement of the agency in the importation of drugs into the inner city were absent in the mainstream elite discourse. As a result, blacks that were attentive to the black elite discourse were receiving racial cues that heightened the importance of an ostensibly nonracial agency when considering the advancement of black interests. Blacks who were more attentive to mainstream political discourse were not influenced by these racialized frames; thus, racial considerations were not employed when making evaluations. We hope these findings inspire more scholarly attention devoted to understanding the different ways that indigenous elites can influence minority opinion. Latinos, for example, experience even greater segregation in political information as they are also divided by language. How might this segregation lead to differences in Latino opinion?

The second point is that measures of mainstream or general political information may not truly capture the effects of blacks' attention to politics. If the messages of leaders within racial minority communities only appear in segregated information environments—indigenous institutions—and not in mainstream information channels, then imposing singular importance on the mainstream environment assumes away any significant consequence of attention paid to alternative, racial-group elite discourse. This is not to say that Zaller was incorrect in his formulation of elite effects on mass opinion; however, it is clear that these effects deserve more contextualization, especially as they pertain to populations whose norms and values are not represented in mainstream media discourse. This contention can also be extended to any group that is underrepresented in mainstream media coverage, such as Muslims or individuals who identify as LGBTQ. It also may lead us to a mischaracterization of the extent of elite consensus or disagreement on political issues, if disagreement is coming only from those outside the mainstream. Thus, we hope more attention is devoted to developing more precise measures of attention to racial elite discourse.

NOTES

1. Douglass S. Massey and Nancy A. Denton. *American Apartheid: Segregation and the Making of the Underclass* (Cambridge, MA: Harvard University Press, 1993).

2. Erica Frankenberg and Chungmei Lee, "Race in American Public Schools: Rapidly Resegregating School Districts," Civil Rights Project, Harvard University, 2002, www.civilrightsproject.harvard.edu/research/deseg/Race_in_American_Public_Schools1.pdf; S. F. Reardon, J. T. Yun and T. M. Eitle, "The Changing Structure of School Segregation: Measurement and Evidence of Multi-Racial Metropolitan School Segregation, 1989–1995," *Demography* 37, no. 3 (2000): 351–64; David Card and Jesse Rothstein, "Racial Segregation and the Black-White Test Score Gap," *Journal of Public Economics* 91, no. 11–12 (2007): 2158–84.

3. Douglas S. Massey, Gretchen A. Condran, and Nancy A. Denton, "The Effect of Residential Segregation on Black Social and Economic Well-Being." *Social Forces* 66, no. 1

(1987): 29–56; Mark Schneider and Thomas Phelan, "Black Suburbanization in the 1980s," *Demography* 30, no. 2 (1993): 269–79; Fredrick C. Harris, *Something Within: Religion in African-American Political Activism* (New York: Oxford University Press, 1999); Donald P. Green, Dara Z. Strolovitch, and Janelle S. Wong, "Defended Neighborhoods, Integration, and Racially Motivated Crime," *American Journal of Sociology* 104 (1998): 372–403; Ruth D. Peterson and Lauren J. Krivo, "Racial Segregation and Black Urban Homicide," *Social Forces* 71 (1993): 1001–26; Amy Schulz, David Williams, Barbara Israel, Adam Becker, Edith Parker, Sherman A. James, and James Jackson, "Unfair Treatment, Neighborhood Effects, and Mental Health in the Detroit Metropolitan Area" *Journal of Health and Social Behavior* 41 (2000): 314–32; David R. Williams and Chiquita Collins, "Racial Residential Segregation: A Fundamental Cause of Racial Disparities in Health," *Public Health Reports* 116 (2001): 404–16.

4. Harris, *Something Within*; Taeku Lee, *Mobilizing Public Opinion: Black Insurgency and Racial Attitudes in the Civil Rights Era* (Chicago: University of Chicago Press, 2002); Michael C. Dawson, *Black Visions: The Roots of Contemporary African-American Political Ideologies* (Chicago: University of Chicago Press, 2001); Oscar H. Gandy, "Race, Ethnicity and the Segmentation of Media Markets," *Mass Media and Society* (2000): 44–69.

5. Susan Herbst, *Politics at the Margin: Historical Studies of Public Expression outside the Mainstream* (Cambridge, UK: Cambridge University Press, 1994); Michael C. Dawson, *Behind the Mule: Race and Class in African-American Politics* (Princeton, NJ: Princeton University Press, 1994); Melissa V. Harris-Lacewell, *Barbershops, Bibles, and BET* (Princeton, NJ: Princeton University Press, 2004); Lee, *Mobilizing Public Opinion*.

6. John Zaller, "Analysis of Information Items in the 1985 Pilot Study," Report to the NES Board of Overseers, Center for Political Studies, University of Michigan, 1986.

7. See Lee, *Mobilizing Public Opinion,* for more on this point.

8. Robert M. Entman and Andrew Rojecki, *The Black Image in the White Mind: Media and Race in America* (Chicago: University of Chicago Press, 2000).

9. Black media are defined here as media directed primarily toward black audiences. The black media in the United States are primarily a source of entertainment news; however, the black media (like many other exclusively black institutions) have regularly become a tool for black elites to efficiently mobilize black opinion.

10. Katherine Tate, *From Protest to Politics: The New Black Voters in American Elections* (Cambridge, MA: Harvard University Press, 1993); Allison Calhoun-Brown, "African American Churches and Political Mobilization: The Psychological Impact of Organizational Resources," *Journal of Politics* 58, no. 4. (November 1996): 935–53; Cathy Cohen, *The Boundaries of Blackness: AIDS and the Breakdown of Black Politics* (Chicago: University of Chicago Press, 1999); Dawson, *Behind the Mule*; Dawson, *Black Visions*; Harris, *Something Within*; Eric L. McDaniel, *Politics in the Pews: The Political Mobilization of Black Churches* (Ann Arbor: University of Michigan Press, 2008).

11. Tate, *From Protest to Politics*.

12. Joel D. Aberbach and Jack L. Walker, "The Meaning of Black Power: a Comparison of White and Black Political Interpretations of a Black Political Slogan," *American Political Science Review* 64 (1970): 367–88. McDaniel, *Politics in the Pews*; Tate, *From Protest to Politics*. Harris, *Something Within*; Tate, *From Protest to Politics*.

13. Herbst, *Politics at the Margin*; Dawson, *Behind the Mule*; Lee, *Mobilizing Public Opinion*; Harris-Lacewell, *Barbershops, Bibles and BET.*

14. Certainly other sources of political communication (for example, black and mainstream radio) may have offered different perspectives and reached different segments of the black population; however, we have no reason to believe that these frames would be vastly different.

15. Peter Kornbluh, "Crack, the Contras, and the CIA: The Storm over 'Dark Alliance'" *Columbia Journalism Review*, January–February 1997.

16. "Dick Gregory Demands Investigation of CIA" *San Francisco Sun Reporter*, October 17, 1996.

17. Larry Reeves, "Black Leaders Demand Probe: Will Clinton Aggressively Press for Quick Resolution of CIA-Crack Connection?" *New Pittsburgh Courier*, September 28, 1996.

18. Kornbluh, "Crack, the Contras, and the CIA."

19. Controls for sex, education, income, southern residence, black interviewer, party identification, and ideology were also employed.

20. Responses to recognition questions about Hillary Clinton, Bob Dole, Al Gore, and Bill Clinton were dropped as less than 5 percent of respondents (between .001 and 3 percent) indicated that they did not recognize these individuals.

21. Responses to the question asking about Jesse Jackson were dropped as less than 5 percent of respondents indicated that they did not recognize these individuals. Only one respondent did not know who Jesse Jackson was.

22. Entman and Rojecki, *The Black Image in the White Mind.*

23. An F-test of the difference in the relative size of the coefficients on the black and mainstream awareness variables also suggests that the two variables are statically distinguishable ($F=4.07$, $p=.043$).

24. We are not suggesting that selection does not occur, but if black political awareness results from social patterns, including racial segregation, that structure contact with environments where black political information is offered, and not from simple information seeking, we should be able to observe evidence of certain types of individuals selecting themselves into these different awareness groups. The most likely and perhaps most damaging pattern of selection would be if highly racially identified blacks simply sought out black political information or perhaps sought out institutions that are more likely to provide this information (black institutions). This does not appear to be the case, particularly when you compare those high in mainstream awareness with those high in black awareness. Racial identification does not seem to vary much with the type or level of awareness; thus, concerns about selective exposure should be eased.

CONCLUSION

Race and Public Policy

JOSH GRIMM AND JAIME LOKE

The recent shooting of a Minneapolis yoga instructor by a Somali police officer garnered national attention, and will likely continue to do so as the case moves through the courts. Already comparisons are rightfully being made between how officials respond and how protesters are treated as compared to police shootings in the past in which the victim was not white. Since the shooting of Michael Brown in Ferguson, Missouri, over three thousand people have been killed by police in the United States, and given the disproportionate suffering of people of color embedded within this statistic, the impact of race continues to be felt.

The chapters in this book discuss a variety of issues: health, wealth, politics, law, immigration, crime, media, and segregation. However, race and public policy permeate all aspects of society—education, employment, discourse, to name a few—and numerous obstacles to equality remain that cut across many of these issues. One challenge that makes addressing these problems particularly difficult is the overlapping influence of local and national entities, particularly as these issues move forward in a volatile political atmosphere. Mayors and city councils in sanctuary cities are drafting legislation to ignore any decrees from the federal level that would force them to turn over undocumented immigrants to authorities. States are passing laws regarding climate-change standards. Laws regarding consent can vary simply by crossing a state border. This geographic variance represents a potentially dramatic, fundamental shift, as conservatives tend to tout states' rights and local authority over a meddling federal government. Regardless of party affiliation, these issues of jurisdiction will need to be settled before permanent change can be made. Yet, it's not just a case of a partisan government; many of these issues need—at the very least—cooperation between local and national officials.

Along those same lines, a particular area's history and how that understanding of history might inform how its population might react to a certain set of circumstances are also important to remember. When discussing the story of the shooting of Justine Damond, it is noteworthy that the tragedy took place just weeks after the controversial, but unfortunately unsurprising, verdict in which the officer who had killed Philando Castile was acquitted of manslaughter. Moving forward, the Castile shooting is going to have a significant impact on how the Damond shooting is perceived, as the local population has a point of reference for comparison. That shared history, that geographic uniqueness, will shape future understanding, consequences, and policy. Understanding those similarities and differences will help inform this process.

Making sure to consider all aspects of race moving forward is also essential. We've spoke about race broadly, and we've delved into certain populations—for example, multiracial individuals. But being inclusive is essential. A great deal of research has been done on the black-white binary because of the extensive amount of data available. However, though much attention has been paid to the "racial poles" of blacks and whites (thus impacting how issues of the "racial middle" in the United States are understood), individuals of other races have unique experiences that cannot be reduced to "patterns typical of Whites or Blacks."[1] The larger, dominant groups determine what characteristics are appropriate and representative for different races and ethnicities. Like whiteness itself, these characteristics become visible and even exaggerated when juxtaposed with an opposite set of characteristics. Just as "Whiteness is rarely named in conversations about race, except when it is discussed as the opposite of Black,"[2] whiteness is transparent in day-to-day activities unless contrasted with blacks, maintaining its privilege. Unlike the visibility of blackness, to "be" or "act" white is something that is rarely addressed—it is, rather, assumed. Henry A. Giroux explains that whiteness becomes "a racial marker, an index of social standing or rank" as it is "both invisible to itself and at the same time the norm by which everything is measured."[3] This "invisible flexibility" allows "Whiteness to move with ease" and "retains its invisibility and race neutrality."[4] This invisibility emerges from, among other things, U.S. history: whiteness was the outright dominant culture, but when it began to be associated with white-power groups and those who opposed civil rights, whiteness went into hiding and became invisible to other whites.[5] Understanding and acknowledging whiteness is particularly important in the current political environment. Richard Delgado and Jean Stefancic explain that whiteness can manifest itself in an "exaggerated form seen in White supremacy and White power groups."[6] Emboldened and unchecked, these groups will serve as a hindrance to public policy progress, particularly through intimidation. Early numbers suggest the start of a troubling trend. Compared with the first half of 2016, the first half of 2017 has seen a 91 percent increase in anti-Muslim hate crimes, with 940 reports of "potential bias incidents" in the months of April and June alone.[7] Given the shift in rhetoric, there also might be a shift toward a more explicit form of racism rather than the more common implicit form.

Moving forward, policy decisions will continue to be informed by the public, particularly with the plethora of communication outlets available. By working to understand the complexity and pervasiveness of racial inequality, perhaps an informed public can continue to create positive change to reduce racism in all of its forms.

NOTES

1. Eileen O'Brien, *The Racial Middle: Latinos and Asian Americans Living Beyond the Racial Divide* (New York: New York University Press, 2008), 2.

2. Stephanie M. Wildman, "Reflections on Whiteness: The Case of Latinos(as)," *Critical White Studies: Looking Behind the Mirror* (1997): 324.

3. Henry A. Giroux, "Racial Politics and the Pedagogy of Whiteness," in *Whiteness: A Critical Reader*, ed. Mike Hill (New York: New York University Press, 1997), 305.

4. Lisa A. Flores, Dreama G. Moon, and Thomas K. Nakayama, "Dynamic Rhetorics of Race: California's Racial Privacy Initiative and the Shifting Grounds of Racial Politics," *Communication and Critical/Cultural Studies* 3, no. 3 (2006): 184.

5. Tammie M. Kennedy, Joyce Irene Middleton, Krista Ratcliffe, Kathleen Ethel Welch, Catherine Prendergast, Ira Shor, Thomas R. West, Ellen Cushman, Michelle Kendrick, and Lisa Albrecht, "Symposium: Whiteness Studies," *Rhetoric Review* 24, no. 4 (2005): 359–402.

6. Richard Delgado and Jean Stefancic, *Critical Race Theory: An Introduction* (New York: New York University Press, 2017): 77.

7. Janice Williams, "Under Trump, Anti-Muslim Hate Crimes Have Increased at an Alarming Rate," *Newsweek*, July 17, 2017, www.newsweek.com/hate-crime-america-muslims -trump-638000.

CONTRIBUTORS

MARY E. CAMPBELL received her PhD in sociology from the University of Wisconsin. She is an associate professor of sociology at Texas A&M University. Her research focuses on the measurement of race and ethnicity in surveys and inequality between and within racial and ethnic groups. Much of her research focuses on individuals with connections to multiple racial groups, including people who self-identify as multiracial and individuals in interracial relationships. Her work has been funded by the National Science Foundation and the National Institutes of Health, and has appeared in journals such as *American Behavioral Scientist, American Sociological Review, Ethnic and Racial Studies, Social Problems,* and *Sociology of Race and Ethnicity.*

JARED K. CLEMONS is a PhD student in political science at Duke University. His research interests include political socialization, African American politics, identity politics, political behavior, and social policy. He is a recipient of the 2017–18 American Political Science Association Minority Fellowship.

SYLVIA M. EMMANUEL is a graduate student in the Department of Sociology at Texas A&M University. She also received her undergraduate degree in sociology at Texas A&M in 2016. Her research interests include race and ethnicity, identity, racism and discrimination, and social distance. She is currently doing research examining the association between the salience of persons of color's ethnic identity and the likelihood of their entering an intermarriage.

SHAUN L. GABBIDON is distinguished professor of criminal justice at Penn State Harrisburg. He has served as a fellow at Harvard University's W. E. B. Du Bois Institute for Afro-American Research and has taught at the Center for Africana Studies at the University of Pennsylvania. He is the author of more than one hundred scholarly publications, including more than sixty peer-reviewed articles and eleven books. His most recent books include *Race and Crime* (fifth edition, 2019) and the coauthored *A Theory of African American Offending* (2011).

JOSH GRIMM is the associate dean of research and strategic initiatives at the Manship School of Mass Communication at Louisiana State University. The main focus of his research is how diversity is portrayed in the media, with an emphasis on race, gender, and sexuality. Most recently, his work has focused on how gay men communicate about PrEP (pre-exposure prophylaxis), with an emphasis on perceptions of susceptibility and barriers. Josh also loves science fiction and horror movies, and he recently published a book on the modern horror classic *It Follows*.

JACKELYN HWANG is an assistant professor of sociology at Stanford University. Her research examines the relationship between how neighborhoods change and the persistence of neighborhood inequality by race and class in U.S. cities. She received her PhD in sociology and social policy from Harvard University and has been supported by the American Sociological Association and the National Science Foundation, among others.

CHRYL N. LAIRD is an assistant professor of government and legal studies at Bowdoin College. She specializes in race, ethnicity, and politics, political behavior, and political psychology. Her work has appeared in *American Political Science Review, Politics, Groups and Identities,* and *American Politics Research.*

JAIME LOKE is an assistant professor at the Bob Schieffer College of Communication at Texas Christian University. Her research interests rest on the intersection of women and minorities, mass media, and the new online public spaces. Additionally, her scholarly work relies on critical media and cultural studies theory in accompaniment to more traditional journalism research.

LORI LATRICE MARTIN is professor of Sociology and African and African American studies at Louisiana State University. Dr. Martin is the author of numerous scholarly books and articles. Her research interests are race and ethnicity, the sociology of sports, and racial wealth inequality. Dr. Martin was born and raised in Nyack, New York, and currently lives in Baton Rouge. She is the proud mother of two sons, Emir and Derrick.

ERNEST B. MCGOWEN III is an associate professor of political science at the University of Richmond. He specializes in political behavior, public opinion, campaigns and elections, race and ethnicity, and political methodology. His work has appeared in *Presidential Studies Quarterly, Public Opinion Quarterly,* and *Journal of Black Studies.*

SRIVIDYA RAMASUBRAMANIAN is associate professor of communication at Texas A&M University. She is also the director of the Aggie Agora Difficult Dialogues on Campus Race Relations. Her research focuses on media studies, intergroup/intercultural communication, cultural diversity, and media literacy. She has received the 2017 Outstanding Researcher Award from the National Association for Media Literacy Education and 2017 MCD Service Award from the National Communication Association for her scholarship.

ELIZABETH ROBERTO is an assistant professor in the Department of Sociology at Rice University. She has broad research interests in social and spatial inequality, a substantive focus on residential segregation, and methodological expertise in computational social science and quantitative methods. Dr. Roberto received an MPA from George Washington University and a PhD in sociology from Yale University.

JACOB S. RUGH is an associate professor of sociology at Brigham Young University, where he joined the faculty in 2012. His research focuses on race, neighborhood space, and immigration, with an emphasis on housing segregation and homeownership. His work has been featured by *The Atlantic, FiveThirtyEight, National Public Radio,* and the *New York Times.* Dr. Rugh received a dual master's degree in public affairs and urban and regional planning and a PhD in public affairs from Princeton University.

ISMAIL K. WHITE is an associate professor of political science at Duke University. He specializes in African American politics, public opinion, and political participation. His work has appeared in the *American Political Science Review, American Journal of Political Science, Journal of Politics, Public Opinion Quarterly, Journal of Black Studies,* and *Race and Social Problems.*

HOLLEY A. WILKIN is an associate professor of communication and public health at Georgia State University in Atlanta. Her applied health communication research program revolves around reducing health disparities in diverse urban environments. Her work approaches health communication from an ecological framework—exploring individual, community, and societal factors influencing health knowledge, attitudes, and behaviors. She earned her PhD from the Annenberg School for Communication and Journalism at the University of Southern California. Her research has been published in several peer-reviewed journals, including *Journal of Communication, Journal of Applied Communication Research, Journal of Health Communication, Health Communication, Health Education Research, Journal of Electronic Communication, Communication Research Reports,* and *Journalism: Theory, Practice, Criticism.*

INDEX

113, 128–130. *See also* undocumented immigrants; *specific immigrant groups*
Immigration Act (1917), 123–124
Immigration Act (1990), 128
Immigration and Nationality Act (1965), 127
Immigration Reform and Control Act (1986), 127, 129
implicit prejudice, 3, 67, 194
income inequality, 46, 146; segregation and, 34–35 (*see also* segregation). *See also* wealth inequality, racial
Indian Removal Act (1830), 144
indigenous communication, 7, 42, 169. *See also* black media
indigenous peoples, 42, 144, 159. *See also* American Indians/Alaskan natives; Native Americans
individual development accounts, 155
indoor pollutants, 84, 87–88
information: mediated sources for, 57–58. *See also* black media; media; political information
Instagram, 57, 58
Institute for Assets and Social Policy, Brandeis University, 143, 157
institutional racism, 4–5, 143
Internet access, 58–61
intersectionality, 71
Iran, travel ban on, 113–114, 131
Iraq, travel ban on, 113
isolation index, 30–32, *33*

Japanese immigrants: forced relocation of, 123; prejudice against, 117; reparations for internment, 159; restrictions on, 119
Jim Crow era, 159, 161, 188. *See also* segregation, residential
Johnson, Andrew, 147
Johnson, Lyndon B., 83, 127, 152
Johnson Act (1921), 119
Johnson-Reed Act (1924), 119, 128
Justice, Department of: data on police stops, 11–12; Police Data Initiative, 24
justice system, 9–10; convict leasing and, 149–151. *See also* crime; police; prisons

"Kate's Law," 133
Kennedy, John F., 127
Kerner Commission, 61
Korean immigrants, 119
Korean War, 125
Kornbluh, Peter, 176
Krysan, Maria, 2, 42

Labor, Department of, 128
labor policies, 156
labor shortages, 123–126
Laird, Chryl, 6
land ownership, 140, 143; by former slaves, 146–147
language: nativism and, 117; segregated political information and, 189
Las Vegas, 82
Latin American immigrants, 117–129, 138n80. *See also* Mexican immigrants
Latinos/Latinx Americans/Hispanics: health disparities, 77–79, 86; Internet access, 58–59; killed by police, 18–20; media representation of, 64, 70; multiracial, 100, 108 (*see also* multiracial individuals); political information and, 189; racial identity, 99; racial profiling and, 12–13; segregation and, 29, 31–33, 36–38, 40–42, 45–47, 189; stereotypes about, 64, 70, 121
Law and Order (television show), 21
law enforcement. *See* police
Lead-Based Paint Poisoning Prevention Act (1971), 87
lead-based poisoning, 87–88
Ledbetter, Calvin, 150
lending industry. *See* mortgage lenders; predatory lending
"Let's Move" campaign, 83
liberal ideology, 2, 130, 171, 180, 185, 187
Libya, travel ban on, 113–114, 131
Lichter, Daniel T., 35
local institutions, 192–193
Lombroso, Cesare, 9
Longitudinal Tract Database, 36
Longmire v. Wyser-Pratte (2007), 98
Los Angeles: access to healthy foods in, 83; alleged CIA drug trafficking in, 167–168,

Los Angeles (*continued*)
172–188; health centers in, 121–122; immigrants in, 121–123, 132; racial segregation in, 123
Los Angeles Times, 176
Louisiana, 145
lower-income neighborhoods, environmental pollutants in, 76, 84–88. *See also* income inequality; poor minority individuals; poverty deconcentration; segregation, residential
Lynch, Loretta, 23
lynching, 121

MacDonald, Heather, 20
mainstream political awareness, 180–188, 191n24
mainstream political information, 167, 169–189; black opinion and, 182–189
Maltese Falcon, The (1941), 123
marginalization, 61, 69, 85, 96
Martin, Lori Latrice, 6
Martin, Trayvon, 22
Marvilla Center (for "Mexicans Only"), 122
Maryland State Police, 10–11
Massey, Douglas S., 28
mass opinion formation, 168–169. *See also* black elite discourse; black political information
McCain, John, 129
McCarran-Walter Act (1952), 125–127
McGowen, Ernest, 6
media, 56–71; access to, 56–61, 66–67, 69; alternative, 68; commodification of, 62–63, 66; community-oriented, 68; deregulation of, 62–63; diversity in, 61–62, 66–68; ethnic, 65, 68, 169 (*see also* black media); intersectionality and, 71; mediatization perspective, 57–58; news coverage of police killings, 1–2, 22, 192–193; proliferation of, 56–57; racial inequalities in workforce, 61–63, 68, 70–71; racially inclusive policies, 6, 66–70; representations of racial minorities, 21–22, 63–70; right-wing, 132–134; segregated political information, 166–167, 169, 188–189. *See*

also digital media; mainstream political information; social media
Media Action Grassroots Network, 69
Media Action Network for Asian Americans, 69
media-activist groups, 69–71
media literacy skills, 69
media ownership, 56, 61–62, 66, 70; corporatization and consolidation in, 62–63
Media Rise, 69
Medicaid expansion, 79–81
metropolitan areas: gentrification, 30, 33, 43–44, 48; residential segregation, 30–35, 38–42, 45, 47–48, 123. *See also* housing
Metropolitan Housing Rule (Portland, OR), 50
Mexican immigrants, 117, 119–126, 133, 138n80. *See also* Latin American immigrants
Mexican Revolution, 119
Miami Times, 104
microaggressions, 96
microbusinesses, 155
Middle Eastern people, 11
Milner, John, 150
Minuteman Project, 129
Mitchell, Jill E., 97
Mitchell v. Champs Sports (1998), 97
mixed-race individuals. *See* multiracial individuals
Molina, Natalia, 121
monoracism, 96
mortgage lenders, 44–46; interest reduction, 156; redlining, 28, 44, 151; soft second mortgages, 154–155; subprime loans, 45, 48, 152. *See also* homeownership; housing
Moving to Opportunity, 48
MSNBC, 2
multiracial individuals, 95–109, 193; discrimination against, 95–103; identity types, 106–107; misrecognition of racial identities, 96–97, 104; public perceptions of, 104–105; race-based public policy and, 103–109; self-identification, 99–100, 105–109

www.ingramcontent.com/pod-product-compliance
Lightning Source LLC
Chambersburg PA
CBHW031131270326
41929CB00011B/1587